# THE LOOM OF ART

# THE LOOM OF ART

GERMAIN BAZIN

CHIEF CURATOR, MUSEUM OF THE LOUVRE

SIMON AND SCHUSTER · NEW YORK

TRANSLATED BY JONATHAN GRIFFIN


PRINTED IN GREAT BRITAIN BY JARROLD AND SONS LTD NORWICH
LIBRARY OF CONGRESS CATALOG CARD NUMBER 62-12408

# CONTENTS

# PREFACE

THIS BOOK is neither a manual nor a history of art, certainly not an encyclopaedia, and still less a treatise on aesthetics: it is a game; essentially a game with images, a play of images. There has been much talk in recent times of the primacy of images over idea. André Malraux has conceived his *l'Univers des Formes* (*The Arts of Mankind*) as a close co-ordination of text and illustration: the text serves as a commentary on the image, but the image comes in obedience to the governing train of thought. The present book has been fashioned out of images that have grouped themselves, by analogy or contradiction, into confrontations, which in turn have come together into larger complexes. It is therefore a work of memory—and of visual memory: but this does not exclude its domination by a directing line of thought; for (as Bergson has shown) since a man preserves within him all his perceptions, feelings and thoughts, memory is simply a faculty of recovering, at exactly the right moment, materials called up by our creative power in answer to some task, action or idea. Here the text came afterwards and is merely added to the images, rather than following them up.

Contrary to the fashion at present prevailing among editors and publishers, I decided that the text should be separated from the illustrations and not interwoven with them. The philosopher who sets out to meditate upon the world does not climb a mountain to get the widest possible view of the world or the universe, but is more inclined to shut himself up in a cell: as Poussin would have said, to grasp the prospect one must forget the aspect, and an act of separating oneself from reality is an essential part of the very effort to attain and apprehend it. In this book, therefore, ten chapters act as prefaces to ten books of images: they are not—any more than are the image sequences—guided by logical deduction, for to the author also the writing of this book was a game—and one that was meant to be free from any too narrow enslavement to the business of commentary or to the discursive style. Its thought, in the description of these complexes of images, sometimes rises to a panoramic view, and at other times, like a tracking camera in a film studio, descends to enjoy and linger over a specialist's close-up examination of a given sequence—these changes being always governed simply by the author's caprice or taste. For everything in this book is the result of a personal choice; and that is its least defect: its only justification is the pleasure experienced in evoking the marvellous world of forms. Uncommitted to any historical scheme, as well as to any preconceived ideas, it was, in short, an exercise of relaxation after the author's labours in writing a manual *(A Concise History of Art)*.

What I should like is for the reader to share my pleasure and to go on with the game I set before him. For this small world of images is full of echoes and reverberations which the reader will discover for himself as he turns over its pages, and to appreciate it one would need to be able to take it in at a glance, placing oneself at its centre as in the circular dioramas of the last century.

If we are looking for human unity, it is in prehistoric times that this will best be found. Civilisations develop later by a series of differentiations—yet not without constantly rejoining those primordial typologies to which Eugn ie d'Ors gave the name of 'aeons'. Thus the ambivalence between figurative art and abstraction (notoriously inadequate terms) continues throughout the length of history down to our own time. The same is true of that between the rectilinear style (or rhythmic expression) and the curvilinear style (or melodic expression). The former gives life to African art, to the Doric style, to Japanese art, to 'Atticism', to Italian Romanesque, to the Early Renaissance, to Poussin, to David; the latter to Polynesian art, to the Ionic style, to Chinese art, to 'Asianism', to French Romanesque, to the *style flamboyant*, to Rubens, the Rococo, Ingres and Delacroix. Every style, when realised in its completest expressiveness by a civilisation, makes explicit some fundamental human value and becomes, to the historian, a transcendent vocable—even though it may sometimes take over strange forms. Was there ever anything more extravagant than Art Nouveau? What can be more surprising, then, than to see it making a sporadic appearance, in the course of history, in a Sung sculpture, a Bernard Palissy dish, or in the Margravine Wilhelmina's dining-room at Bayreuth—and even enlivening Picasso's *Actor*? Of these constants the most remarkable is 'Antiquity', which was defined in the fifth and fourth centuries B.C. and has welled up ever since throughout Western civilisation, adulterated, forgotten, violated, rediscovered, condemned or praised—always reborn in spite of the Pyrrhic victories of its antagonist 'Nature', with which indeed it often comes to terms, though perhaps destined to succumb in the end, along with Nature and with all art, to the final offensive of the *Informel*.

*Plates 65, 398*
*Plate 400*

The work of art, as Gaëtan Picon has said, claims to be like a sun: it doubtless wants to be seen, but only in a dazzle that prevents it from being examined; and since all explanations of a work of art are vain attempts to grasp the unfathomable, they merely accentuate its transcendence (which my generation was so acutely aware of but the rising generation is beginning to abandon, in its desperate anxiety to apprehend works of art by every sort of non-artistic means—psychology, psycho-analysis, philosophy and even history). The arguments in this book do not pretend to 'explain' works of art by some sort of deduction from given elements: they are the result of a quest for knowledge 'directed towards loving'—which to Bossuet was the only valid end of knowledge. While this study of ours tells us nothing about the mechanism by which the work of art (still essentially unforseeable) is produced, all the historical, sociological, aesthetic, psychological, psycho-analytical and even economic facts here accumulated add to the pleasure which it gives us—not indeed as a work of art, but as an essential and transcendent human fact that enables us to know more about our own species. It is, so to say, an accompanying pleasure, one that leads us on to further study and writing without in any way interfering with the delight which to Poussin, that heir of the schoolmen, was the aim of painting, as it was to Matisse later: in the words of St Thomas, '*Id quod visum placet*'.

None the less, only what is outside the work of art can be comprehended; for the work of art as such can only be a source of emotion and can have no equivalent except in another work of art, usually a literary one. But while it is impossible to explain 'why' a work of art appears or 'what' its essence is, one can at least catch glimpses of 'how' it comes into being; and the knowledge of the providential concatenation that produces what is called an 'artistic civilisation' is one essential factor in humanism, that is to say in culture.

'One Law, one Faith, one State' is the well-known formula by which historians have summed up the policy of Justinian. Taken in their social sense, these three words are the axioms of every civilisation; with their capitals removed they become the principles of every personal culture. A civilisation is a body of religious beliefs, philosophical and aesthetic concepts, social functions and technical know-how—an active body made from the collaboration of all the members of a society in which, from the *élite* to the man of the people and from the philosopher to the craftsman, there reigns a spirit of agreement, animating the progress of art, technical skill and thought with a single rhythm so that the humblest object of daily use and the highest speculative flight of philosophy alike bear that imprint which is the *style* of a period.

A culture is that complex of elements older than the individual, of vestiges of the past, which forms the soil for the vigorous plant of the future to grow in and which, at a certain period, enables every man, whatever his condition of life, to achieve a full development of his personality. This extension of culture to the whole social body is, it is true, found only in primitive civilisations, and in the West the Middle Ages were the last example of it. At that time the collective culture was based on Christianity, which allowed each person to 'cultivate' his soul with a view to a beatific final condition that was promised to all: it offered to the humblest manual worker as well as to the intellectual the power to satisfy an instinct for creation—to realise in a work moulded by his hands or issuing from his mind and becoming an object, his personality, active and effective. Classicism broke this essential unity of the social body and made culture the attribute of an aristocracy: in thus cutting it off from its sources, it exposed it to the dangers of academicism, while the people, expelled from creative activity, carried on a stationary art which, until in our own lifetime it was killed by the rise of industrialism, maintained without development forms that had come into being in the Neolithic period and had become, strictly speaking, styleless. Versailles is the temple raised to the monarch-god, in whom an aristocracy complacently recognised the finest example of itself; but the cathedral of Chartres is a people's confession of faith. The stonemasons who worked at Versailles were merely the executants of a plan conceived by an intellectual, and the workman who carved the Ionic capitals of the first storey, having no freedom to impose on them any personal imprint and being rigorously bound to observe a canon that was utterly remote from him, could hardly find in the work any sort of mode of perfection. But the sculptors of the cathedral of Laon or of the Florentine buildings of the fifteenth century never carved two capitals the same; every capital that left their hands represented, step by step, a progress over the last, a stage in perfection, a fresh research, a cultivation in the artist of his personality as a craftsman, and in this he found a vital equilibrium, a joy which, in the Middle Ages, expressed itself as the dynamic impulse that made a cathedral a growing thing.

In the eighteenth century, to some extent, these fortunate circumstances recurred, thanks to the social harmony which prevailed at that time. By insensible gradations a subtle bond between the aristocracy and the people was established, and rarely has a civilisation elaborated by an *élite*—which had become idle and spent its time polishing the art of living to the most delicate possible refinement—so extensively impregnated the products of a period. In this respect royal France, whose culture gradually extended to the whole of Europe, was akin to the Middle Ages—although the culture of the Middle Ages was still more extensive, that of the eighteenth century being almost exclusively urban. There was in the eighteenth century a fresh progress in the minor arts that prosper in the great collective periods, and for this reason we have given them prominence in this book. Although in France the increasing dominance of classicism in architecture forced the craftsman more and more to sacrifice his personality to that of the intellectual who had conceived the monument, in the other countries the decorative profusion of the Baroque and Rococo styles assured the prosperity of all the ancillary crafts. In the art of furniture-making, however, France recovered the optimum conditions for the craftsman's culture as these had flourished in the Middle Ages. The so-called 'cabriolet' chair of the Louis XV period, adapted as it was to all the attitudes of life, to rest and to work and above all to conversation, is a masterpiece of culture: it sums up a whole conception of human life.

This provisional renewal of collective culture was broken off by the nineteenth century, and the rupture then produced has gone on widening until our own day. The very idea of style as the expression of an ideal shared by a whole people is disappearing. In the Renaissance artistic creation became separated from the people: in modern times it becomes distinct even from the *élite*, which—with the exception of a minority of art lovers—has now no dealings with art except as a by-product of concepts elaborated by the preceding generation and accepted painfully after tardy assimilation. Romanticism is condemned in the name of classicism, Impressionism in the name of both, and modern art in the name of all tradition; and the absence of any unity of culture that would enable every man to fulfil himself *in his station* leaves him no chance of accomplishing his destiny except outside all frameworks, that is to say by individualism. This explains the unprecedented literary and artistic inflation characteristic of our time; every individual in whom the dominance of materialism has not stifled creativeness is no longer able to give this impulse an outlet in his life, and therefore seeks to satisfy it in some abstract order. At the same time, since the abandonment of all precepts has simplified the means of art to the utmost and placed them within reach of the greatest number, there is a tendency, thanks to the aesthetic of the *Informel*, towards the reconstitution of a style—of a mode of collective expression which, this time, is world-wide and may prove to be the prelude to that non-'art' art integrated with technology, the art of tomorrow.

Doubtless, too, there will be more and more truth in the disillusioned dictum of Reynaldo dos Santos, a historian of contemporary art who is also a scientist: 'Man is making much more use of the wings of the aeroplane than of his own wings.'

GERMAIN BAZIN
*Les Presles. Le Temple-sur-Lot*
*31st July 1960*

# I PILGRIMAGE TO THE FOUNTAINHEAD

# I Pilgrimage to the Fountainhead

OFTEN A MONKEY IN THE FOREST will seize hold of a stone or a fruit as a projectile or, faced with an enemy, will use a branch as a club, but this use of an auxiliary means of action does not go beyond the weapon and achieve the tool; still less does one ever see a monkey keep the stone or club after use in order to improve its usefulness. Mankind learned logic by working with tools: the genius of man was born of human weakness. In primitive man the need to increase the efficiency of his actions developed the faculties of reasoning; and there is, in the museums of prehistory or early history, nothing so moving as those eloquent glass cases in which each primitive tool is shown along with the activity for which it was meant: one can see that this equipment, only slightly perfected, is still what is used today in the various crafts and professions. This was how the worker learned the elements of mechanics, the same that are still applied today in manual activity based on an indirect force. Long before Archimedes explained its theory, primitive man had discovered and applied the lever, that principle at the origin of all technique, which was to remain fundamental for machinery of every kind until the invention of electricity established the idea of a continuous force.

The lever was something primitive man could observe in the very organisation of his skeleton and play of his muscles. Examination of the principle of indirect force is, in fact, at the origin of all human reasoning, which breaks down thought into successive deductions in order to urge it on towards a conclusion. All art springs from that—language, the dance and the art of forms. Gesture imprints its rhythm on the brain, leading to logic and with it, to dialectic, rhetoric and the art of bringing an idea to birth: the syllogism, with its major and minor premises, is already contained in the first genuine axe, made to be held by a handle and not plied with the hand, as was probably the case with the double-edged axes of the Early Palaeolithic period.

Although we shall never have more than a vague knowledge of the thought of prehistoric man, thousands of examples of the tools he used have been preserved, and these can be interpreted and reconstituted to give us a complete picture of the life of his workshop. We see him step by step inventing the means of self-defence, the weapons for stunning, cutting and piercing, the projectiles for wheeling flight and direct flight, all the tricks and methods of snaring and the combination of a launching device (the spear-thrower, and then the bow) with a projectile (the assegai and then the arrow); and at last he becomes capable of imagining a masterpiece—the boomerang, which returns to its sender after having accomplished its mission of death. Attack at a distance must very soon have seemed preferable to combat at close quarters: the primitive double-edged blade must soon have been accompanied by the hurling stick which, flung with a scythe-like movement against the animal's legs, brought it wounded to the ground, so that all that remained was to close in and finish it off. When the bow appeared, multiplying the range and penetrative power of the projectile, it must have momentarily conferred on the first tribe to use it an unequalled power, enabling it to satisfy instincts of domination. It is a fact that with the use of the bow, the first representations of man fighting against man make their appearance.

We shall never be able to do more than imagine these struggles. That is part of the charm of this period in which history has been submerged for lack of writing. The rivalries between the clan wearing helmets with auroch horns and the bear clan have left no trace in human memory. Since the 'events' which, during the historic period, screen and mask the continuity of human genius have been erased by time, the so-called prehistoric period looks to us like a continuous 'progress' through an ardent, yet patient, search by man for the means of increasing his power, of assuring his livelihood and that of his dependents, and of conquering hostile nature and wild beasts—in a word, of perfecting himself. All we can see, at a distance of millennia, is this vast pacific effort; and I think this forgetting of the fratricidal struggles, this 'oblivion of history', is what, from the very beginnings of the historical epoch, engendered the myth of a Golden Age, of an original state of perfection.

Perhaps indeed there is some historical truth underneath this myth: in prehistoric times, when human life was so precarious and men very few, who was there to oppose them? What was there to fight for, when there was nothing to conquer? From time to time a more numerous family may have chased another out of some rocky shelter; but peace between men may on the whole have been assured by the need of defence against the common enemy, the wild beast; and a social grouping by families or small clans was not very suitable for engendering the power instinct that torments the masses and produces leaders. The theme of the Golden Age appears along with writing itself, in Sumerian literature: it doubtless contains a real echo of an earlier peaceful human condition, for which there arose a certain nostalgia after the terrible struggles that must have resulted from the coming of agricultural civilisation. This had brought with it the possession of riches and the accumulation of wealth, and then the more backward peoples fell upon the more civilised, to seize from them the fruit of the labour: the struggle between the mountains and the plains began—certain peoples conceived the idea that it was easier and nobler to live by the lance than by the plough, so forcing the labourer himself to take up the sword. Centuries of poetry, beginning with Hesiod and Virgil, have made us see in agriculture the incarnation of peaceful existence, and it is to the hunter that we assign the attributes of cruelty; but it cannot have been like that at the beginning, when the hunter had, first and foremost, to fight against the wild beast. War appeared with the farmer: he had something to defend—his barns. Paradoxical as it may seem to us moderns, it was farming that gave rise to urban civilisation. The co-ordination of the infinitely complex activities of agricultural life demands a communal organisation, under some sort of leadership, and therefore the creation of a political system; and the possibility of storing the produce of the harvests brings with it the necessity of building a wall to protect them from the covetous. Jericho, the oldest city in the world, built at the verge of the agricultural era in the sixth millennium, has a rampart.

The memory of a time when the wild beast was man's only enemy remained, however, indelibly carved upon our traditions. The vanquishing of a wild beast, not of a man, was long to remain the sign of power: in the Asiatic dynasties that created the whole apparatus of absolute monarchy, the essentially royal attitude is that in which the sovereign is seen taking aim at some real or mythical animal—a bull, a dragon, an antelope or a lion. The chase was a royal perquisite: among the Achaemenids, the Assyrians or the Sassanids, wild beasts were brought up in menageries for the princes' hunt. In Roman Africa big game hunting was strictly regulated, especially the hunting of the lion, which the Egyptians had raised to the rank of king of beasts;

*Plates 53–56*

the wild animals of the forests were sacred; they were the servants of the gods, and their immolation at the games in the amphitheatre had a ritual character; it was forbidden to kill them, and the task of capturing them fell to soldiers only; the lion hunt was indeed an imperial monopoly, to be exercised only in the name of the sovereign; during their visits to Africa the emperors reserved for themselves the accomplishment of this rite; even Hadrian, that philosophic emperor, went lion hunting in Mauretania. The kings of France at the end of the *ancien régime* saw no reason to let this rite lapse: indeed, it was their principal occupation. The chase remained until 1789 a feudal privilege, one of those that excited the most hatred: the Frenchman killed his king to be able to kill the hare, as if there was no human dignity possible without the conquest of wild animals. This ancient power instinct rises up again from the depths of the ages in the soul of every countryman out with his gun—who, as he shoots a quail, feels within him the soul of Gilgamesh strangling the lion. Although anyone in France may now go out shooting, the President of the Republic has not abandoned the regal privilege of making hecatombs of game; and pictures of the bag laid out at evening after a presidential shoot at Rambouillet remind one of what can be seen in Assyrian bas-reliefs. Elizabeth is never so much Queen of England as when, setting an example to the nobility, she goes hunting.

Among the peoples of the early civilisations there was perhaps another confused memory of the period when man was still face to face with the wild beast and resembled it. This was what might be called the ritual of hair and beard, which associated physical strength, or even power and wisdom, with abundance of hair. The Israelite warriors were observing it when they let their hair grow before going into battle, and Samson lost his strength together with his hair when Delilah treacherously cut it off. Among the Assyrians, the Achaemenids and the Egyptians the beard, genuine or false, was a royal or priestly attribute. Among the Egyptians, who were clean-shaven, this false beard was so precious that they enclosed it in a gold case. The rationalism of the classic Greeks found expression in their smooth faces; yet for them too the beard was still an attribute of wisdom, whether political (Pericles), philosophic (Socrates), poetic (Homer) or divine (Zeus). In Hellenistic and Roman times the growth of hair in majestic waves about the face was an attribute of the sacred power of the gods, and it seemed natural that the curling heads of Ocean should give birth to living creatures or to plants. The hair is the part of the human body that binds its owner to the primordial instincts, to the forces of the forests, to the hidden powers of the universe. It was an attribute of the 'wise man' which the first Christian missionaries to China were careful not to neglect.

*Figure p. 15*
*Plate 52*

Primitive men surely did not devour one another any more than wolves do: and it is tempting to suppose that there was a Golden Age in which our ancestor gradually invented the implements of the hunter, of the carpenter, of the potter and, soon, of the smith. What an idyllic picture it presents—and what a degree of organisation! Can we not already see the genius of industry in that very England which, many centuries later, brought into the world modern mechanical civilisation? Neolithic deposits of flint implements worked in accordance with all the principles of rationalisation of the Taylor system have been discovered at Peterborough. The method of organising labour advocated by Adam Smith in the eighteenth century is even more clearly evident in the Spiennes deposits in Belgium, where various hut floors have yielded flint implements in their successive stages of manufacture! The universal character of that stone-using civilisation proves to us that discoveries were being transmitted across the world at a period when national frontiers were not there to hinder the spread of progress.

Very soon the workman brought to the fashioning of tools designed for action a care in their execution—the microliths in particular are one of its most remarkable expressions—which is evidence of a striving for an unnecessary formal perfection: for what Riegl would call a 'will to art'. Take for instance a certain Palaeolithic spear-point in the Copenhagen Museum, which is

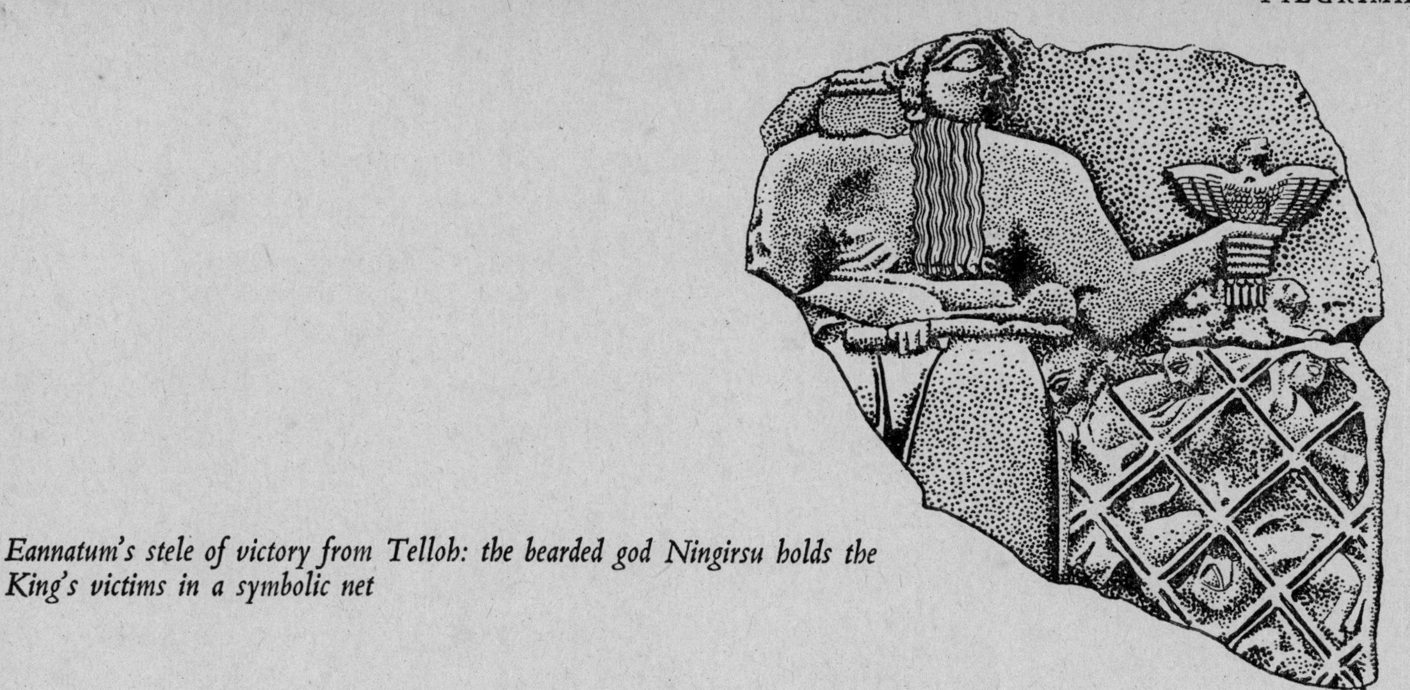

*Eannatum's stele of victory from Telloh: the bearded god Ningirsu holds the King's victims in a symbolic net*

carved out of a hard stone with such finish that it has the beauty of an antique cameo: how can one suppose that the workman in this case was not thinking of making a work of art rather than a tool? This taste for the beauty of objects in stone was destined to become an end, not a means, when these were still employed traditionally as ritual objects in a more developed civilisation. The use of stone during hundreds of millennia impregnated humanity so strongly that it never altogether ceased to worship stones. The bethels, or sacred stones, all over the world bear witness to this; and the era in which this cult of stone seems to have been most developed is the Megalithic, when for his tools man moved from polished stone to bronze and then to iron. No doubt, in the earliest civilisations, what has been called the law of frontality derives from the need to see that the statue still has the divine rigidity of the monolith, the essential virtue of stone, which among the religious archetypes carries with it the attributes of eternity; right down to the end of their history—that is to say, to the beginning of our own—the Egyptians retained this style, which was ritual rather than aesthetic. The Romans, who were so deeply attached to religion and kept up all the human ideas of divinity from the most distant ages, still honoured a *Jupiter lapis*, represented in the form of a flint. When stone tools are kept for ritual purposes their execution is given particular care, as in the case of the knife from Gebel el-Arak and even the flint axe and knife found in the funerary temple of Snefru in Egypt, which dates from the Fourth Dynasty, that is to say from historic times. All over the world one finds traces of this ritual. Among the Aztecs, who did not discover bronze until shortly before the conquest, the use of stone tools was utilitarian: they were executed in flint or obsidian, that is to say more or less sumptuously according to their purposes. Polished obsidian, which was also used for mirrors, could be given a cutting edge like that of a razor; scalpels of this stone served for the ritual blood-letting and, at the time of the conquest, sacrificing priests were still using such knives to immolate the human victims on the summits of the pyramid temples.

*This refinement gives the cult objects a jewelled quality, akin to the most delicate manifestations of a more sophisticated art: for instance, on an Egyptian knife, a handle of carved ivory fitted to a stone blade (1); the conjunction, in a Chinese dagger, of enamelling, with a jade-fine blade of polished stone (2); and incrusted niello-work in a Mycenean sword (3)*

*Plates 1, 2*

Such veneration for implements lasted on even after the Stone Age into the Bronze Age: the double-axe of bronze and sometimes even in gold became one of the principal cult objects of the Cretans. To primitive man the tool is not a machine, it is a god; a craftsman confers a soul upon the object created by his hands, giving to it the attribute of 'spirit' which is within him, and which he believes to have come from beyond him.

*Plates 3, 14*

Stone, wood and clay provided man with the first materials for his tools. Wood, an organic material, has the precariousness of everything that is close to life, and stone is indestructible; but clay, fragile though it is, has left innumerable evidences of men's industry. It is safe to say that in

Neolithic times there existed what may fairly be called a clay civilisation: earth supplied man not only with his food but also with the material of his gods. There was a method of fashioning idols by adding clay pellets, one after another—a method so simple that it was used all over the world by the most distant civilisations: our illustration groups together examples of it which, though from dispersed sites, might be taken to be from the same hand. The salient parts of the body—eyes, nose, ears, breasts—are formed of pellets stuck on to the body, while certain emphases or ornaments are achieved by incisions into the still damp clay. In Mesopotamia, in the El Obeid civilisation and in Palestine, everything necessary for living was made of earth—not only the vessels indispensable for daily life, but the fisherman's sinkers and those small weaver's spindles which, surviving in their thousands, bear witness to a textile art of which everything else has disappeared. One finds there even the tools one would least expect to see made of this material—axes and sickles. In Mesopotamia, Iran and in India at Mohenjo-daro, clay also supplied man with the docile material suited for taking the impressions from his seals, those signs of his beliefs and of his property instinct. Jehovah drew the body of Adam from clay, and for the creation of man the Mesopotamian god Ea even used the potter's wheel.

*Plates 23–33*

One might almost say that, if all the rest of his activity were to vanish, man might still be known by his pottery. It is the systematic classification of vases that has enabled archaeologists, studying various obscure civilisations, to reconstruct their chronology; and the strange property possessed by baked earth, of preserving traces of the terrestrial magnetism prevalent at the place where and the moment when it was placed in the oven, has helped in this reconstitution of time, while it has also, in return, aided the geologists who are trying to trace back the history of the earth.

*Plates 34–41*

The first decorations on pottery, which imitated basket-work, show that the use of baskets as receptacles is even earlier. These were rendered watertight by an inner skin of clay or of gum, so that it was possible to cook in them, heating the water by putting hot stones into them. The transition from basket-work to pottery is perceptible all over the world, in China as well as in Crete, and in the Neolithic of the West; but nowhere is it more apparent than in the civilisation of the 'Basket-Makers', who preceded the Pueblos in America. No doubt the art of pottery was discovered by accident—by the negligence of some housewife who, having left a clay-lined basket close to the hearth, returned to find a pot, baked by the fire which had consumed the basket-work. This transmission of ornament from one art to another is one of the first examples of a certain idleness in the human imagination, which is slow to think out forms corresponding to the techniques it invents—an idleness that was later to give the gauge of railways the width of a pair of horses drawing a coach, and to give the Greek temples forms derived from wooden buildings. The first designs on pottery came from impressions made by textiles or cords on the clay before baking; and the constancy with which not only the same designs but the same shapes are found throughout the world is remarkable—particularly the bell shape, derived from a flared basket, of which many specimens are still found today in popular basket-work in various places. Decoration probably moved from weaving to basket-work, from basket-work to ceramics and from ceramics, sometimes, even to work on stone—as in the case of the strange ornamentation of the Zapotec palaces at Mitla in Mexico, where the walls seem to be covered with hangings woven in stone for giants.

*Plates 34–36*

The pots were first modelled with the hand, then on a turntable (a simple horizontal board) and finally on the potter's wheel—which remained unknown on the American continent. Painted decorations followed those impressed or incised. In Mesopotamia, in the archaic civilisations before the arrival of the Sumerians, and at Susa in the Elamite civilisation, the more or less stylised decoration is continuous like a script—no doubt a sacred script. Secularised on the arrival of the Sumerians, pottery lost its decoration and stone became the principal means of expression.

*Plate 12*

Being light to transport, though fragile, pottery has always been one of the chief articles of export, and so a privileged carrier of forms from people to people. Already in Neolithic times

*Plates 37–41*

impressed-ware was exported by barge across western and northern Europe. The dissemination of the forms of Greek art was carried on across the Mediterranean by vases more than by statues: Cyprus, Corinth and then Athens flooded the ancient world with their forms, and the majority of the Greek vases that have survived come from Italian soil. From the Cretans down to the decadence of the art in the fourth century, ceramics provided the Greeks with a remarkable field for artistic experiment, making possible the invention of the noblest curves and the solution of the problems of adapting decoration to the shapes of objects. From the fourth to the sixth century painting on pottery was still more advanced than sculpture. Later, when this art had long been in decline, the Romans made a kind of red pottery ornamented in relief (called Arezzo Ware from Arezzo in Tuscany, its chief centre of manufacture), and the sherds of this pottery are found everywhere where the Romans passed, from Scotland to India, particularly in the times of Augustus and Tiberius. In the second half of the first century A.D., when Aretine production had gone down, other sources of export arose in various parts of the Empire, and the products of potters in Lorraine or the Rhineland are found even in Africa, Sicily, Sardinia and Italy itself. Africa exported lamps, whose manufacture was no doubt bound up with the production of the oil. In the Middle Ages Persia was to sell its famous lustre-ware to the whole of the Islamic world, and certain wrecks, which sank in the Persian Gulf with their cargo of dishes and vases, still bear witness to the intensity of this trade: there lie complete series of the various types of Persian pottery, which archaeologists dream of exploring. In Palestine there are sites, like that of Tel el-Hesy, where a cross-section of the strata yields a view of the pottery made by man from Neolithic times right down to the Arezzo Ware and even to the Arab vases.

*Plate 38*

One of the materials provided by Nature must have fascinated man at the time of the earliest civilisations—that marvellous metal which, on the American continent, he knew even before the commoner metals, since it could be picked up in its pure state: gold. The Sao people, of the shores of Lake Chad, believed there was a time when gold was alive: when it was drawn from the soil it flew into the air, but could be caught in flight, and a single bit of it was enough to light a whole house. Gold, the incorruptible metal, could assure a man's passage into eternity; and no doubt it was for the after-life, more than for this life, that those splendid adornments found by amazed archaeologists in the tombs of Ur and in that of Tut-ankh-amun were fashioned. Man lived, during millennia, only for his tomb. One striking sign of that poverty of imagination which we have already observed in the human mentality is that man could not picture to himself the life beyond except as a reproduction of the life on earth. There was a time, indeed, when he considered it merely as the prolongation of this life—a view which in China, Siberia and Mesopotamia led to those hecatombs of servants, dogs and horses which have given us a glimpse of funeral rites of a cruel magnificence. But a day came when man had more confidence in the virtues of the image made by his hands: then real sacrifices ceased, and the tombs were filled not with real bodies but with imitations. China shows this progress clearly in its different stages: after the human sacrifices of the Shang tombs, one finds in the Chou tombs holocausts of animals only, and the Han tombs are content with statuettes. In this way art came to the help of man, delivering him from a heavy tribute of blood paid to the next world. This was the moment when the artist became conscious of being really a godlike creator, since the imitation which he made of things and living creatures had the value of reality. The Egyptians thought that the dead man had his survival guaranteed as long as there remained a copy of him, and therefore the images of the dead man, as also of his attendants and servants were multiplied. In spite of this power attributed to the copies, consumable goods, those tangible realities, were not neglected either: libations were relied on to sustain the dead, but since the loyalty of the descendants was doubted, stocks were laid up in an attempt to make sure. At Meydum there has been found the tomb of a dignitary called Hemaka, who served one of the First Dynasty kings: it contains a vast cellar of forty-two rooms filled with provisions; one

*All the ancient civilisations have revealed a similar abundance of gold and other precious metals buried in the tombs: at Ur (42, 46); Minoan sepulchres (44, 45); South American tombs filled with solid gold statuettes (43)*

*One of the latest discoveries of this kind is that of the Liu Li Ko tombs in China, which once contained a whole squadron of war-chariots, apparently placed there in battle order (51)*

*Figures in Egyptian tombs, cast in the same mould and repeated* ad infinitum, *seem fixed for all eternity (48)*

of them held 2000 jars of wine closed with clay stoppers. This, allowing a consumption of one jar per week, would have meant that the dead man would go short of the wine indispensable to his survival before half a century was out. Such poverty of imagination, characteristic of Egypt to the very end, shows that there was even at that date a certain doubt of the efficacy of the copy, for otherwise a jar painted or—better—carved on the wall would have guaranteed our man his wine for eternity.

*Plate 51*

The gold gleaming in the depths of the tombs aroused the covetousness of robbers and led, all over the world, and from prehistory onwards, to the violation of the sepulchres. When the Spaniards landed in America and gutted the tombs of the Incas or Aztecs, other plunderers had been before them. The pharaohs employed many devices against this scourge in vain: are there not in Egypt, in certain villages, families of tomb-robbers, who are thought to have carried on this 'profession' from father to son since Antiquity? The Chinese emperor Shi Huang Ti after having built for himself a magnificent tomb in which the regions of the world were delineated in precious stones and the rivers and seas represented by streams of mercury set in motion mechanically, and where candles were supposed to burn for a thousand years, had it fitted with a whole arsenal of bows already strung and crossbows at the ready, hidden in the mass of the tumulus. Vain precautions: few royal tombs remained inviolate anywhere in the world; even that of Tut-ankh-amun had had visitors, the famous tombs of Pazyryk in Siberia were found in disorder, nor were those of Mycenae respected.

*Plate 52*

The present controversies about figurative and non-figurative art have raised the question which of the two was the world's first art. Does abstract art derive from the figurative through progressive stylisation, or has the abstract sign gradually taken on life? Since many of the objects were of perishable material and have disappeared, the problem can be resolved only imperfectly on the evidence that we have. The oldest idols that have come down to us, the fertility statuettes of the Aurignacian period, which have been found dispersed widely over the West, appear to be sometimes strongly naturalistic (the *Venus of Willendorf*), more rarely stylised (the *Venus of Lespugue*); but our ignorance of the chronology leads us to treat as contemporary images that are no doubt centuries apart. If one leaves out of account the clumsy stylisation that characterises the exercises of children (and we have no example of this that goes back to the earliest times), the so-called 'abstract' forms surviving from prehistoric periods suggest a cunning elaboration rather than a spontaneous act. Has not the movement we have seen happening in our own time, from the naturalism of the Impressionists to the *Informel*, passing through Cézanne's interpretation of Nature, through Cubism and through abstract art, reconstituted under our own eyes all the stages of that elaboration? Though the motif of both of them was probably magic, the realism and the abstraction of primitive art imply contrary attitudes. It seems more natural to suppose that at first, attempting a crude sympathetic magic, man attributed the greatest power to the strictest likeness between image and object: the Egyptians retained in its pure state this imitative conception taken over from Palaeolithic art, and perhaps it was transmitted to them from other parts of Africa where the realism of Magdalenian art continued until the Roman period. If one leaves aside certain Aurignacian statues that are stylised into primary masses, one is forced to conclude that abstract art, which appeared in the Mesolithic Age, is contemporary with the birth of the agricultural civilisations—that is to say, with an advanced stage of civilisation at which men, emerging from the tribal state, were organising themselves in social groups with a complex structure, while the fertility of the earth, which they had learned to master, was developing in them a feeling of the presence of personalised divine powers going beyond the simple play of natural forces. Worringer saw in abstract art a mystical tendency dictated by the desire to escape from a hostile external world. Against this theory there is the fact that the finest abstract art appears in Neolithic times, at Harappa and Susa, in the form of decorations on vases which show that man

*Plates 4–10*

*Plate 4*

*In his determination to 'catch' the animal whole, the sorcerer-artist of the hunter epoch projects its real form on to rock-face or engraved stone in a kind of trance which identifies him with the living creature he depicts (6)*

*The will to abstraction is particularly expressive in certain works of art where a realistic head is placed on a body that is distorted, no doubt, for reasons of magic (10)*

*Evolution of a theme: the garland-dancers*

*Siyalk III (4th millennium)*

*Siyalk III*

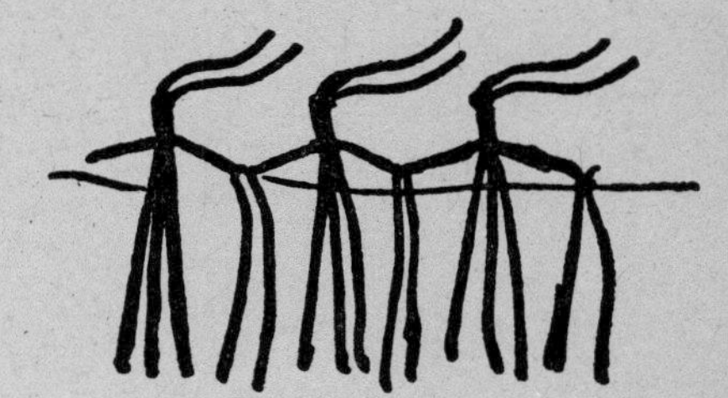

*Rana Ghundai I, Zhob Valley*

*Samarra (5th millennium)*

*Arpatchiya, Upper Tigris (early 4th millennium)*

*Tal-i-Skau*

*Amri, Sind (end of 4th millennium)*

*Q'alat-i-Gird, Hilmand Valley (3rd millennium)*

*Mohenjo-daro (3rd millennium)*

had mastered a regular keyboard of signs and figures, passing from one to another with virtuosity and conferring upon the most abstract signs, derived from animal forms, a joyful vitality—already a proof that art can be closest to reality when least constrained to imitate it. In any case, abstract art arises from the feeling that the real world cannot be reproduced—which means that the world is a sort of mystery, a hidden truth, only revealed in so far as it emerges to the visual surface in signs and symbols: the more generalised these are and the more potential being they include, the greater is their charge of force, so that, unlike the Magdalenian painter, the potter of Susa believed the efficacy of the signs he traced on the sides of his vase to be all the greater because it evoked—or invoked—reality without reproducing it.

In the pebbles of the Mas d'Azil, as well as in the Sahara paintings or the pottery of the Susa region, it is easy to classify the forms in accordance with a progression from figure to sign—an evolution which seems more natural than the opposite would have been. The sign seems indeed to be a sort of graphic summary of the naturalistic form. This script of image-signs can be either

*Painted pebbles from Mas d'Azil*

rectilinear or curvilinear. The somewhat limited repertoire of these two kinds is found in widely dispersed examples with remarkable resemblances—a fact which has sometimes led archaeologists to believe that influences have been transmitted over vast distances. What connection is there between the 'angular men' of the Rhodesian paintings and the prehistoric rock engravings of the desert regions of Egypt, and the similar men on the Dipylon vases? And what is the explanation of the enormously wide diffusion of the reversed spiral, which across time and space link Honan and Crete, Scandinavia and the Amazon? The attempt to interpret the symbolic value of these signs has given rise to many theories, often contradictory. As regards the spiral, it is still disputed whether, in the West, its originators were the peoples of the Aegean or of Central Europe; it implies a predilection for everything that suggests gyration; some have seen in it a stylisation of the waves of the sea, while others claim that it could also be the sign for the thunderbolt, which, it is true, the Cretans venerated; but how can it be so similar in Honan and in Crete? May it not, in both places, have passed from basket-work to pottery, as it can be seen to do in America? A series of them together gives the 'running-spiral' motif; is it not in fact analogous to the Greek-key pattern? In the two cases, is not the same form being interpreted curvilineally and rectilineally? The rectilinear style, which breaks down a form into sections, represents an analytical way of thought, while the curvilinear, which unites what is separate, arises from the spirit of synthesis. The two styles are found in their elementary state in Cuneiform writing: the point of the *calamis* traced angles or strokes in the soft clay, while the rounded, uncut end of the reed served to form circles and half-circles. In the language of the Babylonians geometrical emblems have an exact value which has been transmitted through the millennia, right down to our own times. The circle is perfect number, sky, and the symbol for the cosmos: it was to keep this universal meaning right up to the central plan churches of the Renaissance and the cupolas of our Parliament buildings. Its contrary, the square, is the earth, and serves to express every idea of limitation: it was to be the form given by the Romans to their camps, and in France the *pré-carré* is still the symbol for assured possession of a piece of territory. As for the staff, that symbol of unity, it has given us the sceptre, emblem of power exercised by one man, and its last metamorphosis is, in our days, the marshal's baton. All these archetypes, laid down in the collective psyche from the earliest times, are still alive, deep within us.

*Plates 11, 15*
*Plates 16–22*

## *Tool-maker*

It was from using tools that mankind learned logic. The need to make his activities more efficient by some material aid developed in primitive man the faculty of reasoning and gave rise to the idea of progress, urging him on to study the various materials (wood, carved stone, polished stone, metal, clay) and ceaselessly to improve not only their practical fitness but also the quality of the workmanship. Hence the 'will to art'.

*1 Egyptian Predynastic flint knife with ivory handle, 4th millennium* B.C.

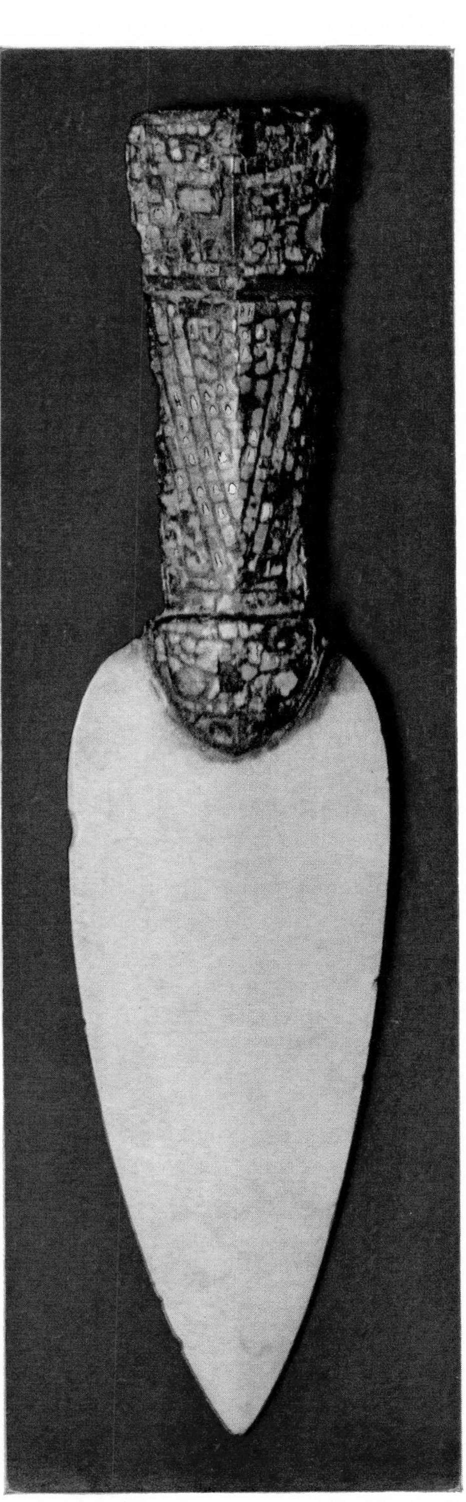

*2 Chinese Shang Dynasty spearhead, 13th–12th century* B.C.

*3 Mycenaean dagger with gold handle, c. 1500* B.C.

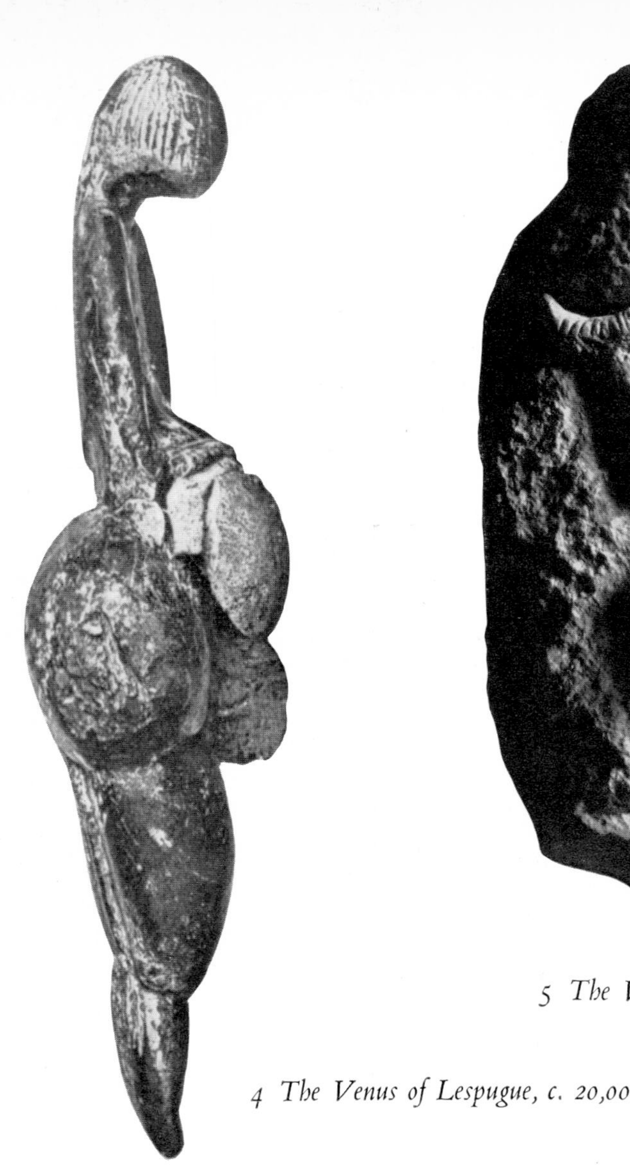

4 *The Venus of Lespugue, c. 20,000* B.C.

5 *The Venus of Laussel, c. 20,000* B.C.

# *The Two Paths*

From the beginnings of Man two paths are apparent, between which the evolution of forms has oscillated down to our own time: the naturalist image and the abstract image. Since many objects made of perishable materials have disappeared, it is not possible to say whether abstract art was derived from the representational by gradual stylisation, or the abstract sign was gradually clothed with life. Neolithic examples, as well as those of the present day, suggest that abstract art is parallel to the attitude of mind which seeks to capture the forces of the world by a positive conquest yet feels their hidden mystery.

6 *Prehistoric cave-painting, Lascaux, c. 20,000* B.C.

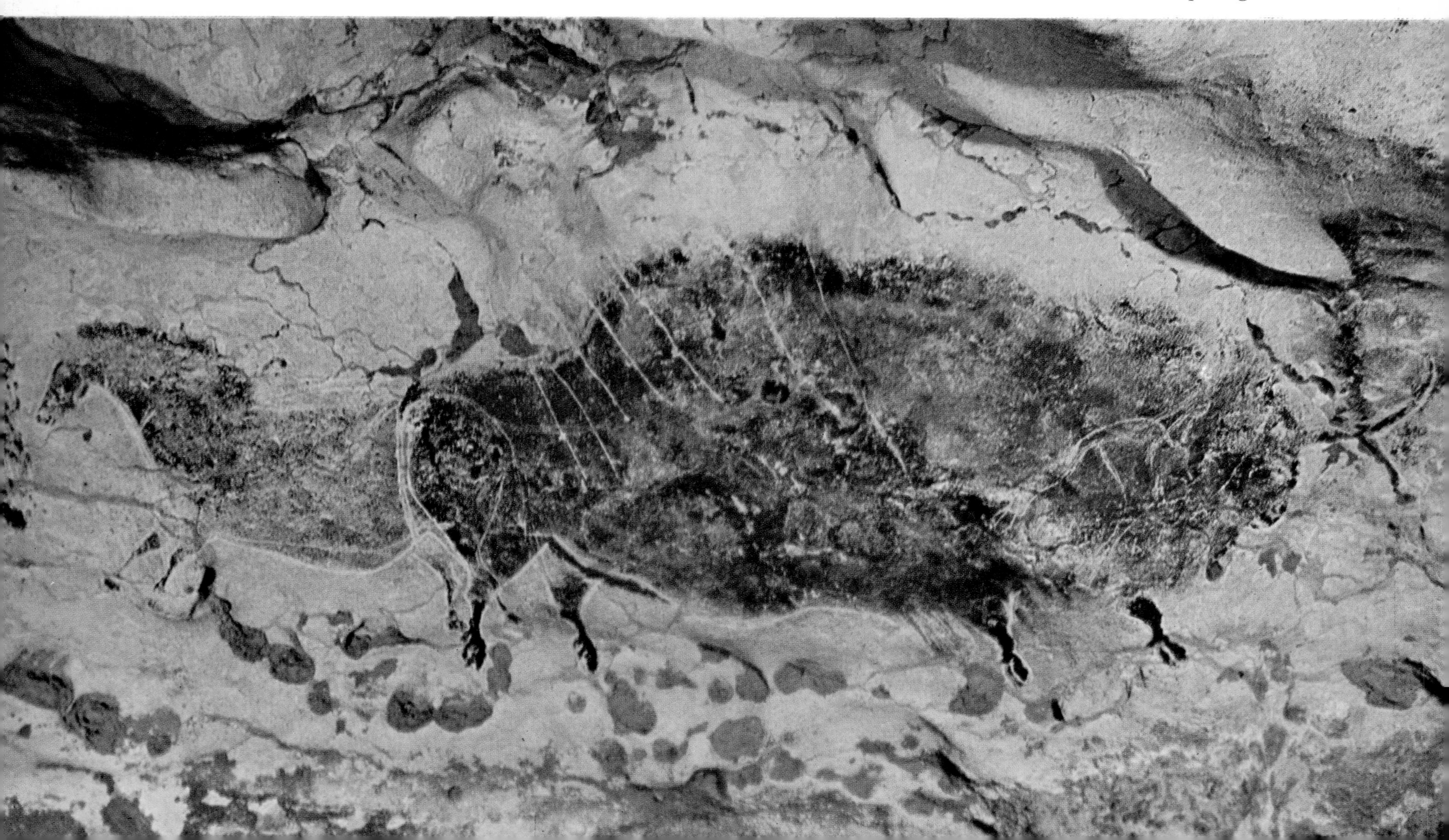

*8 Carved door-slab from Castelluccio tomb, 1900–1800* B.C.

*7 Cycladic idol from Pharos, c. 2000* B.C.

*9 Prehistoric rock-relief from Sers, Upper Palaeolithic*

*10 Etruscan bronze votive figure, 4th century* B.C.

# Rectilinear Style

The rectilinear and curvilinear styles imply two opposed but complementary attitudes: one tending towards a feeling for the discontinuous, the other towards continuity. The somewhat limited repertory of these two classes recurs with remarkable constancy all over the world: for instance—in the rectilinear style—the 'angular man' and the stiff zigzag, which indicate a predilection for rhythmic expression of a kind that suggests a spirit of logic—but also of aggressiveness.

11 *Cave-painting at Ghat, 1900–1800* B.C.

12 *Painted goblet from Susa, c. 3500* B.C.

13 *Arizonian bowl, c.* A

14 *Minoan gold double-axe, c.* 1500 B.C.

15 *Attic vase of terracotta, 8th century* B.C.

## *Curvilinear Style*

The spiral—whether its authors in the West were the Aegean peoples or certain peoples of Central Europe is still disputed—implies a predilection for whatever suggests gyration. Some have seen in it a stylisation of the waves of the sea, others maintain that it might also be the sign for the thunderbolt. It is one of the primordial forms, invented by many civilisations far apart in time and space.

*16 Carved lintel at New Grange, c. 2000* B.C.

*18 Belt-shrine from Moylough, Ireland, 8th century* A.D.

*17 Chinese Pan-Shan jar, 3rd millennium* B.C.

*19 The Stele of Vallstenarun, 8th century* A.D.

20 *Omalian pot, 4000–3500* B.C.

21 *Amazonian Ware pot*

22 *Minoan spouted* pithos, *1900–1700* B.C.

# *Idols from Clay*

In Neolithic times there was a clay civilisation—no less: the earth, which nourished Man, supplied also his gods. Idols were fashioned by successive additions of clay lumps, a method so simple that it was used all over the world by communities remote from one another in time and space. Decoration was done by incising or by applying more clay.

*'erracotta figurine from Mohenjo-daro,*
*-2000* B.C.

*24 Japanese clay figurine, 2nd–1st century* B.C.

*26 'Pretty lady' from the Valley of Mexico, c. 1500* B.C.

*27 Clay idol from Tlatilco, Mexico, c. 1500* B.C.

*28 Funerary figure of the Sao culture, Africa, 10th–16th century* A.D.

*25 Egyptian Predynastic statuette, 4th millennium* B.C.

*29 Female statuette from Susa, late 3rd millennium* B.C.

*30 Sumerian demon figure, 3rd millennium* B.C.

*31 Idol from Sāri Dêhri, India, 2nd millennium* B.C.

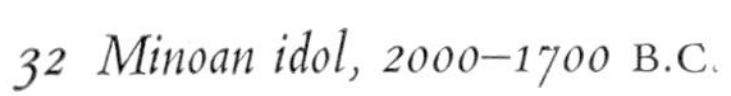

*32 Minoan idol, 2000–1700* B.C.

*33 Clay figurine from Mohenjo-daro, 2500–2000* B.C.

*34 Chinese late Neolithic pot, late 3rd millennium* B.C.

## *The Experiment of Pottery*

From the Neolithic period onwards, pottery was a particularly fruitful field for artistic experiment—the search for shapes and the search for decorations. These seem at first to have been derived from textiles and from basketwork, then to have taken flight independently, adapted themselves to their object, and finally become enriched with figures. Being light to transport, though fragile, pottery was from the first one of the chief exports and so a vehicle for the spread of forms from people to people.

*35 Large pot-beaker from the Netherlands, c. 1750* B.C.

*36 Storage jar from Malta, 1600–1500* B.C.

*37 Cypro-Phoenician bichrome jar, 8th century* B.C.

*38 Roman vase, Arezzo Ware, 3rd century* A.D.

*39 Cycladic vase from Lerna, 2000–1700* B.C.

*40 Greek black-figure vase, late 6th century* B.C.

*41 Minoan flask with octopuses, 1500–1450* B.C.

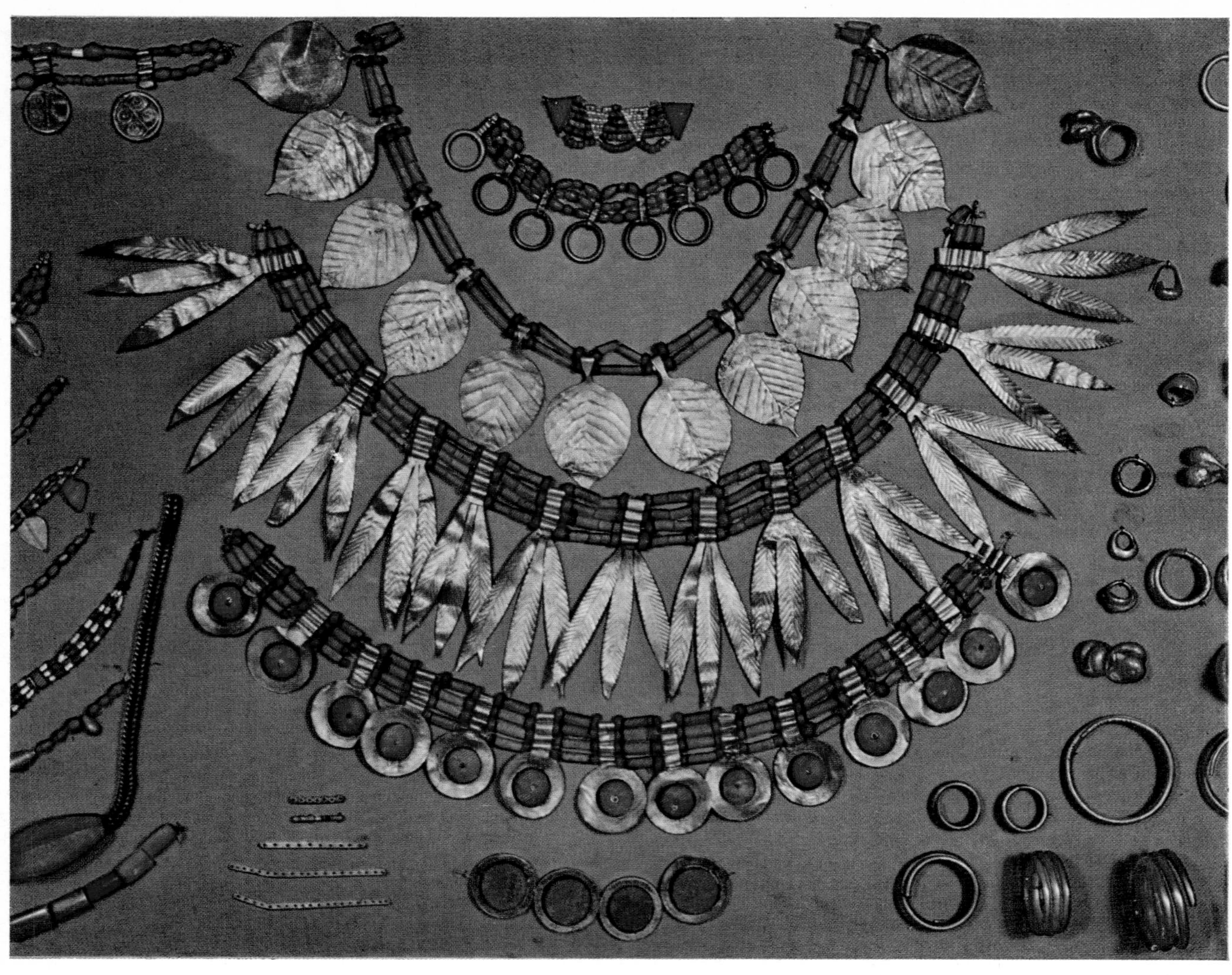

*42 Head-dress of a queen of Ur, c. 2500 B.C.*

*43 Quimbaya statuette from Columbia*

*44 Minoan treasure from Aegina, c. 1600 B.C.*

# *Symbol of the Eternal*

One material supplied by Nature must have fascinated the men of the earliest civilisations: gold. On the American continent, it was known to them even before the common metals, because there it could be picked up unworked. Gold, the incorruptible metal, was called upon to assure Man his passage into eternity. Those splendid forms discovered in the tombs by dazzled archaeologists were certainly made for the after-life more than for this life.

*46 The 'Ram caught in the thicket' from Ur, c. 2500* B.C.

*45 Mycenaean gold death-mask, 16th century* B.C.

*47 English Bronze Age gold ornamental belt plates, c. 1450* B.C.

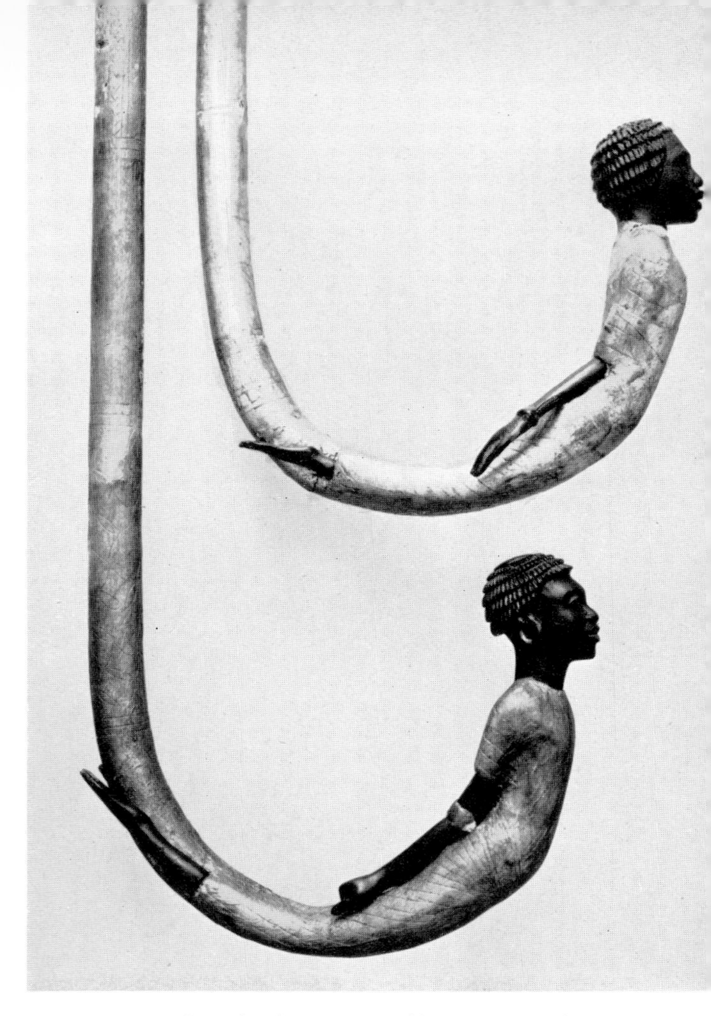

*49 Ceremonial sticks from Tut-ankh-amun's tomb, c. 1350* B.C.

*48 Egyptian wall-painting from Thebes, 19th Dynasty, 13th century* B.C.

*50 Relief of King Antiochus I from Nimrud-Dag, 280–260* B.C.

# *Faces from the Beyond*

For thousands of years to prepare one's tomb was the first object of life. A certain slowness in imagining any other world than the natural one is suggested by the fact that, for a long time, men saw the life beyond death merely as a prolongation of this life: hence the hecatombs of slaves, dogs, and horses, whose remains are evidence of cruel and grandiose funeral rites. At length belief in the virtue of the image made by his hands released Man from this blood-tax, paid to the dead man to ensure his survival.

51 *Chariot burials, China, 4th century* B.C.

52 *Gold lid over the mummy of Tut-ankh-amun, c.* 1350 B.C.

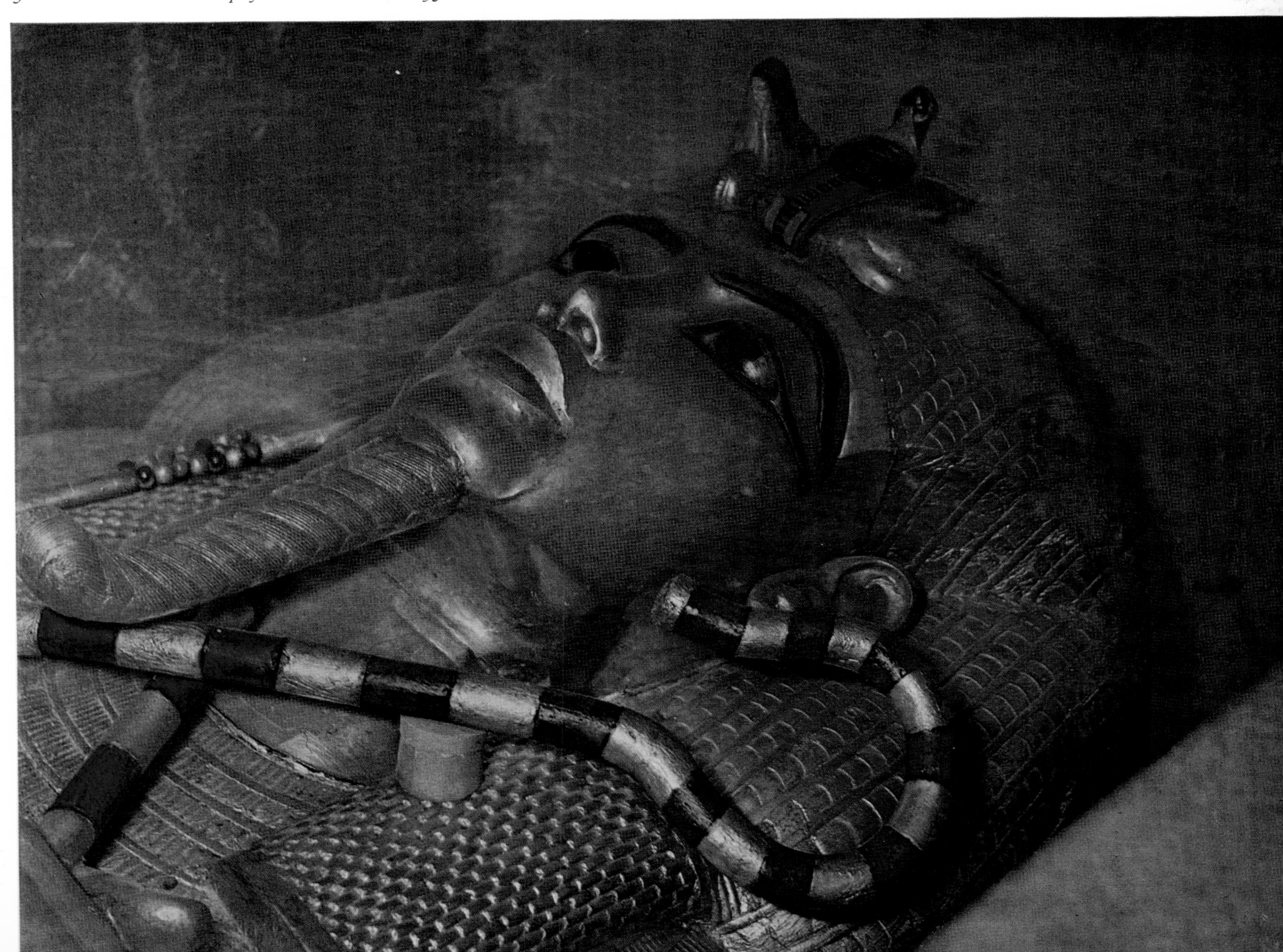

# The Royal Act

The memory of the time when animals were the only enemy has remained inscribed indelibly upon our customs. For ages the sign of power has been the conquest not of a man but of a beast, and a sovereign's royal act the killing of some animal, real or mythical.

*53 Carving from the Lion Gate at Malatya, c. 1000* B.C.

*54 Relief from the palace of Darius, Persepolis, 6th–5th century* B.C.

*55 Sassanid silver plate, 4th century* B.C.

*56 Medallion from the cup of King Chosroes II,* A.D. *590–628*

# NOTES ON THE ILLUSTRATIONS TO CHAPTER I

In the case of museums and galleries, where no photographer is mentioned, the photograph is the copyright of the institution concerned.

1 *Flint knife with ivory handle. Gebel el-Arak, near Denderah. Egyptian, Predynastic period. Musée du Louvre, Paris.*
*Photo: Maurice Chuzeville, Paris*

2 *Spear-head with jade blade and bronze socket inlaid with turquoise. Unprovenanced. Chinese, Shang Dynasty, 13th–12th century* B.C. *British Museum, London.*
*Photo: Eileen Tweedy*

3 *Dagger with gold handle engraved with spirals. The inlaid blade shows three leopards between rocks. From Routsi near Pylos. Mycenean, c. 1500* B.C. *Archaeological Museum, Heraklion.*
*Photo: Hirmer*

4 *Venus of Lespugue (Haut-Garonne). Upper Palaeolithic. Musée de l'Homme, Paris.*
*Photo: Pasquino*

5 *Venus of Laussel (Dordogne). Upper Palaeolithic. Private collection, Bordeaux.*
*Photo: Archives Photographiques, Paris*

6 *Cave-painting at Lascaux (Dordogne). This left wall of the 'nave' shows bison and mare, the former marked by seven engraved arrows. Upper Palaeolithic.*
*Photo: Peter Bellew.*

7 *Idol from Pharos, Cycladic Islands. Late 3rd millennium* B.C. *Musée du Louvre, Paris.*
*Photo: Christian Zervos, courtesy Editions Cahiers d'Art*

8 *Carved door-slab from the Castelluccio rock-cut tombs, Sicily. Early Bronze Age, 1900–1800* B.C. *National Archaeological Museum, Syracuse.*

9 *Rock relief from Sers (Charente), showing fighting goats. Upper Palaeolithic. Musée des Antiquités Nationales, St Germain-en-Laye.*

10 *Female votive figure. Bronze. Etruscan, 4th century* B.C. *Musée du Louvre, Paris.*
*Photo: Hürlimann*

11 *Cave-painting from Ghat, Fezzan. Neolithic.*
*Photo: Archives of the Frobenius-Institute, Frankfurt*

12 *Large painted goblet. Susa, Persia. Susa A style, c. 3500* B.C. *British Museum, London.*
*Photo: Edwin Smith*

13 *Black and white bowl. Arizonian Ware, Pueblo III, c.* A.D. *1400. British Museum, London.*
*Photo: Edwin Smith*

14 *Golden votive double-axe. Arkalochori, Crete. c. 1500* B.C. *Archaeological Museum, Heraklion.*
*Photo: Hirmer*

15 *Colossal vase of terracotta, showing the lying-in-state of the dead and funeral procession. Greek, Attic Geometric style, 8th century* B.C. *Metropolitan Museum of Art, New York.*

16 *Carved lintel of the Megalithic tomb of New Grange, Ireland, c. 2000* B.C.
*Photo: Bord Fáilte Eireann (Irish Tourist Board)*

17 *Jar with spiral design. Chinese, Neolithic, Pan-Shan culture, 3rd millennium* B.C. *Museum of Eastern Art, Oxford.*
*Photo: M. R. Dudley,* A.I.B.P., A.R.P.S.

18 *Detail of a belt-shrine, from Moylough, showing the buckle counter-plate. Irish, 8th century* A.D. *National Museum of Ireland, Dublin.*

19 *Stele of Vallstenarun. Viking, 8th century* A.D. *Statens Historiska Museum, Stockholm.*
*Photo: Antikvarisk Topografiska Arkivet, Stockholm*

20 *Omalian pot from Vaux-et-Borset (Liège). Neolithic, c. 4000–3500* B.C. *Royal Museum of Art and History, Brussels.*
*Photo: A.C.I. Brussels*

21 *Pot of Amazonian Ware. Redrawn from Heloisa Alberto Torres, 'Arte Indigena de Amazonia'.*

22 *Spouted* pithos *with three handles. Clay. From the Old Palace of Phaistos. Kamares style, Middle Minoan II, c. 2000–1700* B.C.
*Photo: Hirmer*

23 *Terracotta figurine with 'pannier' head-dress. Mohenjo-daro. Indus civilisation, 2500–2000* B.C. *National Museum of Pakistan, Karachi.*

24 *Clay figurine. Mamam, Japan. Late Jōmon period, 2nd–1st century* B.C. *T. Nakazawa Collection.*

25 *Mother and child. Clay statuette. Egyptian, Predynastic period, 4th millennium* B.C. *British Museum, London.*
*Photo: Edwin Smith*

26 *'Pretty lady' figure from the valley of Mexico. c. 1500* B.C. *British Museum, London.*

27 *Clay idol. Tlatilco, Mexico. c. 1500* B.C. *Museum of Archaeology and Ethnology, Cambridge.*

28 *Funerary figure. Terracotta. Africa, Sao culture, 10th–16th centuries* A.D. *Musée de l'Homme, Paris.*

29 *Female statue. Terracotta. Susa, late 3rd millennium* B.C. *Musée du Louvre, Paris.*
*Photo: Eileen Tweedy*

30 *Demon figure. Clay. Sumerian, 3rd millennium* B.C. *Musée du Louvre, Paris.*
*Photo: André Vigneau, courtesy Editions 'Tel'*

31 *Clay idol. Sāri Dêbri, India. 2nd millennium* B.C. *Boston Museum.*
*Photo: Courtesy Boston Museum of Fine Arts, Boston*

32 *Clay idol. Piskokephalo, Crete. Middle Minoan II, 2000–1700* B.C. *Archaeological Museum, Heraklion.*
*Photo: Hirmer*

33 *Clay figurine. Mohenjo-daro. 2nd millennium* B.C. *National Museum of Pakistan, Karachi.*

34 *Pot. Chinese, late 3rd millennium. Musée du Louvre, Paris.*
*Photo: Archives photographiques*

35 *Large pot-beaker. Stroërzand (Guelders). Late Neolithic, c. 1750* B.C. *State Museum of Antiquities, Leiden.*

36 *Large storage jar decorated with overlapping scales. Tarxien temples, Malta. 1600–1500* B.C. *National Museum, Valetta.*

37 *Cypro-Phoenician bichrome jar. Citium, Cyprus. 8th century* B.C. *Ashmolean Museum, Oxford.*
*Photo: Eileen Tweedy*

38 *Roman vase, Arezzo Ware. 3rd century* A.D. *British Museum, London.*

39 *Vase. Lerna. Middle Cycladic (2000–1700* B.C.*). Corinth Museum.*

40 *Black figure vase, showing Athene bearing arms. Greek, late 6th century* B.C. *British Museum, London.*

41 *Lentoid flask with octopuses, from Palaikastro, East Crete. Late Minoan I, c. 1500* B.C. *Archaeological Museum, Heraklion.*
*Photo: Josephine Powell*

42 *Head-dress of a queen of Ur and gold ornaments of Queen Schub-ad. Royal Cemetery, Ur. Assyrian, 3rd Dynasty of Ur, c. 2500* B.C. *British Museum, London.*

43 *Quimbaya statuette. Gold-copper alloy. Cauca Valley, Columbia, South America. British Museum, London.*
*Photo: Eileen Tweedy*

44 *Treasure found on the island of Aegina. Possibly of Minoan manufacture. British Museum, London.*
*Photo: Eileen Tweedy*

45 *Gold death-mask of a prince, called the Agamemnon mask. Mycenae. Shaft Grave 4, 1650* B.C. *National Museum, Athens.*
*Photo: Hirmer*

46 *'Ram caught in the thicket.' Polychrome figure on a wooden core. Ur, 3rd Dynasty, c. 2500* B.C. *British Museum, London.*

47 *Gold ornamental belt plates. Bronze Age tumulus burial of Bush Barrow, England, c. 1450* B.C. *British Museum, London.*
*Photo: Malcolm Murray*

48 *Wall-painting of the ante-room of Queen Nofretiti at Thebes. Egyptian, 19th Dynasty, 13th century* B.C.
*Photo: Hirmer*

49 *Gold heads of ceremonial sticks from Tut-ankh-amun's tomb. Egyptian, New Kingdom, 18th Dynasty, c. 1350* B.C. *Cairo Museum.*
*Photo: Griffiths Institute, Ashmolean Museum, Oxford*

50 *Stone relief, from the West Terrace at Deziosis (Nimrud-Dag), Iran, showing King Antiochus I (280–260* B.C.*) and Apollo Mithra. Seleucid.*
*Photo: F. K. Doerner and Theresa Goell*

51 *Chariot burials. Liu Li Ko, China. 4th century* B.C.
*Photo: Chinese People's Association for Cultural Relations with Foreign Countries*

52 *Pharaoh Tut-ankh-amun. The golden lid above the mummy of Tut-ankh-amun. Egyptian, New Kingdom, 18th Dynasty, c. 1350* B.C. *Cairo Museum.*
*Photo: George W. Allan*

53 *Carving from the Lion Gate at Malatya. Syro-Hittite period. Ankara Museum.*
*Photo: Josephine Powell*

54 *King fighting a lion. Bas-relief from the eastern gate of the palace of Darius, Persepolis.* In situ. *Achaemenian, 6th–5th century* B.C.
*Photo: Roger-Viollet, Paris*

55 *Sassanid silver plate. Shapur II (*A.D. *309–79). Freer Gallery of Art, Washington.*

56 *Central medallion of rock-crystal from the cup of the Sassanid King Chosroes II,* A.D. *590–628. Louvre, Cabinet des Medailles.*
*Photo: M. Rigal, Paris*

# II MAGIC WORLDS

*Chinese bronzes: Bird*

## II Magic Worlds

IN SPITE OF THE VICISSITUDES of history, the fall of empires, religious wars and the decline, of peoples into decadence, it can truly be said that the civilisation which blossomed in the Middle East in the fourth millennium has continued to our days, after having covered at its maximum the area which we have named the West. Its principle has been the pursuit of the external world, envisaged as an objective reality which human thought seeks to master by knowledge as well as by power.

In the process of conquering the rest of the inhabited world, the West, expanding beyond Europe, found itself at the end of the fifteenth century in contact with other civilisations, ruled by what modern ethnologists have called the 'primitive mentality'. In this the aim of mental activity is to introduce itself into a thought or mind conceived as universal, not so much in order to gain knowledge of it as to insert human life into that play of forces, to make them work to its advantage without allowing this connection to disturb the harmony of the world. The human soul feels itself one with the soul of the universe; life consists, for the human community, in letting oneself be carried along by the cosmic stream; and reason, whose first act is always to divide subject and object, is here not the master faculty. By a kind of divination, by directly seizing hold of the mystery, the soul can rejoin the primordial unity, centre of those beneficent or malevolent forces which man evokes, provokes or conjures with the aid of what for him is science—magic.

Only fifty years ago, before the present age in which objectivism, that invention of the West, conquered the whole world, the various civilisations which had remained apart from European influence displayed all the stages of that primitive mentality, from the elementary animism of the Polynesians and the negro tribes to the refinements of the Confucian religion. Some of these peoples had in fact managed to reach a high degree of culture, but their natural flourishing was stunted by the limitations set by the primitive mentality—which explains why some of them declined, like the Maya, well before the Spanish conquest, and why others, like the Chinese, were blocked in a long stagnation. Others, again, have perpetuated that state of mind in its most elementary forms down to our own times—but not for long now, to judge from the rapidity with which Africa, that last stronghold of magic, is surrendering to the principles of Western civilisation.

In this division of the world India, the West of the East, appears as a kind of intermediary or arbiter; for in the metaphysical field, its thinkers had arrived, by the exercise of intuition, at certain conclusions comparable to those produced by Western logic.

For those peoples, the gods are still incarnations of the energies dominating the world: they are demons—that is to say, blind forces—rather than gods. Such, certainly, was the Chinese

*Plates 57–62*

religion, at least in its official form which kept very close to popular superstition: a religion without a god, though peopled with gods and demons innumerable, to whom were added the spirits of the ancestors, all recognising one master only—that vague, almost amorphous entity, Heaven. Nowhere else, perhaps, has the mechanist character of a religion based on animism been so pronounced: the universe was thought of as a vast piece of clockwork, of which the Son of Heaven, the Emperor—and, by delegation, the priests and princes—were charged with keeping the wheels going by means of a ritual whose aim was to preserve the harmony of the world. Through the obscure religion of archaic China—of which we know almost nothing, yet can imagine a certain amount inductively because of the enormous conservatism of the Chinese—we catch glimpses of a humanity bound beneath the yoke of terror. In the ritual bronzes of the Shang and Chou periods the concept of the monster—that is to say the hybrid, which the Greeks so hated—attains a metaphysical status unknown in any other civilisation. On the sides of the *ih*, *lei*, and *chüeh*, the mask of the *t'ao t'ieh* burgeons in a hybrid proliferation of bear, ram, dragon and owl; as René Grousset has put it, the monster, 'diffused through matter and glimpsed in flashes only' manifests an 'omnipresence, always ready to resolve itself into terror', and 'two societies, bowed under a régime of blood, could see nothing, when they wished to plumb their destiny, but a mask of *t'ao t'ieh* threatening from the midst of the cloud'.

The history of China under the ferocious hegemony of the Ch'in can be summed up in the number of heads cut off: in 331 B.C., 80,000; in 318, 82,000; in 307, 60,000; in 293, 240,000; in 275, 40,000; in 274, 150,000; and finally, in 260, the record was reached—400,000 (and that after a promise to spare the lives of enemies). In those times when soldiers could only get their pay on producing heads, the leaders used to throw their enemies into cauldrons, drink the loathsome brew and compel the victims' relatives to drink it. A contempt for human life is, in fact, the characteristic of those primitive civilisations in which man, as an individual, is nothing—a mere piece of grit in the world's wheels, yet enough to upset the giant mechanism if he does not respect its laws. In those times the only measure of excellence was force, of which the clearest manifestation is cruelty.

Archaic Chinese bronzes of the Shang and Chou periods are explosions of symbols. The bellies of these vessels team and crawl with monsters which, not yet being differentiated in this pantheistic world, exchange their forms; geometric elements lie side by side like the broken coils or rings of some chopped-up reptile, and yet the arabesque creates no unity from these littered fragments: enwrapped in the jerky *lei-wen* (the sign for 'cloud and thunder') the *chüeh* extrude from that boiling world—fleetingly—stylised motifs drawn from the buffalo, or birds or from the ram, while from the turbulent curves the mask of the *t'ao t'ieh* stands out, sneering.

Specialists have tried to decipher this mysterious language, to make inventories of this monstrous bestiary, these memories of a cosmology in which, no doubt, the animal embodied the supernatural. The struggling forces of a cosmos in gestation have never been expressed with such power in so small a space by any people, unless by those of Central America—between whose carving and that of the Chinese there are analogies which have long been noticed by scholars and have given rise to various hypotheses. The human soul, in those lands of excess which make up much of Central America, is weighed down by the exuberance of Nature, and the grim struggle with the demoniac went on without respite. On this strange continent, which for so long pursued its solitary destiny in the history of the world, among peoples whom a brutal conquest threw suddenly from prehistory to the light of day, only to cast them at once back into nothingness, God was never visualised as anything but a demon. In no other territory does the sign of blood blaze so violently as in the American. The Sun, if he is to pursue his journey, must have his daily ration of human blood; Tlaloc, the god of rain, is no less exacting—the beneficent showers can only be attracted by the tears of sacrificed children. Nowhere else has sympathetic magic driven the

*Serpent*

*T'ao-t'ieh*

*Winged dragon*

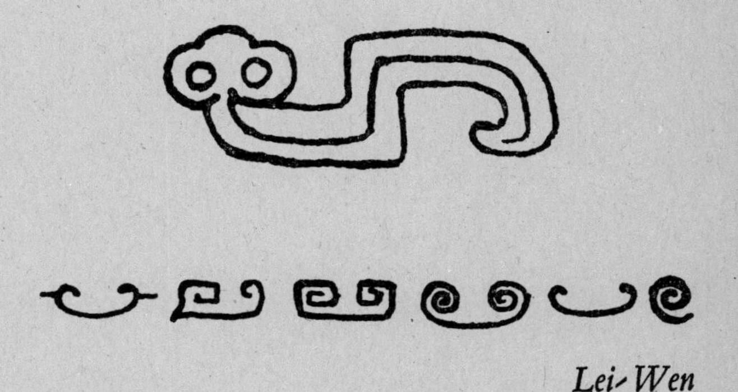

*Lei-Wen*

*The wild beast roaring is, together with the serpent, the dominating figure in pre-Columbian art (84, 86)*

priest to actions more horrible. Did not the maize harvest require that a man be flayed alive as a symbol of the threshing? Boys and girls were hurled into the *cenotes*. Violent death, either in battle or as a prisoner of war on the *latars* of the conqueror, was alone able to guarantee an after-life. The priests, swathed in the skin of the flayed victim, sprinkled the idols and sanctuaries with fresh blood, then hurled the palpitating remains down from the pyramids to an assembled people enjoying ecstatic communion by eating the dead.

*Plate 85*

Formally, the pre-Columbian works of art are made up of a composite agglomeration of fragmentary elements locked together without any continuity. The Mayan and Aztec system of writing gives us the key to this. Unlike Egyptian writing, which aligned pictographic and ideogrammatic signs in a rational succession, Mexican writing heaped the signs together in such a way as to form what amount to rebuses of images. Such writing was entirely characteristic of that primitive stage of thought which was first called 'pre-logical' and then 'paralogical': incapable of the operation of deduction, which breaks down into analyses and reconstructs into syntheses, the mind can apprehend the world only in a complex of appearances that are both successive and simultaneous. The introduction of a principle of continuity, of an orderly succession, into the chaos of phenomena belongs to a type of thought which, whether rational or intuitive, is capable of projecting intellectual lines of force into the discordant multiplicity of the world.

*Plates 30, 48*

All the gestures in an Egyptian low-relief are linked together by a continuous pattern; and Egyptian or Sumerian monsters are constructed out of elements chosen rationally—the motive for their assembling seems to be, in the one case, the search for architectural balance and, in the other, a law of innate form. But in an Aztec relief there is no linear continuity that one can follow: its unity is constantly being broken by sudden gaps, and it is a chaos of forms borrowed from different fields, with the death's-head grinning over it all. We know enough about Mexican thought to be sure that its world is a demoniac, heterogeneous and inorganic one in which change is not development but merely comes in obedience to abrupt mutations. It is easy to imagine the pessimism such a conception must have involved (indeed, the speech made over a Mexican child on its entry into the world was a recital of miseries); for optimism arises among men from the possibility of introducing order into the world, within a medium whose forces obey laws that govern a recurrence of phenomena.

The analogy—indeed it sometimes appears to be identity—between pre-Columbian carving and that of the Chinese ritual bronzes is one of the most mysterious problems of art history. Some people have looked for an ethnological or historical cause for this formal similarity, but the sites have been ransacked by treasure-seekers over too long a period with little profit to science, and our knowledge is still embryonic, so that the more prudent specialists have given up the attractive hypothesis of a 'shipwrecked junk', though not the hypothesis of a migration from Asia across the Behring Straits in the far-distant past. Not enough attention has been given to the fact that the works of art that present these formal affinities across so wide a spacial gap are separated also in date by several centuries. And yet is it not possible that similar conditions of life—aided perhaps by a remote ethnological connection—may have created effects that appear synchronous though they are widely separated in both time and space?

Carving of this demoniac character, pushed as far as it is in Shang and Aztec art, must, or so it seems, have come at the end rather than the beginning of a stylistic development. Although life was already, to the Maya peoples, something that had to be paid for at the price of blood, it is now known that they carried out those sacrifices with restraint and within the limits of what must have seemed strictly indispensable, whereas the Aztecs literally wallowed in orgies of blood, into which they dragged the conquered Mayan peoples. The demoniacal significance of the non-co-ordinated style of sculpture which we have described seems to be confirmed by the fact that in the art of the ancient Mayan Empire—which has sometimes been compared with Greek art—the

*On a Maya bas-relief one can trace the windings of a dancing arabesque that suggests some of those that occur in Romanesque art (85). In Aztec art this melodic line becomes broken up into sections*

various formal elements are unified by principles of order, and the work of art is governed by laws of rhythm, cadence and proportion. Earlier still, about 1500 B.C., the recently excavated productions of the so-called 'middle civilisations' of Central America, for instance the graceful and witty clay figurines of Tlatilco—show the smooth and calm forms characteristic of prehistoric civilisations—another confirmation that the appearance of the demoniac in human life is connected with the organisation of men in hierarchical groups with autocratic leaders and the organisation of war. The development of cruelty in response to a philosophy of 'might is right' may be a symptom of decadence, which later men would have to overcome, yet be unable to reject altogether.

*Plate 27*

Although from the Shang to the Ch'in period China appears to us to have been possessed by demoniac forces, the later work of the philosophers brought to it a humanism which was to temper, or rather to compensate, these instincts of violence—so far as this is possible in the extreme climate of Asia. Chinese thinking was able, in the shelter of Confucian conformity, maintained as this was by a shrewdly devised mechanical ritual, to evolve towards lofty metaphysical speculations, while exquisitely refined ways of life were elaborated, favourable to the growth of the arts. Yet this calming influence, due to the two philosophers Lao-Tse and Confucius (who are thought to have been contemporary and to have lived in the sixth or fifth century B.C.), was not immediately felt: the last echoes of the archaic fury found other expression in elegant and flamboyantly sinuous forms during the period of the Warring States and of the Ch'in Dynasty, and then, quite suddenly and without warning, there arose in the Han period (202 B.C.–A.D. 220) a realistic art. Our Western minds are so used to the logical evolution of forms (the best examples being Greek and Gothic art) that we cannot help assuming the existence of some vanished intermediary—perhaps in some perishable material—which would show this naturalism in its archaic stage. But such a rationalist way of thinking is our own and may not apply everywhere: in India too a naturalistic art seems to have arisen, fully formed and without warning, out of the unknown. When man reconciles himself to Nature, it always means that he is in harmony with himself: the naturalism of Han art corresponds to the achievement of the emperors of that dynasty in establishing order for the first time over the whole of Chinese territory. A joyful vitality animates the compact forms that stir across those incised or stamped plaques, although in their terracotta funerary statuettes the Chinese sculptors were already attempting that pure definition of volume in which they were to excel for centuries.

After the period of the Six Dynasties with its political fragmentation and the advent of Buddhist art with its spiritualising influence, the empire reconstituted by the T'ang Dynasty (A.D. 618–906) brought three centuries of artistic affluence, during which all the arts flourished, especially painting, which was to become, so to say, the 'major art' of China, and to give rise to aesthetic speculations on the part of the painter, to art criticism and to the collector's passion. In this the emperors shared, and some of them were not above actually practising the art. We possess treatises on painting that are earlier than the oldest surviving Chinese paintings: 3 date from before the T'ang Dynasty, 8 from that period or from the Six Dynasties, and there are 24 from the Sung, 10 from the Yuan, 58 from the Ming and 182 from the Tsing. The most famous of them, which codifies the principles of academic teaching, is the *Mustard-seed Garden Painting Manual.*

*Plates 75–78*

T'ang monumental sculpture in the round, with its smooth volumes and the grandeur of its simplifications, exhales a spirit of imperial power; but the funerary figurines done in terracotta by obscure craftsmen bear witness, with their fluent grace, to the importance women had acquired, alongside the warrior, in that advanced society.

*The chronology of these T'ang statuettes is hard to establish; but a certain summary definition of forms, reminding one of the abridged realism of Han art, must surely belong to works dating from the beginning of the Empire (64), while the coquetry, the mannered grace, of some of the figurines must indicate a later period (63)*

One might have expected Chinese art, having suddenly taken with such enthusiasm to the imitation of Nature, to find itself paralysed as regards its power to create pure forms; for this has happened in the West, where, in each period, art has submitted to the dominance of forces derived from the 'logistic' spirit which the men of our civilisation bring to everything they do. But, on the

*Compared with a Shang cauldron, a vase like that in plate 67 shows the fierce energy of the Chinese becoming restrained within the harmonious rhythms of a form that has been mastered. The sorcerer gives way to the artist*

*The beauty of the celadon ware continued until the Yuan epoch (66); then the material became opaque and regular and, no doubt through an excessive interest in finished execution leading to monotony, lost its mystery*

*The oldest paintings that have survived (77, 78) show, against a background of one colour, graceful figures that suggest the terracotta figurines from the tombs. Landscape and the study of animals developed in the Sung period, under the influence of philosophic speculations, especially of the Tao doctrine with its effort towards union with the energy diffused through the universe (75, 76)*

*A Sung statue like that in the Metropolitan Museum of Art (65) seems almost to have been designed to adorn some monument by Guimard or Van de Velde*

contrary, that was the moment when, thanks to the arts which we in our academic classification have called 'minor', the Chinese realised those amazing flights of imagination in the fields of form, material, colour and ornament which make the art lover who holds in his hands a Han jade or a Sung celadon feel that any other object is barbarous. Supported by men of letters, a refinement of all the senses—including that of touch, which has remained so coarse in the West—gave the craftsman that intuitive feeling for the absolute. This was the same quest for an essential unity that drove the Tao or Tch'an anchorites to look for the secret of reality in the simplicity of Nature. One Time contains all things. The speculations of the sages passed into the hands of the potters; they also, from the T'ang period onwards, animated the paintings, in which the forms of animals, plants, water, clouds, mountains and human beings seem to take their life from a single small drop of reality, fresh as dew and equally evanescent.

For nearly two millennia many different races had mingled in the Chinese crucible, to form valuable alloys; but to this process the Mongol invaders dealt a fatal blow: and yet, as always, the violent shock from outside crystallised the internal tendencies that were making for disruption. The very refinement of Sung art, so beneficial to both painting and the minor arts, led to a degeneration of sculpture into a mannerism strangely suggestive of Art Nouveau. Chinese art slowly debased itself, and the success it was destined to have in Europe precipitated this decline.

Into Asia, where the violence of Nature's forces had convinced men that they were born to a life of hopeless suffering, Buddhism brought the radiant face of compassion. The privilege of bestowing on the Far East the image of a divine man belonged to India, that land flowing with deities. To the peoples of this great region Sakyamuni carried the one hope that seemed permissible to them in their essential pessimism—that of a deliverance from life; but the Mahayana schism later transformed the original rigour of this doctrine of Stoic renunciation into a message of love, incarnate in the Bodhisattva who, touched with infinite pity for the suffering of living creatures, were represented as remaining suspended on the threshold of Nirvana, waiting, still in the cycle of rebirths, until all the world's living creatures should have been saved.

*Plates 68, 72*

Round about the beginning of the Christian era there appears, in the figures or figurines of the Buddhist monasteries and sanctuaries of Hadda and Gandhara at the cross-roads of the Orient and the classical world, a new expression: till that moment all that men had known of the divine was the fear of it; now they discovered saintliness. It was a radiant moment in history, one that seems suspended above periods and peoples. To engender it, to produce that complex blend of impenetrable divine aloofness with a redemptive love realised in compassion, the spirit of India and the genius of Greece had to meet. So powerful was the gift for art comprised in the Greek genius that, before its death, it laid down at the limits of the known world a ferment destined to give shape to mysticism, its very opposite. Then, upon the faces of the divine beings, there flowered that mysterious smile which was to propagate itself throughout the East: India, having created the spark to kindle it, would be the first to welcome it; and each people would give it a form of its own—sensual in Indochina, tender in Indonesia; but it was in China, in those caves of Lung-Men and Yun-Kang (plundered in our own time as though to make possible a fresh diffusion of Buddhism throughout the world) that it was destined to reach its greatest spiritual heights. The sweetness it poured forth was so beguiling that, to later generations, the meekness of the Boddhisattva appeared feminine, and Avalokiteçvara the Compassionate became metamorphosed into the goddess Kwan-Yin.

India abandoned the Buddhism it had created, to return to the more vitalistic Vedanta beliefs; nor did Buddhism go very deep with the Chinese, who assimilated it into their own philosophico-religious complex: paradoxically perhaps it was to find its firmest roots in the most remote parts of the Orient—the burning lands of Indochina and Indonesia, demon-ridden Tibet and the warlike empire of the Rising Sun.

The excessively 'artistic' spirit of the Japanese, in their island Land's End of the Far East, inclined them towards a formal perfection symbolising that of the soul, while their poor understanding of the things of the heart made them single out from the countenance of the Buddha not so much the gift of love as the sublime detachment—which indeed was not free from the pride that stiffened the race of the Samurai. Just because Japan owes its art to China, one can measure in this case how far a single morphological ancestry can engender radically divergent styles: the Japanese received the Chinese impulse without being prepared for its reception by a solid native tradition, and its forms, which they adopted, did not at the deepest level correspond to their temperament. The ease with which, later on, they assimilated the Western cult of objectivity provided them with a way out from what had been a misunderstanding—from a state of tension which had, however, produced much that was truly poetic. The most original expression of the Japanese spirit is unquestionably to be found in the portraits of feudal lords of the Kamakura period and in the cavalcades painted by the Tosa school, in which one sees, reborn for a moment, the same proud quality of line and modelling—the expression of a warrior temperament—that had already given life to the mysterious terracotta figures of the prehistoric period.

*The smile of compassion that lit the faces of Chinese Buddhist statues of the Wei and Sui periods hardens, in the Japanese Buddha of the 7th century (81), into an enigmatic expression conveying withdrawal*

*The 12th-century portraits seem cut out by a sword-blade (83). Conflagration, that symbol of violence gashes with its glare the paintings and the lacquer-work (82). The very sages have a frowning air (80)*

*The terracotta figurines of the Jōmon period, which have recently come to light, contain a premonition of the aggressiveness of that warlike race (79)*

*Plate 63*

Our knowledge of so-called primitive art is rendered very tentative by the fact that the first attempts at art by man have not come down to us, either because they were carried out in perishable materials, or even because they were essentially ephemeral. Masks and tattooing were perhaps the first stage in artistic creation: before he could believe in the magical efficacy of a figure made by his hands, man may well have thought of 'transfiguring' himself into one of those mythical beings which he would later embody in fetishes. More than any other artistic creations, these masks and costumes have lost their meaning, now that they are deconsecrated and turned into inert *objets d'art* in museums; for they were essentially bound up with another art, the dance, which must have been of paramount importance in the early days of humanity. There was a time, it seems certain, when the representative of a higher world, evoked by his double, could have real force only in movement and had therefore to borrow the movement of life. The first Sudanese to reveal to men from Western Europe the secret of African civilisation, the sage Ogotommête, used to say: 'The society of the masks is the whole world; and when it bursts out in some public place it dances the march of the world, it dances the system of the world.' It was only later, surely, that motionless images, painted or carved, were themselves thought of as able to round up the forces to be harnessed. The sight of the mechanism of the bodies of animals with which he was closely bound up by his hunting, and the co-ordination of his own movements with a view to more effective action, no doubt taught man the first of the arts—rhythm. The spectacle of growth everywhere must also have convinced him of the fundamental importance of movement in any magical act: William Fogg observed that certain curves in African sculpture correspond very closely to those known by mathematicians as exponential or logarithmic—the curves that govern various forces of growth in, for example, plants, shells and the horns of animals. A negro sculpture, in appearance a block of wood or a tree-trunk, may in fact be a battery of energy.

In Polynesia there is a single word, *Tahunga*, for the priest and the craftsman. To carve, to paint, and to procreate are synonymous. In the Marquesas Islands the artists, as they make their effigies, recite the Song of Creation, which deals with the history of their tools and materials, and at the same time carry out rites of purification and observe sexual taboos, thus surrounding themselves with a whole network of protective magic against maleficent influences.

But now that the objectivist civilisation conceived by the West has spread, under our eyes and in the course of this century, to all parts of the globe, these survivals of a society wholly regulated by a belief that the world of appearances and the beyond are one and the same are finally disappearing. The idea of artistic creation as such is essentially a Western one, and it is possible that in the near future, when man has moved still further away from the belief in magic, whose intense poetry he can still feel, these objects from Africa and Oceania, bearing witness to a dead world, will no longer, except to a few specialists, seem anything but childish stammerings, because they will no longer be more than a single dissociated element out of a whole composed of figures, gestures, instruments, dance and music—in a word, out of the *drama* which gives them their value.

The art of Oceania is its painting, and seems to derive from tattooing, in which some of the tribes of this region became *virtuosi*. The painter's instinct sometimes took over the tools of the sculptor for its satisfaction, carving the wood into perforated forms and engraving upon these the melodic labyrinths and spirals in which it delighted—and which it also used in the painting of the body. The energy of line and colour in this art sometimes suggests that of the Cretans. Is it inspired by the waves of the sea? Or, perhaps, by the impenetrable tangle of the virgin forest? Some artists in New Ireland and New Guinea have transposed into painted wood-carving the vital exuberance of a natural life that knows no seasonal pauses: in their swirling forms one can almost hear the strident cry of the bird whose flight streaks the shadow and the shafts of sunlight with its many-coloured flashes. And in fact, to some of these peoples the bird, the carrier of the soul, plays a primary part in their religious beliefs.

*Plates 93–97*

It is in Africa that the dance has been brought to its highest degree of expressive power, and the influence of the negro rhythm on contemporary music has certainly been even greater than that of the African fetishes on the Fauve and Cubist painters. The manner in which negro sculpture made its way into the aesthetics of the West has, no doubt, somewhat falsified our understanding of it: we have tried to see in it a geometrical organisation of forms, answering to a search for plastic order, when in fact its jagged lines and whirling volumes are much more closely related to the throbbing of the tom-tom and to the syncopations and melodic snatches of a music in which rhythm predominates over tune. Has not the study of races according to blood-groups shown us that the races of blood-group 'O', which are dominant in Oceania, are 'melodic', while the races of blood-group 'B', common in Africa, are 'rhythmic'?

*A comparison between a Melanesian mask (96) and a negro one (90) brings out the difference between the two civilisations: the one rose from the Beyond, the other from the depths of the forest. The negro fetish seems to have been hacked out in abrupt volumes and planes (91), while in the Polynesian statue the forms are springy and tend to unity (97). The two primordial styles, the rectilinear and the curvilinear, set these two regions of the world in opposition to each other*

There is still much to be learnt about the negro art which extends over the whole of Western Africa, and it resists the attempt to reduce it to unity. It seems that, in Africa as in Europe, there have been both a sophisticated art, elaborated by advanced political régimes, and a popular or tribal art confined to relatively small communities. Sophisticated or imperial art is beginning to emerge from excavations in Nigeria where the Nok, Ife, Gobba and Tada sculptures strew the centuries with evidence of so fine a plastic art in bronze that it has led some authorities to suggest a Greek influence, and renders the blossoming of the art of Benin less inexplicable. These sculptures do indeed seem related to the Mediterranean aesthetics of idealised naturalism, and we must turn to the fetishes of the tribal populations of Guinea, the Ivory Coast, the Congo and the Cameroons to find the 'primitivism' usually suggested to us by the phrase 'negro art'.

*Plate 92*

*Plate 89*

*Plate 91*

One of the most astonishing adventures in the epic of forms is that great movement which, starting somewhere in the depths of Asia, brought as far as the West the zoomorphic art practised by all the peoples who, for centuries, swept in all directions across the steppes from Mongolia to Podolia. To these nomads, these herdsmen and hunters, the animal which supplied them with almost all the elements of life was naturally the incarnation of Nature, the model to which they looked for the basic data of their art—an art applied to objects in metal serving for their own adornment or that of their chariots or their horses' harness. Sometimes they represented their model realistically; more often they interpreted it, creating an imaginary biology by combining several different species. Yet it is noteworthy that these composite creatures rarely have the monstrous, indeed terrifying, character they had among the Chinese: the Scythians, Sarmatians, Sacians, Sogdians and Ordos seem to have tried to express the vital energy of the chimaera, rather than its magic. In the course of their wide-ranging migrations they tapped the antithetical zoomorphic

*Plates 102–104*

blends of Mesopotamia and the hybrids of China, and brought elements of both to the West; but their originality lies in the biological interlacings which they created and in the virtuosity with which, taking advantage of the ductility of metal, their favourite material, they contrived to reduce the animal shape to ornament without losing the feeling of a living thing—thanks to the self-renewing curves and counter-curves that lead the expansive power of the form back upon itself; and in the continuity of these sinuous curves, so different from the spiked and jagged archaic Chinese monsters, one may see the remote beginnings of the *style flamboyant*.

*Plate 103*

Carried as far as the Baltic and the Atlantic by the barbarian migrations, this art split into two. On the one hand, the Visigoths, Germans and Franks made it more and more dry and stylised by mingling it with the abstract vocabulary derived from the theme of the circle (wheels, helices, roses, daisies, swastikas) which is to be seen on the oldest Sumerian seals. On the other hand, the Scandinavian peoples took up the spirit of the nomadic art and brought it to a kind of apotheosis. Through the Angles and Saxons it reached the British Isles, where it ended up in the illuminated manuscripts of the Northumbrian and Irish monks. Among the Vikings, a seafaring people with a horse cult, it inspired the decoration of their ships, and this—when they were converted to Christianity—survived in their earliest churches. Romanesque art inherited this world of forms seething up from the depths of Asia and gave it its ultimate and most monumental expression.

*Plate 105*

Moslem art delved, to some extent, into the same inspiration; or rather, the same current coming from the eternal Orient, eddied back upon Moslem art through other channels. But the resulting art was very different. Islam has never made its decision between symbol and representation. The old belief that the Koran forbade the representation of living creatures is erroneous. Had such a prohibition existed how many Moslems would have been sinners! In fact, throughout the great Moslem civilisation, which has embraced so many different peoples, the tendency to abstraction co-exists with figurative art just as in the West.

*Plates 98–101*

The remains of the eighth-century frescoes adorning the palace of the caliphs of Damascus at Qasr al-Amra, the paintings of the Abbassid harem at Samarra, the fourteenth-century paintings and the stucco reliefs in the Alhambra at Granada prove that there was a Moslem art of secular imagery comparable to that of the West. The ban on representing living creatures applies only to religious buildings: there it is strict. The great mosque of Damascus and the Dome of the Rock at Jerusalem, built by the Omayyad caliphs, display no animal or human creature: at Damascus the only life is vegetation, executed in mosaic and perhaps symbolising the ideal garden or Paradise promised to the believer. The frieze of the castle of Mschatta near Damascus illustrates perfectly this distinction between secular and religious art: various animals and monsters, and even a few small human beings, are to be found in the course of the frieze, but at the part of the façade where the mosque is they disappear and there are only flowers.

*The Persian miniature of the 13th and 14th centuries retains the spirit of those primitive paintings in which the human or animal form is dominant (101)*

At the same time these secular images must themselves be interpreted differently from those of the West. Islam's rare attempts at sculpture reveal a fundamental incapacity for thinking of form in three dimensions. A sort of timid swelling, an ineffective attempt to make the relief emerge from the surface, is all that these works display: whether their vocabulary was representational or not, the sculptors of Islam never created more than open-work screens—as it were, nets to catch fantasy and let reality escape. The famous frieze of Mschatta, though executed with the drill and in the form of an embroidery, retains all the supple, living rhythm that characterised the 'plastically' executed friezes of Palmyra and Baalbek; but in the hands of the decorative artists of Samarra or Cairo this work became dry and was reduced to the geometrical arabesque. This difficulty of conceiving the world in terms of relief may be partly a Semitic heritage, the consequence of visual habits acquired through nomadic life in limitless deserts, and partly due to a religious prohibition. Such explicit prohibitions as are to be found in the theological texts, relate precisely to figures

*The rare carvings in stucco from the Seljuk period show the artist's inability to capture in flight that elusive thing, relief (99)*

*Whether in Iran, in Egypt or in Spain, the pierced decorative work becomes in the end a kind of lattice, which lets only a disjointed image of reality filter through (100)*

casting a shadow, because these alone are considered capable of embodying reality—so that, in representing them, man's motive would be the insensate desire to compete with the Almighty.

Thus Islam's prejudice against the representation of living bodies is a *negative* result of the ancient belief in the magical power of the image. What is forbidden to Moslems is not the representation of figures, but naturalism. In Iran, where the strictly Arabic heritage was exposed to strong native traditions, the consumption of images was high, among the poets as well as among the miniature painters, painters on pottery and craftsmen in bronze; but the tendency to lyricism disembodied the images, and flowers, gazelles, tigers, hunters and princesses are—in the Persian miniatures, the most naturalistic of the Modern arts—creatures of dream. From the primitive beliefs in life as undivided the Moslems retained that poetic style which makes all things exchange their virtues: one poet compares a gazelle's wound to a red rose and, in another poem, the rose to the gazelle's blood; and the charm of Moslem art is its way of making creatures and things float in a dream-world where nothing is delimited and all takes place in an atmosphere of transience and impermanence. The Moslems admitted the real as a fiction only: not much inclined to linger over the world of the senses, and hostile to the evocation of the supra-sensible, they rejected illusionism and merely kept illusion.

*It is in the Persian carpets that the image-making impulse of the Ancient East secretly survives (98)*

# *Explosive Symbolism*

The archaic Chinese bronzes of the Chang and Chou periods are like explosions of symbols. The sides of the vessels that were used in the magic rituals of the early Chinese civilisations teem with monsters whose forms are interchangeable—indeed exchanged—in that still undifferentiated pantheistic world.

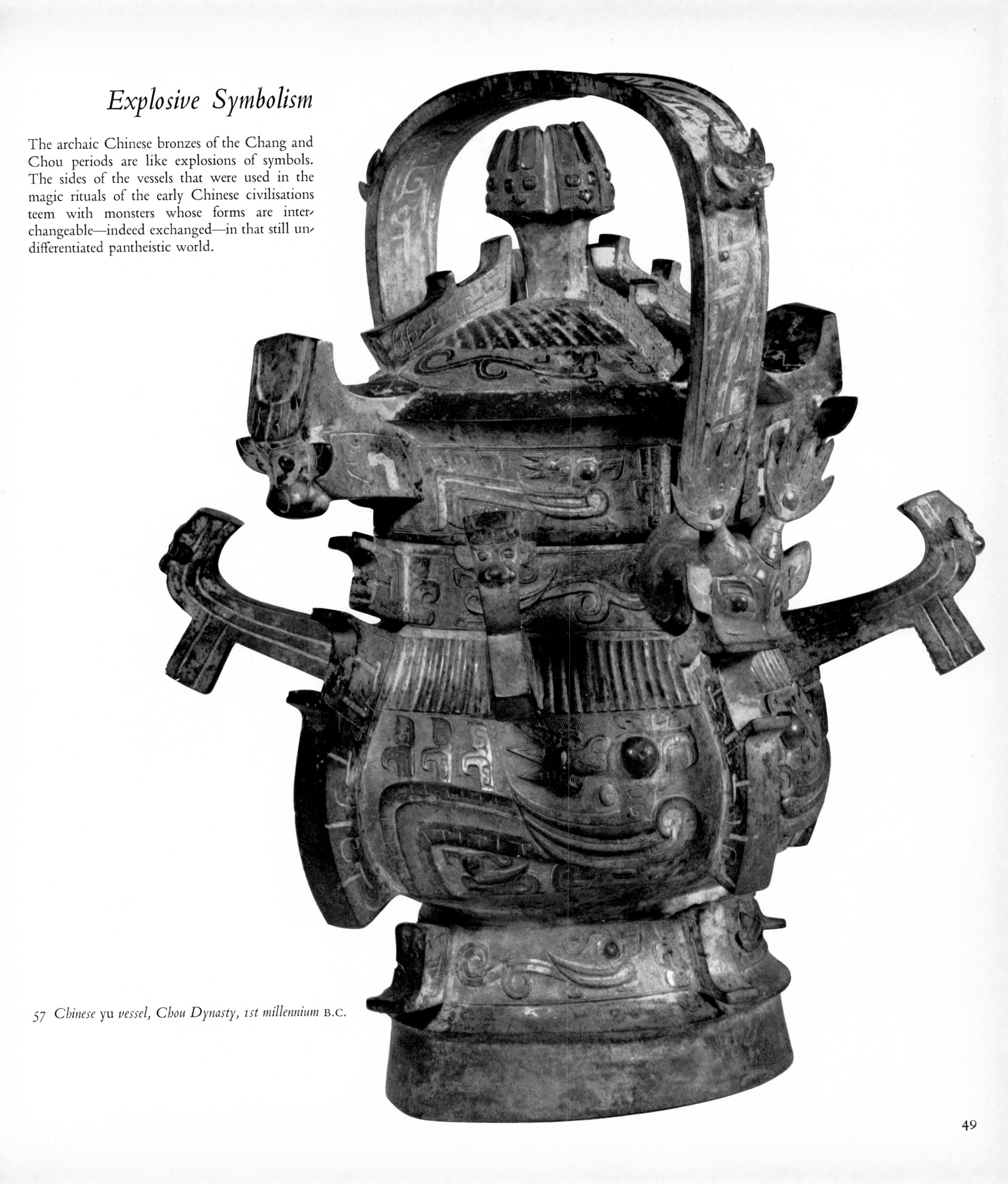

57 *Chinese* yu *vessel, Chou Dynasty, 1st millennium* B.C.

# *Magic Book of Beasts*

The monster-ridden Book of Beasts on the Chinese vases of the Chang and Chou periods takes us back to a cosmology in which, without question, the animal embodied the supernatural. No people has ever so powerfully expressed the conflicting forces of a cosmos in process of birth.

58 *Chinese* huo *vessel in the shape of an elephant, Chou Dynasty, 1st millennium* B.C.

61 *Chinese vessel in the shape of a tiger, Chou Dynasty, 1st millennium* B.C. ▶

60 *Chinese bronze finial, Chou Dynasty, 1st millennium* B.C.

59 *Chinese* fang tsun *vessel, Chou Dynasty, 1st millennium* B.C.

62 *Chinese bronze chariot fittings inlaid with gold and silver, 5th–4th century* B.C. ▶

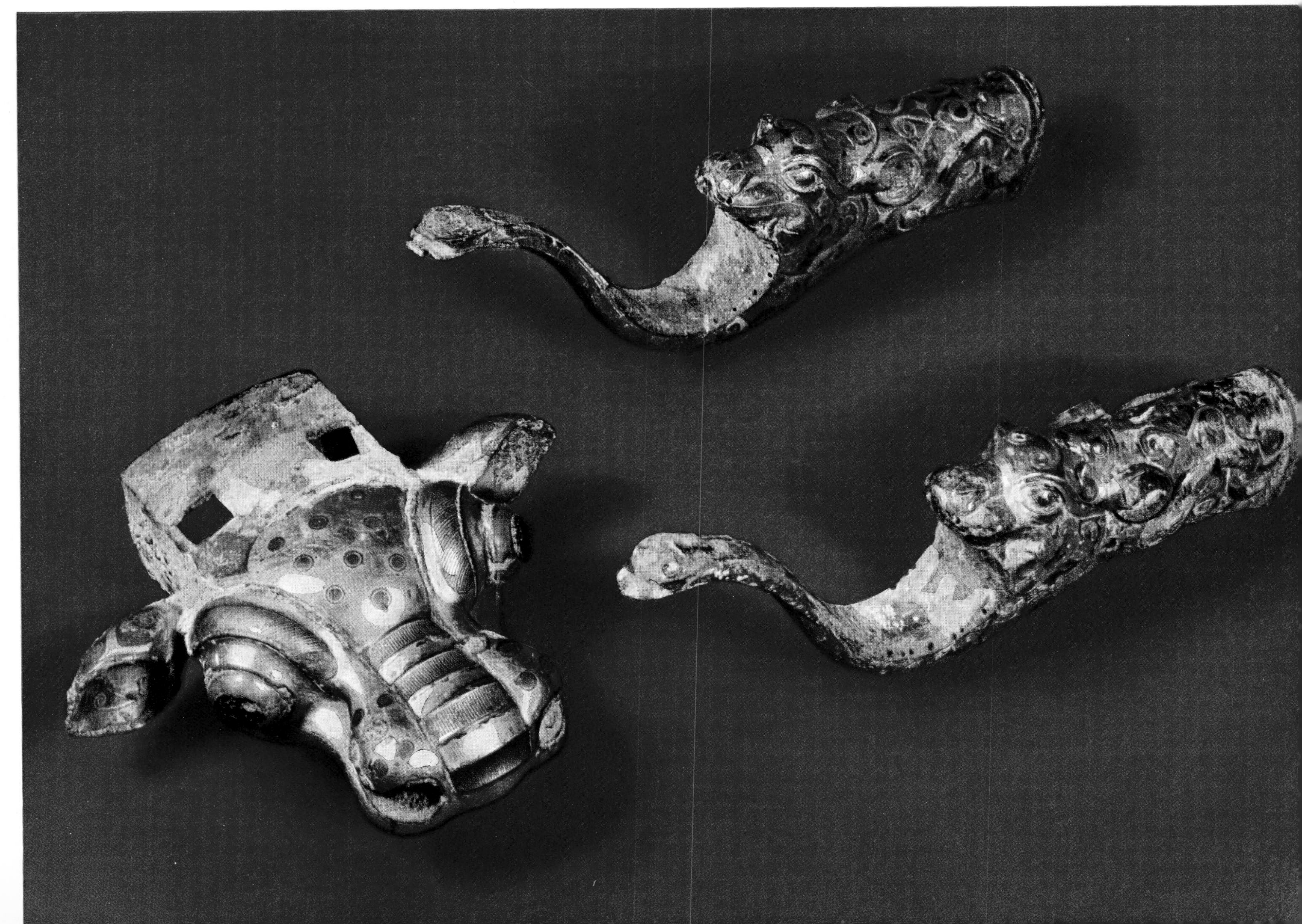

*63 The Lady at her Toilet, T'ang Dynasty, 7th–10th century* A.D.

*65 Chinese marble figure, Sung Dynasty, 10th–13th century* A.D.

*64 Chinese pottery figure, T'ang Dynasty, 7th–10th century* A.D.

# *Power and Refinement*

After prehistoric times the introduction of a humanistic philosophy tempered—or rather counterbalanced—in the Chinese their primitive instincts of violence. Supported by the stable power of the empires, Chinese thought elaborated exquisitely refined ways of living and forms from which art benefited. The astonishing speculations upon form, materials, colour and ornament embodied in works of art of the T'ang and Sung periods make the art-lover feel that all other objects are barbarous.

*67 Eumo painted vase*

*66 Yuan celadon vase*

68 *Genius with flowers, from Hadda. Hellenistic, 3rd–5th century* A.D.

69 *Birth of Buddha, Gandhara school, 2nd century* A.D.

70 *Maya's dream and the nativity, 2nd century* A.D.

71 *Siddhartha in meditation, 6th century* A.D.

# *The Face of Pity*

Into Asia, where the violence of natural forces had made men feel that they were born to a destiny of suffering without any remedy, Buddhism brought the radiance of mercy. To India, that land teeming with gods, belonged the privilege of giving to the East the divine man. Mahayana Buddhism (the Great Vehicle) with its doctrine of mercy gave rise, on the faces of the Bodhisattava of Hadda, Gandhara, the Indus Valley, and later of China in the Wei period, to the mysterious smile that expresses redemptive love flowing out in compassion.

*73 Buddhist wall-painting, Afghanistan, 5th century* A.D.

*72 Head of Buddha, Gandhara school, 3rd–4th century* A.D.

*74 Chinese relief showing Apsaras, 4th–6th century* A.D.

# Impermanence

Chinese men of letters cultivated a refinement of all the senses, including that of touch (which is so gross in the Western peoples), and this gave the Chinese craftsman his intuition of the absolute. The search for an essential unity, which drove the Taoist and Chan hermits to look for the secret of things in the simplicity of Nature, produced the paintings of the T'ang and Sung periods, in which the forms of the animals, plants, water, clouds, mountains, and men are given life by a mere droplet of reality, cool and evanescent as dew.

*75 Misty landscape. Painting on silk, Sung or Mi Fei Dynasty*

*77 Attributed to* KU K'AI CHIH: *Admonitions of the Instructress, 4th century* A.D. ▶

*76 Wild geese. Chinese, Sung Dynasty, 10th–13th century* A.D.

*78 Attributed to* CHOU WEN CHU: *Palace Ladies,* A.D. *907–60* ▶

人咸知脩其容莫知飾其性性之
不飾或愆禮正斧之藻之克念作
聖
出其言善千里應之苟違斯義
同衾以疑

## *Presence*

The Japanese are much closer to reality than the Chinese—though profoundly influenced by them. The most original expression of the Japanese spirit is to be found in the portraits of feudal lords of the Kamakura period and in the paintings of cavalcades of the Tosa school: in these the pride of line and modelling, expressive of a warlike temperament, which already animated the mysterious prehistoric figures, is for a moment reborn.

*79 Japanese clay figurine, Jomon period, 4th–3rd century* B.C.

*80* BUNSEI: *Portrait of Yuima, dated* A.D. *1457*

*81 Japanese wooden Miroku statue. Late Asuka period, mid 7th century* A.D.

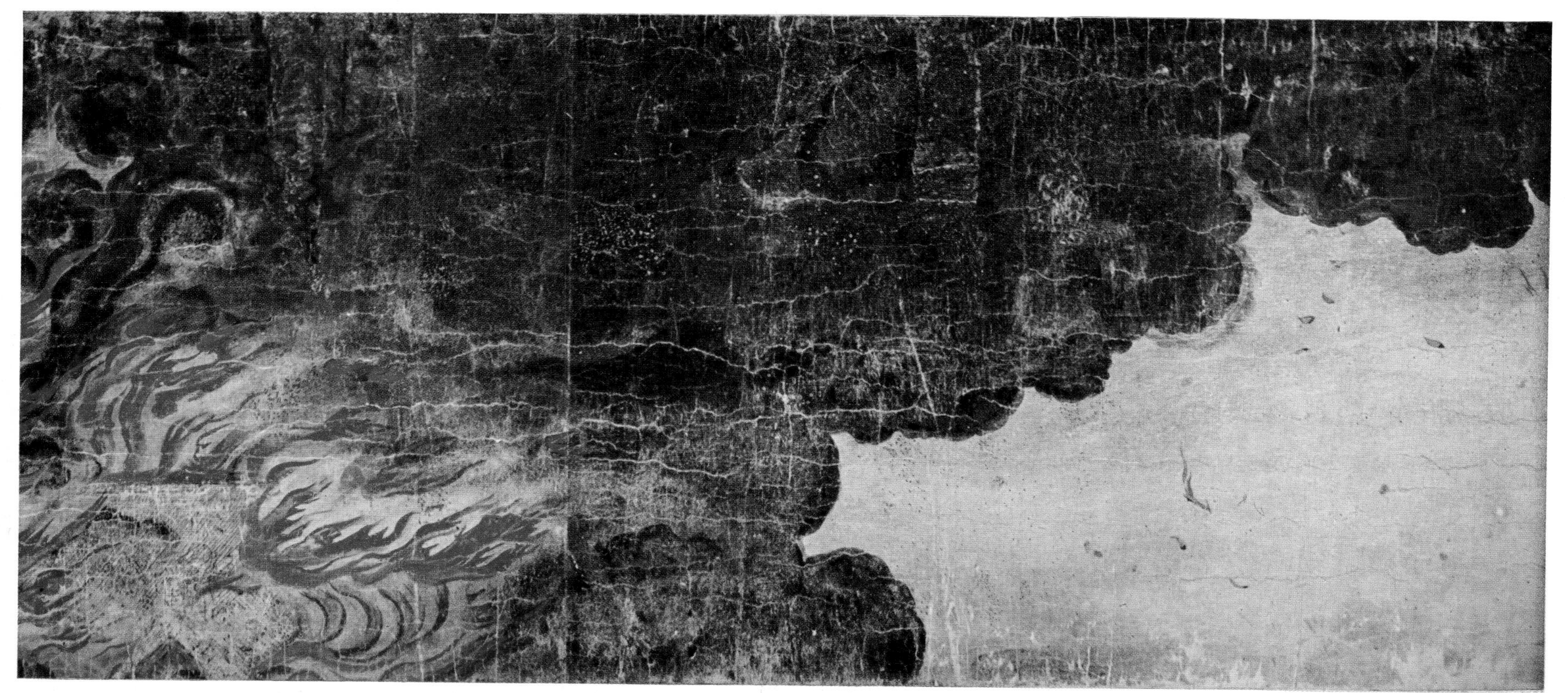

*82 Ben Dainagon scroll, Japanese, Late Heinan period, 12th century* A.D.

*83* FUJIWARA TAKANOBU (A.D. *1142–1205*): *Portrait of Shigemori* ▶

85 *Lintel from Menche, Maya culture, c.* A.D. *680*

84 *Peruvian jar, Mochica culture, c.* A.D. *500*

86 *Mexican jaguar mask, Olmec culture,* A.D. *500–1000*

## *Demoniac Powers*

In the extreme climates of Central America, where the souls of men are overwhelmed by the exuberance of Nature, the grandiose struggle between man and the demoniac knew no respite. God never appeared except with the face of a demon. Rhythmic discontinuity, resulting in a jerky and peremptory style, expressed a primitive way of thinking, to which reality was revealed only as a complex of simultaneous phenomena, with no principle of continuity or of succession projecting any intellectual lines of force into that discordant multiplicity.

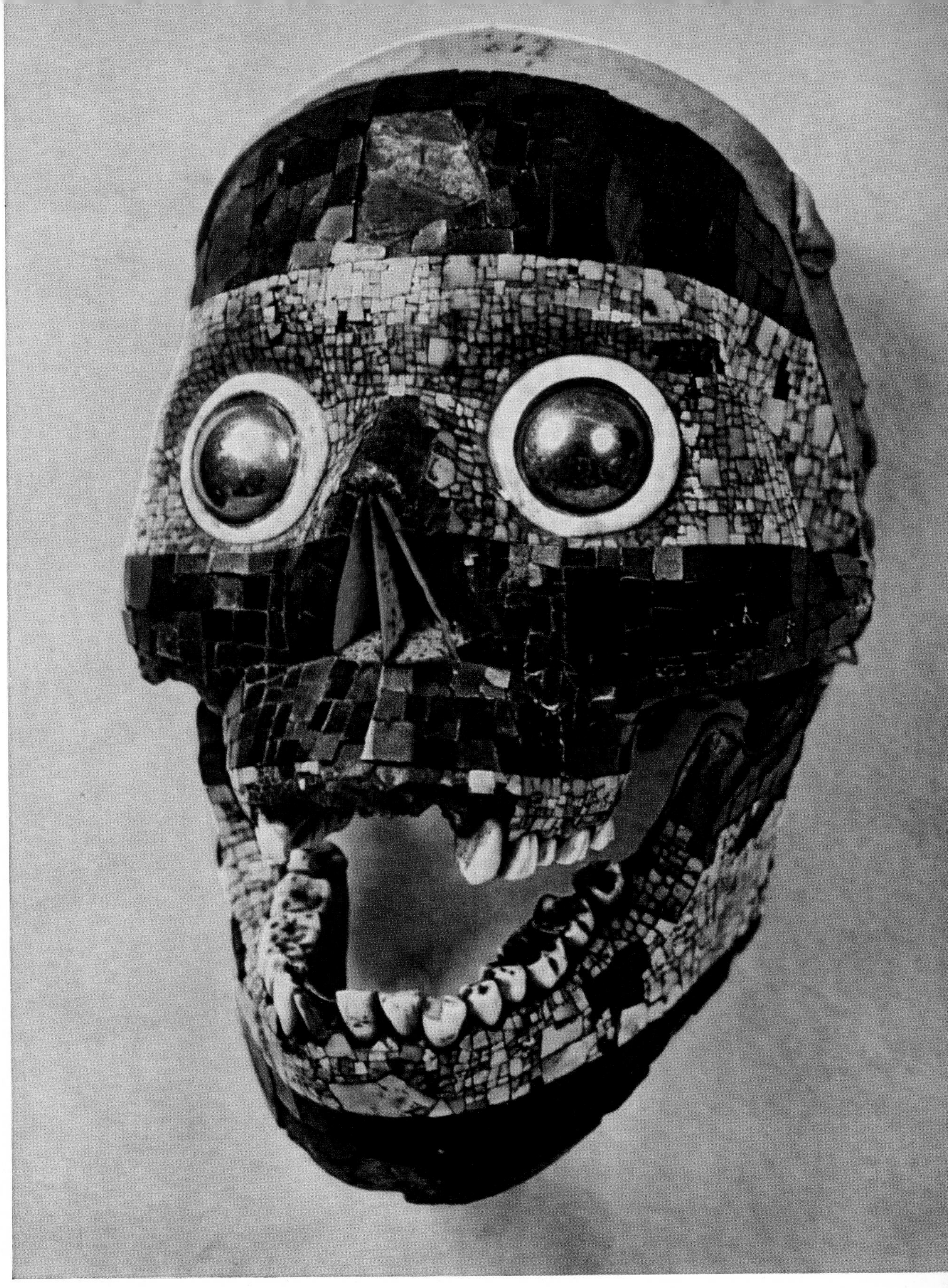

88 *Skull overlaid with turquoise and obsidian, Aztec culture, 14th–15th century* A.D.

87 *Toltec ruins at Tula, c.* A.D. 1000

# *Africa*

Two aspects of African art should be distinguished: one elaborated under some ancient empires, a sophisticated form whose remains are being brought to light by excavation; and a popular or tribal form which is more widespread. Negro sculpture seems to be a sort of accumulator of energies, condensing in its harsh and geometrical forms savage rhythms that find expression in the dances of those peoples, reminding us that the dance—with its correlative the mask—was surely the first of the arts.

*90 Wooden dance-mask, Dogon tribe, W. Africa*

*89 Leopard, ivory studded with copper. Benin culture, W. Africa, 18th–19th century* A.D.

*92 Woman's head, Ife culture, W. Africa, pre-13th century* A.D.

*91 Statue from Cameroon, W. Africa*

# Polynesia

The chief art of Oceania, its painting, seems to be derived from tattooing, in which certain peoples of that part of the world are virtuosi. The painter's instinct sometimes feels led to take up the carver's tools, cutting the wood into fretted forms upon which are engraved the melodic labyrinths and spirals that are also used to adorn the body: these express the vital exuberance of a vegetation whose fertility knows no seasonal pauses.

*93 Polynesian lintel*

*94 Sun-disk from New Guinea*

*95 Gable mask from New Guinea*

*96 Melanesian dance-mask from New Britain*

*97 Polynesian temple figure*

# *Between Sign and Image*

Islam has never made up its mind as between sign and image. In point of fact, in the great Moslem culture that groups together so many different peoples, the tendency towards abstraction coexists with representational art, as it does in the West. The rare Islamic attempts at sculpture in the round show a deep-seated inability to conceive three-dimensional form: the forms developed by Moslem art are simply nets to catch fantasy and let reality escape. Things and living beings float in a world of dream, where nothing is defined and everything becomes transient, impermanent.

*99 Iranian stucco head, Seljuk period, 12th–13th century* A.D.

*98 Silk animal rug, Persian, mid 16th century* A.D.

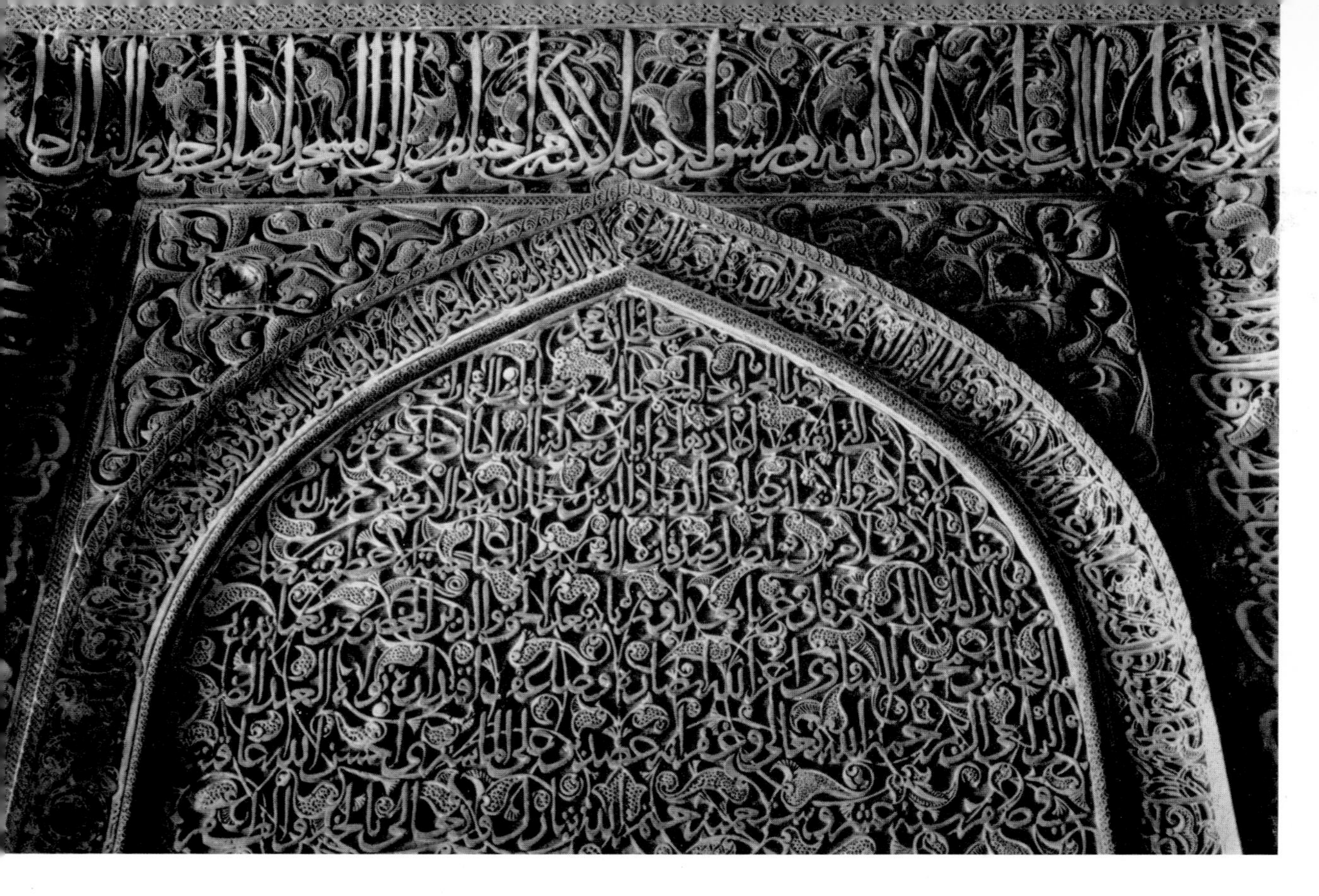

*100 The Mosque at Masjid-i-Jami, Isfahan. Detail of pulpit,* A.D. *1310*

*101 Jonah and the Whale, Persian, 14th century* A.D.

*102 Scytho-Greek gold brooch, 5th century* B.C.

# Zoomorphic Art

One of the most astonishing adventures in the epic of forms is that great movement which, starting in the depths of Asia, carried with it, as far as the West, the zoomorphic art practised by the whole group of peoples who for many centuries swept across the steppes in every direction from Mongolia to Podolia. It found its way, eventually, into the art of the Vikings and into Romanesque art. To these nomads, both shepherds and hunters, the incarnation of Nature was the animal, which supplied them with almost all the elements of life.

*103 Gold belt-buckle, Siberian, 4th century* B.C.

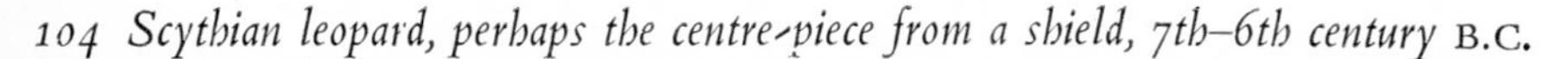

*104 Scythian leopard, perhaps the centre-piece from a shield, 7th–6th century* B.C.

*105 Figure-head from the Gokstadt Viking ship, 10th century* A.D.

# NOTES ON THE ILLUSTRATIONS TO CHAPTER II

57 *Bronze* yu *vessel. Chinese, Chou Dynasty. Freer Gallery of Art, Washington.*

58 *Bronze ceremonial covered vessel of the type* huo, *in the form of an elephant. Chinese, Early Chou Dynasty. Freer Gallery of Art, Washington.*

59 *Bronze ceremonial wine vessel of the type* fang tsun. *Chinese, Early Chou Dynasty. Freer Gallery of Art, Washington.*

60 *Bronze finial. Chinese, Chou Dynasty. British Museum, London.*
*Photo: Eileen Tweedy*

61 *Bronze vessel in the form of a tiger. Chinese, Chou Dynasty. Freer Gallery of Art, Washington.*

62 *Bronze chariot fittings inlaid with gold and silver, from a tomb at Chin Ts'un, near Loyang, Honan Province. Chinese, 5th–4th century* B.C. *British Museum, London.*
*Photo: Eileen Tweedy*

63 *The Lady at her Toilet. Statuette. Chinese, T'ang Dynasty. Signora P. Varzi Galliate Collection.*

64 *Pottery figure. Chinese, T'ang Dynasty. Museum of Fine Arts, Boston.*

65 *Marble figure. Chinese, Sung Dynasty. Metropolitan Museum of Art, New York.*

66 *Yuan celadon vase. Chinese,* A.D. *1279–1368. Fitzwilliam Museum, Cambridge.*
*Photo: Eileen Tweedy*

67 *Painted vase. Chinese, Six Dynasties period. British Museum, London.*

68 *Genius with flowers. Hadda. Hellenistic, 3rd–5th century* A.D. *Musée Guimet, Paris.*

69 *Birth of Buddha. Stone relief. Gandhara school, 2nd century* A.D. *Freer Gallery of Art, Washington.*

70 *Maya's dream and the nativity. Limestone relief. Ammaravatai, 2nd century* A.D. *British Museum, London.*

71 *Siddhartha in meditation. Stone relief. Lungman, 6th century* A.D. *Museum of Fine Arts, Boston.*

72 *Head of Buddha. Stone. Gandhara school, 3rd–4th century* A.D. *British Museum, London.*
*Photo: Edwin Smith*

73 *Buddhist wall-painting, on a vaulted roof in one of the monks' caves in the valley of Bamiam, Afghanistan. 5th century* A.D.
*Photo: Flinker and Klimburg*

74 *Apsaras holding bowl in right hand, flying right. Stone relief. T'ien Lung Shan Cave 2, northern Ch'i. Chinese, Six Dynasties, 4th–6th century* A.D. *Fogg Art Museum, Harvard University, Cambridge, Mass.*

75 *Misty landscape. Painting on silk panel. Chinese, Sung or Mi Fei Dynasty. Freer Gallery of Art, Washington.*

76 *Wild Geese. Detail of painting. Chinese, Sung Dynasty. British Museum, London.*

77 *Attributed to* KU K'AI CHIH: *Admonitions of the Instructress. 4th century* A.D. *British Museum, London.*
*Photo: Eileen Tweedy*

78 *Attributed to* CHOU WEN CHU: *Palace Ladies. Chinese,* A.D. *907–60. University Museum, Philadelphia.*

79 *Clay figurine. Yamanashi-ken, Central Japan. Jōmon period, 4th–3rd century* B.C. *National Museum, Tokyo.*

80 BUNSEI: *Portrait of Yuima. Ink on paper, dated* A.D. *1457. Yamato Bunkakan Museum, Nara.*

81 *Miroku statue. Wood. Japanese, Late Asuka period, middle of 7th century* A.D. *Koryu-ji, Kyoto.*

82 *Ban Dainagon scroll (detail). Ink on paper. Japanese, Late Heinan period, 12th century* A.D. *Mr Sakai Collection, Tokyo.*
*Photo: Anna Wachsmann.*

83 FUJIWARA TAKANOBU (A.D. 1142–1205): *Portrait of Shigemori. Silk. Japanese, Kamakura period. Jingo-ji, Kyoto.*
*Photo: Anna Wachsmann*

84 *Red and white jar. Peruvian, Mochica culture, c.* A.D. *500. Museum of Archaeology and Ethnology, Cambridge.*

85 *Lintel from the Ancient Maya ceremonial centre at Menche, Yaxchitan, Guatemala. c.* A.D *680. British Museum, London.*

86 *Jaguar mask. Mexican, Olmec culture,* A.D. *500–1000. Robert Woods Bliss Collection, Washington.*
*Photo: Gisele Freund, Paris*

*87 The Toltec ruins at Tula, Mexico. c.* A.D. *1000. Photo: Brehme, Mexico*

*88 Skull overlaid with turquoise and obsidian with eyes of iron pyrites. Mexican, Aztec period, between* A.D. *1342 and 1521. British Museum, London. Photo: Irmgard Groth-Kimball.*

*89 Leopard. Ivory studded with copper. African, Benin civilisation, 18th–19th century* A.D. *British Museum, London. Photo: Edwin Smith*

*90 Wooden dance-mask of the Dogon tribe, West Africa. British Museum, London. Photo: Eileen Tweedy*

*91 Statue from Cameroons, West Africa. Musée de l'Homme, Paris. Photo: E. Sougez, Paris*

*92 Woman's head. African, Ife, pre-13th century* A.D. *Ife Museum, Nigeria. Photo: Guillemot, Connaissance des Arts*

*93 Polynesian lintel. Museum für Völkekunde, Bâle. Photo: Hans Hinz*

*94 Wood carving representing a sun-disk. Lake Sentani, New Guinea. Museum für Völkerkunde, Bâle.*

*95 Gable mask. Wood. Middle Sepik area, New Guinea. Formerly in the collection of Hanns Krenz, Berlin.*

*96 Dance-mask from New Britain, Braining Group, Melanesia. Hamburg Museum.*

*97 Polynesian temple figure. British Museum, London.*

*98 Silk animal rug (detail). Pershian (Kasan), Safavid period, mid 16th century. Metropolitan Museum of Art, New York.*

*99 Stucco head. Iranian, Seljuk period, 12th–13th century* A.D. *Metropolitan Museum of Art, New York.*

*100 The Mosque at Masjid-i-Jami, Isfahan. Detail of the pulpit (Mihrab) by* ULJAITU, *1310. Persian. Photo: Courtauld Institute of Art, London*

*101 Jonah and the Whale. Tempera painting on paper. Persian, 14th century. Metropolitan Museum of Art, New York.*

*102 Scytho-Greek gold brooch. Unprovenanced. 5th century* B.C. *City Museum and Art Gallery, Birmingham.*

*103 A horse being attacked by a lion. One of a pair of cast gold belt-buckles from Peter the Great's Siberian collection. Sarmatian, c. 4th century* B.C. *Hermitage Museum, Leningrad.*

*104 Chased gold leopard, Kelermes in the Kuban, possibly the centre-piece from a round shield. Scythian, 7th–6th century* B.C. *Hermitage Museum, Leningrad.*

*105 Figure-head of a horse from the Gokstad Viking ship. Wood. Late Viking period, 10th century. Universitets Oldsaksamling, Oslo.*

# III THE GREEK MIRACLE

## III The Greek Miracle

THE MOST ASTONISHING THING about the Greek miracle is that it happened twice. The first time has a dawn freshness. Not so very long ago Crete, the birthplace of Zeus, was for archaeology little more than the largest island in the Aegean; but by now, rushing in to follow up the luck of Evans's trowel, the archaeologists have brought to light a whole world—one that gives us a new consciousness of the part played by the pre-Hellenic peoples in the common progress of the first millennia B.C. Before that, only the peoples of Egypt and Mesopotamia seemed to count: nowadays Crete, though apparently deriving much (in the religious field especially) from Mesopotamian civilisation, is usually given a very high place; for it seems to have been, during a thousand years, the great centre of expansion for civilisation in the Mediterranean, spreading the principles of human progress into all the islands of the Aegean and westwards too, even as far as the Iberian coasts. But Cretan civilisation is less accessible to us than those of Egypt and of Mesopotamia, because of the still disappointing results of the attempts to decipher the written texts.

What is there we do not know about Egypt? Have we not recently seen a judicial error committed by a tribunal on the banks of the Nile more than two thousand years ago end in a revision of the verdict because of fresh facts unearthed in recent excavations? As for Mesopotamia, we know a great deal, and would know much more if the thousands and thousands of bricks bearing inscriptions, which have been extracted from the *tells* and *tepes*, were not waiting in the archives of our museums until there are enough specialists in the world to read them. But of mysterious Crete our evidence is largely confined to inscriptionless objects. In this field archaeology does not so much assist history as create it; and it is marvellous to see these silent documents become so eloquent as a result of patient and cautious collation. Although there is not a single written document, we can recognise in Minoan civilisation a strong social structure comprising the three elements essential to a balanced economy: agriculture, industry (metal-working) and a commerce that, based on a powerful fleet, provided the products of farm and forge with markets and supplied the country with useful imports. We know next to nothing of the political organisation, but can guess that it already rested on the city state and that—or so it seems—there was never a centralising power in the island. That the Cretan spiritual life had an Asiatic origin is suggested by the inspiration which the Minoan artists found in the representation of the Great Mother, the goddess of fertility in her many metamorphoses as cosmos, moon, sun, stars, plants and animals.

All this would remain somewhat vague and even lifeless if we were unable to feel, in spite of the silence of history, what the spirit and mentality of these peoples were like; this is something that the work of art alone can yield up to us—not so much by its religious or symbolic content as by its strictly plastic quality, its very form. Minoan art, surviving in objects of relatively small dimensions (I prefer not to say, of 'minor art'), astounds and enchants us by a formal rightness, a balance between naturalist inspiration and urge to stylise, which make it truly pre-classic, free from the ideogrammatic schematisation of primitive art (still apparent in some Greek art), and therefore, even at the start, closer to Hellenic classicism at its height than to the 'archaic' phase which immediately preceded it. It was an art almost without evolution: for a whole millennium, as though absorbed in its own play, it always attained purity of volume and contour and musicality of rhythm without ever losing its life-giving contact with Nature; and it disappeared without experiencing a decline. This innate harmony reveals in the Minoan already the feeling of a secret correspondence between man and Nature—as Christian Zervos says: 'A consciousness of being, within the peripheral immensity, a central present from which his speculations, enquiries, anxieties, supratemporal desires and the infinity of his imagination radiate.'

*Plate 32*

This harmony between microcosm and macrocosm is perhaps happier than that achieved by the Hellenes, to which it was the prelude; for the balance it attains is a richer one than that of classicism, which was too soon tempted to enclose the world's infinity within the categories conceived by the intellect. Compared with the Egyptians and the Mesopotamians, the Minoans seem to have been people released from metaphysical terrors—and this although they had retained that close network of magical relations with the world within which primitive man had lived, no doubt having persuaded themselves that, through some right disposition of their souls, they had managed to make these relations propitious to the hedonistic *Weltanschauung* that was, in turn, to be the strength of the Greeks in their conquest of the spiritual values.

The absence of the demoniac from Minoan religion is surprising in a primitive people, if such they were. It is attested by the quality of the art itself, even more than by the extreme rarity of images of demons. As I pointed out above, the demoniac style is characterised by a discontinuous plastic handwriting that projects a chaotic cosmogony in broken, convulsive and almost seismic rhythms: it reveals a mentality unfitted to transcend the composite and attain composition, a mentality that confuses unity with agglomeration, the multiple with the heterogeneous, and finds in the arabesque—when the formal lineaments do succeed in joining up—a precarious harmony immediately threatened by the explosive force of the unruly powers which it contains. Nothing is more foreign than this to Minoan art which, before Hellenic art and without recourse to the chain of realist servitudes to be found in Egyptian art, was able to bind together all the diverse elements in a work, by subjecting it to the principles of balanced rhythm, cadence and order—so attaining without apparent effort, by a happy collaboration with Nature felt as beneficent, that reduction of the multiple to unity which the Greeks were only to realise by bending the world to reason.

*Plates 57, 58, 85*

*Plates 22, 41*

In the deep-seated harmony and youthful strength of an art that appears to us never to have been senile, we believe we catch a glimpse of the way of life of prehistoric humanity, in the most civilised form that it ever took, but at a moment when social structures that were still simple—and later only slightly differentiated—allowed men to enjoy a spontaneity, freedom and naturalness in their material and spiritual works which they later lost. Perhaps one of the most fruitful among the plethora of ideas suggested by Strzygowksi is his accusation that societies with a strongly marked political hierarchy stifle creative liberty—though he spoils the idea by giving it a purely geographical application, based on racial prejudice. Certainly political power, by forcing art into its service, obliges it to evolve in a closed cycle and produces academicism: the art of the New Kingdom in Egypt, that of Assyria, that of the Romans, that of the papacy of Urban VIII and that of the reign of Louis XIV would be enough to prove this; architecture benefits, but the arts which in precisely these periods are contemptuously called 'minor' can be seen to wither, for they are part of daily life and are the spontaneous expression of a people's gift of plastic creation. And what is one to say of the terrifying annihilation of all artistic culture produced by modern authoritarian régimes with their wide imposition of a lowest common denominator? It is quite remarkable how consistently the most creative cultures rest on a way of life that is judged anarchic by historians of power politics—one in which political power is contained in relatively small and often rival units: for example, the city state in pre-classical and classical Greece, the feudal fragmentation of the Middle Ages and the city states of Renaissance Italy. In other parts of the world, too, examples abound: China produced the highest spiritual values of its civilisation when broken up under the dynasties which preceded the vast T'ang Empire; the Aztec Empire impoverished the creative forces of Central America, academicising the vital art of the Maya cities; and the Inca Empire likewise sterilised the civilisations of the Andes.

Through the beauty of these Minoan forms one can feel a 'state of grace' in that people, which is at the source of the 'Greek miracle'. Great is the impatience of the historians to see inscriptions give up their secret and verify their hypotheses; but a poet may well dread such an unveiling of the Cretan mystery. Is there not, after all, a danger that the pragmatic evidence supplied by the epigraphists, in informing us of the great deeds of certain princes, would dim the creative freshness of a whole people still virgin of history? What need have we to know the annals of the Minoans when we possess their eternal message? The Minoan cities show traces of several catastrophes which ruined them: we prefer to impute these crimes to Nature and make the Plutonian forces responsible. What a Golden Age Christian Zervos (to whom we owe such a fine study of Cretan civilisation) offers us to dream of when he convinces us that 'this people seem never to have invaded a country, weapon in hand'. We may well fear that the first properly Cretan inscriptions to be deciphered will bring us the boastings of some hero proud of having plundered, set fire to and reduced to slavery the neighbouring city. Will the shadows which history brings with it tarnish one day the pure brightness of Minoan civilisation?

Crete, however, was not alone in the Aegean: all the little islands known as the Cyclades appear to us to have been, between 2600 and 1100, a garden flowering with the works of man. There have been civilisations of which history says nothing, but of which man had preserved a memory and the archaeologists have now unearthed many witnesses—for example the pre-Columbian and the Etruscan civilisations, of which our imagination, keen to receive the message of all men, can catch some glimpses. From the Minoan civilisation itself the suggestion of a powerful structure, based on many pieces of evidence that fit together, glimmers through the silence. The more clues we have about a mystery, even though they are not enough to solve it, the more attractive it becomes. But only initiates are allowed access to mysteries; and who can initiate us into the myths of the civilisation of the Cyclades? The finds are still too fragmentary: they have yielded merely a certain number of stone or terracotta vases and those idols which we feel to be fresh evidence for the cult of the Mother Goddess that spread over the whole Mediterranean before Hellenic times; a few drawings, besides, lead us to guess at the existence of a sun cult; and we can see that these men were seafarers. And that is all. The very nature of these objects makes them, in a way, defy analysis: our eye slides over their pure forms, thoroughbred curves, smooth surfaces and polished volumes without coming up against any flaw through which the scalpel of analysis can edge in; in this limpidity all escapes us; there is no confession of clumsiness left behind by the tool, no failure in the leap of the line or in the definition of the volume to give us information on the craftsman's intentions—so much so that even chronological classification is difficult. Hardly any development can be discerned in this collection of documents: must one believe that this civilisation attained these perfect forms at a stroke, and then perpetuated them through so many centuries?

*Plates 7, 39, 128*

What sort of archaeologists could they be who have not felt their hands trembling as they drew from the ground such superb objects? Certain Chinese artists of the great periods—later, though, than those of the Cyclades—were alone able, working in jade, to achieve such silent eloquence by the simple play of material, contour and volume. Is it even possible to use the word 'abstract' of an art in which long elaboration has not weakened the tremor of life it owes to the natural sources on which it draws? Surely the curve of the wine-vessels (*oinochoai*) known as 'duck-head vases' owes its generous firmness to the fact that it is inspired by a woman's bosom—a fact often made clear by the breasts showing below the neck or by a line indicating a necklace. Leaving aside the accidental and crossing the threshold of appearances, the artist pierces more deeply into Nature, even to the essence of things, in the region inhabited by those whom the Ancients—not without dread—called 'the Mothers'. As for the famous marble idols, these, always within the same cycle, present a diversity of forms that reveal in their creators a true taste for plastic speculation leading them to extract from the feminine body some of the finest arabesques and most beautifully moulded volumes to which it has ever inspired men. The freshness of their natural inspiration makes itself felt everywhere—in the faint undulation of a knee, in the first maturing of the breasts, in the curve of a leg—and yet the face never emerges from its hieratic significance to break the incantation of the absolute with an individual accent. It is when this inspiration verges on naturalism, as in the case of the flute-players and harpists, that these small statues suddenly lose their power as idols and seem to be emptied of their potential of truth.

*Plate 39*

*Plate 7*

The palace of Knossos, though affected by several earthquakes, suffered one catastrophe that was certainly due to human agency—its final ruin by fire in about 1425, of which stones and frescoes still bear the traces. Already in the course of the preceding century the greater abundance of weapons in the tombs gives us warning that, for the peaceful Minoan era, the end is at hand.

In the clash of arms prehistory debouches—if not into history, at least into the epic, that child of the marriage between history and myth. A new human type appears—the hero, the man who acquires his glory from bloodshed, pillage and burning. Many centuries later the echo of the great power politics of the Achaeans, as they forced their way across the Aegean to the coast of Asia Minor, was to inspire the Homeric poems, in which for the first time we see the human condition depicted side by side with that of the gods. The most precious of the victor's spoils is always the culture of the vanquished: from the Minoans the Myceneans borrowed ornamentation and imagery which they 'enriched' with scenes of war; but in the hands of the Mycenean potter the inspired arabesques and ripe curves of Cretan art dwindled into stylisation; the pure impulse of creative enthusiasm was stifled by the rough discipline of the camps; and the procession of olive-gatherers full-throatedly singing of their joy in life gave place to the dreary march rhythm of the columns of hoplites.

It is the fate of power to succumb to power, and in the twelfth century the Myceneans fell beneath the blows of other conquerors perhaps already supplied with iron weapons superior to their bronze ones—the Dorians. About their beginnings we know even less than about those of the Myceneans. With them Greece entered upon five centuries of what have been called 'the Greek Middle Ages', an obscure period swept by the ebb and flow of a whole series of peoples and of artistic forms between Asia and Greece, during which the future Greek art slowly ripened, its impulse beginning in the eighth century with the so-called 'Geometric' style. Three centuries of 'archaism' were required to recreate the 'miracle'. Strictly speaking this notion of archaism, invented by modern aesthetics, implies a tendency to move from an imperfect to a perfect state—implies therefore progress: in this sense it is really applicable only to the West and its original manifestation is in Greek art. In prehistory there is no 'archaism', any more than there is in Sumerian or Egyptian or Minoan art, or in that of the Indus Valley. The first civilisations experienced a sort of state of grace, in which they discovered a naïve naturalism or a spontaneous gift for abstraction: slow experiment with forms, in which naturalism emerges gradually from a stylisation that is an artistic as well as a spiritual restriction, appears with Greek art. To stylise

*Plate 45*

presupposes a preceding formal condition to which the action is applied. Whereas Minoan art seems to have been born spontaneously like a flower in the morning of a world, Greek art, feeling its way, borrowed forms from all sides and experimented with them: no doubt the lively analogy between the animal friezes on the pottery of the Rhodian school and the painting on some of the pottery of Susa or of Mohenjo-daro is due to the phenomenon of 'convergence', but how can one suppose that the same is true of the geometrical stylisation applied to the human form itself, which we find on the Dipylon vases and in the paintings of the Levant, Spain and Rhodesia? What vanished intermediary binds together these forms from such widely separated places, in which what would seem the more primitive may sometimes be chronologically later? The friezes of monstrous animals on vases of the Corinthian school confess quite openly their descent from Babylon: the Kouros type derives from Egyptian sculpture, and has not a Doric style been discovered on the banks of the Nile? A common denominator binds these disparate forms together—the impulse towards truth, the urge to break the magic circle that constricts thought, and the restraints that prevent the free blossoming of forms.

*Plates 11, 15*

*Plate 37*

*A classical work like the Apollo of Piombino (111), however elaborate, still allows something of its Egyptian ancestry to show through*

At no moment has this attitude, this turning towards a conquest of the world of the senses, been more marked than in the sixth century, the so-called archaic period. It was the moment when Heraclitus and the physicists were seeking the truth about the world in the data supplied by the senses, while the philosophers of the Eleatic school were establishing the system of reasoning which was to be the instrument of Greek thought, culminating in the balance for which the name of Socrates stands. '*Achille immobile à grands pas*'—Zeno's concept summed up in Valéry's immortal line—brought to the world that light of the mind which has never since then been extinguished, even in the darkest ages of theological fanaticism. The art of the sixth century expresses this hunger for the world, this passionate desire to conquer the human form and to experiment with the rendering of life in its spontaneity—and this not in the statues, which took a long time to break through the Egyptian rigidity, but in low-relief and, still more, in painting, which preceded the sculptured form by fifty years and was the pilot genre of Greek art (as sculpture was for that of the Italian Renaissance). The paintings are lost to us, but how great must their power have been for so much to have survived in the imitations made of them by artisans, by the potters of Attica! A wonderful appetite for life keeps all these human or animal forms in a whirl, sets Perseus scurrying away like a hare before the Gorgon (whatever heroic mythology may say), leads onward the Dionysiac throng, and makes Achilles and Ajax gasp as they bend over their game of dice. This permission given to man to enjoy his human condition, to be a man and one who thinks, just as naturally and with the same pure impulse as an animal is an animal—and yet with that shade of irony, that Homeric laughter which means that one is free to disbelieve if one wishes (just because one is a man and well aware that uncertainty balances on the tightrope between the thinking being and the object thought of)—all this intoxication dominated by reason and at last exercising itself in the freedom of the human spirit had already given life to the mocking smile of the Knossos 'Parisienne', to the arc made by the acrobat over the bull and to the joyous lads on the steatite vase from Hagia-Triada, going out to pick the olives as though on a jaunt (in a flash their roar of laughter tears apart two millennia of darkness). What a cataclysm it was that could extinguish this liberating laughter, so that so many centuries had to pass before it could flower again in the smile on the faces of the archaic Attic figures!

*At whatever point of the Mediterranean the archaic Greek art alighted, this smile blossomed: it was (so it seemed) an article of export, a message of Hellenic optimism. One example (113) is from Sicily. And although the smile itself vanished from sculpture in the 5th century, its graceful curves still give life to the elegant sinuosities of the Ionic order (114, 116) Unquestionably the finest expression of that Olympian balance is the bronze statue of Poseidon (106), which rose from the waters off Cape Artemision (Euboea) in the twenties of this century*

All the diverse elements that Hellas drew from recent or far older experiments culminated in the fifth century—in that balance of faculties in a living whole which is known as classicism. A rationalism belonging to a different time, not to that one, hides from us the true nature of that harmony: it was in the fifth century, not in the sixth, that intuition, sentiment and sensation made one with intellect in what may well be called a sovereign order. The Parthenon—of which it has been said that it was a Doric temple with an Ionic spirit—still remains its unsurpassable example:

'Agreement with the world and with the inner man, extraversion and introversion, here set forth the image of their harmony', says Gilberte Aigrisse, the author of a discerning study on Jungian lines, *Psychanalyse de la Grèce classique*. This time the artists came before the thinkers: on the east frieze, under the chisel of Pheidias, Athena welcomed Dionysos into the assembly of the gods, whereas it was in the next century that Plato introduced the soul's quest into Greek thought and that Aristotle himself, though strictly a physical scientist, tried to define the nature of man.

'Work done so quickly yet made to last so long, the beauty of the work that, when scarcely finished, already gave the feeling of the antique, a thing so fresh that, even in our time, it seems to date from only yesterday: such is the indefinable flower of youth that shines in it and retains through the centuries a pristine aspect. . . . In this work there seems to flow an ever-renewed breath, a soul that could never grow old.' That is what Plutarch thought of the Parthenon, and it still remains true, even after the explosion of the Turkish powder magazine, the Venetian bombardment, the spoliations by Lord Elgin and the orthopaedic restorations by the archaeologists. Because unity is based on the relation of the part to the whole, the whole remains implicit in every one of its fragments. So it is that, in the so-called Temple of Concord at Agrigento, the line of the flutings has remained impeccable even though the forces of the weather, spending their fury on the building for twenty-five centuries, have reduced the poor-quality limestone of which it is made almost to natural rock again: the mason executed the drums of the columns with such care that their rightness of proportion survives in the eroded form, and this stonework by man will never return to raw stone as long as a core of it is left to contain its soul.

*While painting seems to have been in advance of the other arts (to judge from that imitative art, the decoration of vases), there was a rigid parallelism between sculpture and architecture. The incised lines of the figures of the Parthenon frieze (108) answer to the rhythm of the fluted columns. The smooth and stylised figure of the Charioteer of Delphi (107) reminds one of Doric capitals*

*Plates 109, 110*

Classicism was elaborated under the city-state system, in those small democratic communities where the majority vote tamed men's minds into accepting measure, compromise and a sense of proportion. Then Alexander, conquering the world, changed Hellenic society, converting it to the idea of power based on force and so on lack of measure. His conquests brought the Greeks again into contact with that Asia which they had had to overcome in order to be themselves, threw open to them the great high places of an earlier Nature worship, built cities only to melt them together into States, mingling Greek and non-Greek peoples in a new fraternity and transferring from the free citizens to the prince not only government but the direction of the arts: as later with the caliphs, each dynasty had its royal workshops. The town grew larger in proportion to the power to which it was subjected, and the archaic and classical *polis*, which consisted of a large village grouped about a temple and a few public monuments, was transformed into the royal city complete with town-planning. The end of power is glory and its instrument is war: out of fourteen Seleucid kings ten died soldiering. The drama of death invaded monumental sculpture in the form of battles with giants or fights with barbarians, bringing in its wake the whole of life—sufferings, deformities, old age, but also the pleasures of the senses, youth, love and luxury (Hellenistic man was a man of passions, and his passion led to disordered action). Olympus came down again to the level of the hero, and the hero to the level of man; power sought embodiment in excess of physical strength and authority adopted that as its external form; Dionysos I (Soter) of Syria made the muscles of a pugilist a royal symbol.

*The frieze of the Pergamon altar is the most expressive surviving example of a battle-scene, with its explosion of passions let loose (120)*

*Hitherto the business of art was to honour the gods and heroes; but now it occupies itself with describing every kind of human misery—deformities (119) as well as vices (117)*

Meanwhile classical taste kept itself alive in the form of small objects—the intaglios carved in semi-precious stones, cameos, and the coins, which became an attribute of power.

*Plate 127*

The seal makes its appearance as early as the third millennium—cylinder-seals in Sumer, stamp-seals at Harappa. As a sign of ownership it was supposed to have an incantatory power, dooming the thief to the vengeance of some supernatural guardian. Later on, worn on the owner's finger, it was adorned with a motif designed to bring good fortune. Right down to the end of Antiquity the art of the intaglio continued to flourish; it flourished in Crete as early as the Middle Minoan period, and at Mallia workshops have been discovered, complete with stocks of raw materials, steatite, rock-crystal, bone, and objects at all stages of fabrication: here, too, by their art of including within so small a carved surface a form that is both vital and perfect, the Minoans anticipated the Greeks, and with them the animal, caught in its instinctive life and movement, replaces the Babylonian monster. From the fourth century onwards, in Greece and then in the Roman world, this art became so highly appreciated that the Roman collectors formed cabinets (*dactyliothecae*) comprising thousands of precious stones or carved stones. Caesar's was famous; and Verres, when he saw a ring of this sort on anyone's finger asked to have a look at it and did not return it: if he liked the impression on the wax of a letter which he received, he did not fail to have the seal given to him. This mania is easy to understand when one examines, in our museums, those delicate marvels in amethyst, calcedony, sardonyx or steatite, of which Gisela Richter has made so fine a study. The most famous artist in this medium was Dexamenos, a citizen of the isle of Chios in the fifth century. One is stupefied by the sovereign rhythm, faultless proportions and perfect definition of form in this miniature art, when one reflects that all these fine shades of relief were done in concave—that is, in reverse.

*Plate 128*

*The largest known Greek cameo is the so-called 'Tazza Farnese' which belonged to Lorenzo de' Medici: it is a dish, 20 cm. in diameter and 7.5 deep, cut from a sardonyx, with a Medusa's head on the reverse side and a mythological scene in the bowl. It dates from the 3rd or 2nd century* B.C. *(123). The largest Roman cameo, known as the 'Sainte-Chapelle Cameo', belongs to the Cabinet des Médailles in Paris: it is probably the work of Dioscorides, an engraver of gems who lived under Augustus and Tiberius (126)*

The art of minting is a closely related one. In it the Greeks will never be surpassed and nowadays enlargement enables us to appreciate the monumental quality which was included in that shut-in circular form which proved so favourable to the expression of classicism and was later to be used by the Renaissance artists in painting, sculpture and architecture. The finest, most classic forms were minted by Syracuse. Coins alone would suffice to trace the history of the styles of antiquity and even, through the portraits on them, of the men of the ancient world. Alexander and his successors gave a special impulse to this art by throwing into circulation through an abundant coinage the ingots accumulated by the Persian kings and the plate from the temple treasuries. Coins became the carrier of forms about the world: in the Hoggar there has been found a tomb of a queen containing a sheet of gold which bore the imprint of a coin of Constantine; and finds in South Africa have brought to light again Phoenician, Egyptian and Palestinian issues. A coin of Menander, dug up in Pembrokeshire along with one of Vespasian's, calls to the mind's eye some Graeco-Roman merchant whose trading took him from India to Great Britain; and coins from Northern India have been found in Scandinavia. Sometimes coins were a means of importing bullion and were melted down to be given a new imprint: thus the coinage of the Indian emperor Kusharra was made from *aurei*, and in the Goupta period Roman coinage gave its name to the Indian, the *denarius* becoming the *dinar*. Each period was now to have its international monetary standard emanating from the greatest financial power; the *stater* of Alexander was succeeded by the *daric* of the Persian Empire, then the Roman *aureus*, and in due course the Venetian *ducat*, the Florentine *florin*, the French *louis* and *napoleon*, and in our days the *dollar*. In the design of these coins the foreign peoples followed their instinct and indulged in considerable fantasy: out of the classicism of the Roman coins, the Gauls made those whirlwinds of signs which seem to enclose a volcano within a few centimetres; and as for the Byzantine coinage, the Scandinavians had only to carry on the principles of stylisation already to be found there. The art of coinage died with Antiquity: one has only to compare one of the formless Saxon coins of Edward the Confessor with a coin from Gaul to appreciate the decadence. Whatever people may think, this art was not reborn: it had a moment of renewed life in the medallion, with Pisanello, but these were larger pieces half-way to sculpture; this art of highly compressed form belonged to the ancient world, and only the Greeks were endowed with sufficient formal sense to make it blossom.

*Plate 136*

*Plate 129*

*Plates 130, 131*

*Plate 133*

*Plate 134*

A history of forms, in the strict sense, could almost leave out the Romans—at least if one did not count architecture: this is their chief contribution although this is obscured for us by the decadence of the sculpture that covers its remains. In spite of the number of ruins with which the world is dotted (even in Pondicherry a Roman town has been discovered), Roman architecture has come down to us so disfigured that an effort of imagination is required to restore its splendour

—a splendour nowhere less apparent than in Rome, that city trampled by the centuries, unless one admits the Papal art of the seventeenth century as a real renaissance of imperial Roman art. It is to Africa, to Leptis Magna, with the *frons scaenae* of the theatre of Sabratha, or to Asia Minor, to Petra, Palmyra and Baalbek that we must go to find the Roman style still almost intact—although there is something almost Greek about the spirit of the monuments in these two last towns, with their decoration closely bound up with structure. The principle of Roman architecture rests, in fact, on a separation between structure and decoration: the engineer presides over the composition of the volumes as a whole, which are realised in brick, and on to them the decorator claps a pseudo-architecture of marble or stucco. This principle of ornamentation stuck on to a brick building was foreign to the Greeks and derives from Asia: it was to be found in the Assyrian palaces, where low reliefs in gypsum clothed walls of clay, and in the Hittite palaces; it was used by the Parthians and Sassanids concurrently with the Romans; later it was continued by Byzantium, and tenaciously maintained by the Italy of the Middle Ages, and even of the Renaissance, to blossom afresh in sixteenth- and seventeenth-century Italy—while the Greek principle of ornamentation derived from structure and realised along with it was reborn in France (which, from the Romanesque period onwards, carried on its application rigorously until the eighteenth century). The 'noble lie' of ornamentation is the essence of Baroque architecture—of which the Romans were in fact the inventors (for the Hellenistic world seems to have known the Baroque style only in sculpture, and to have come near to Baroque architecture only by enlarging classical monuments—that is to say, by imposing a lack of measure upon something whose essential value was measure).

*Plate 151*

The planning and execution of public and private programmes, corresponding to a rational organisation of daily life, society, comfort, public education and politics and embracing that sense of grandeur and luxury which it was part of imperial policy to propagate, brought with it a magnificent development of architectural technique in the Roman world—all the more so since the liberalism of Rome took care, by fostering municipal and provincial authorities, to maintain (far more than the Hellenistic princes had done) a certain autonomy which made of the Empire a kind of federation of city states.

Greek art satisfies thought, Roman art daily life. In the figurative field, side by side with an official style derived from the Greek canons, now petrified in an academic solemnity, the narrative style of the triumphal bas-reliefs—and, even more, of painting, mosaic work and sculpture drawn into the service of private patrons—made of Roman art an art of expression or illustration, without precedent in Antiquity except in the far-off art of Egypt. But the Romans, conquerors and administrators of a world, despised art as a minor activity fit for artisans, even those Greek works which they collected with passion: the diatribes of Cicero on this point are well known, when he called works of art 'toys to amuse children' and to make slaves forget their servitude. Even Virgil admonished his countrymen thus: 'Romans, remember that you are the rulers of the world. Your arts are these: to maintain peace, to pardon the conquered and to overthrow the proud.' Really the Romans were only developing a germ present even in Greece, one that led, during the decadence of the ancient world, to the distinction between liberal arts and mechanical (or servile) arts. When he left behind him the civilisations based on magic, the artist, becoming laicised, lost his prestige to the philosopher, the poet and the rhetorician, and even to the grammarian. This set the final seal on the victory of the arts derived from writing over those that flow from the image.

*Roman art, in its official manifestations, continued Greek classicism, transposing it into formalism (147, 148); but at the same time, in order to reflect everyday life, it turned realistic and, in particular, took to portraiture. Whether it is the ruler of the world (146), a patrician of Pompeii (145), or a boxer (144) who is being represented, the human face expresses the same will to power, the same anxiety to dominate reality*

There is one civilisation, the Etruscan, which has proved much more important for the future of Western art than its place in the history of forms would lead one to expect. Etruscan art passed through several phases: from the fifth to the third century B.C. it was hardly more than a marginal derivative of Greek art, presenting the usual phenomenon of marginal areas lagging behind originative ones; in the fifth century it carried on archaic Greek styles, and it did not assimilate Attic classicism until the fourth and third centuries. Later, when it became part of provincial Roman culture, it degenerated into popular art, but this decline provides us with a living example of genesis of neo-primitivism—that is to say, of a regressive primitivism born of a developed style. In dying, indeed, Etruscan art bequeathed to Rome a certain inclination towards realism, reinforcing that of the Latins: portraiture, that essentially Roman genre was the result. But the artistic destiny of that mysterious people did not stop there. Excavated Etruscan vases and statues gave the Florentines of the fifteenth century the feeling of a kind of ancient Tuscan fatherland distinct from the Roman fatherland. Their artists may have drawn their inspiration from the actual works, but it seems rather as if there was a spontaneous renaissance of the Etruscan spirit in the style of the second phase of fifteenth-century Florence, when the task of conveying form was left to the outline alone so that the artists were led to galvanise line to an almost neurotic energy. The paintings of Pollaiuolo suggest those of Tarquinia and such carvings as the astonishing dancing Satyr on a funerary urn from Orvieto; and who can miss the Boticellian grace in the Hermes of Veii?

*Plates 142, 143*
*Plates 138, 139*
*Plate 137*
*Plate 140*

Those works which are born from a soil and then buried deep in it form a seed-bed for later crops. The artistic produce that had grown on the lands of the antique world was to render fruitful the harvests of the future, at least in all the territories preserved from the devastating action of Islam—that is to say, in most of Western Europe and, until the fall of Constantinople, in the Byzantine Empire.

## *The Olympian*

With the 'Greek miracle', art emerges into the sunlight; Greek men and gods, Greek thought and the Greek idea of beauty are suddenly accessible to us where those of previous cultures remain dark and hidden. Poseidon still expresses majesty in human form. Apollo, the male principle, shines forth from the sturdiness and strength of the Doric order, while all the grace of Aphrodite seems contained in the delicate volutes of the Ionic.

*106 Poseidon, Greek, c. 450* B.C.

# *Doric – the Imperishable Form*

All the experience of Hellas, whether recent or immemorial, converged in the fifth century B.C. into that balance of faculties within a living whole which is called Classicism. Intention, emotion, and sensation became one with intellect in a sovereign order. The formal perfection still radiates even from mutilated or eroded forms: the perfect proportions of this stone worked by man, whether a temple or an image, will survive as long as there remains a kernel to contain its essence.

*107 Charioteer of Delphi, c. 470* B.C.

*108 Female figure from the Parthenon frieze,* ▶ *446–432* B.C.

*109 Temple of Concord, Agrigento, Sicily, 450* B.C.

*110 Part of a column from the Temple of Concord*

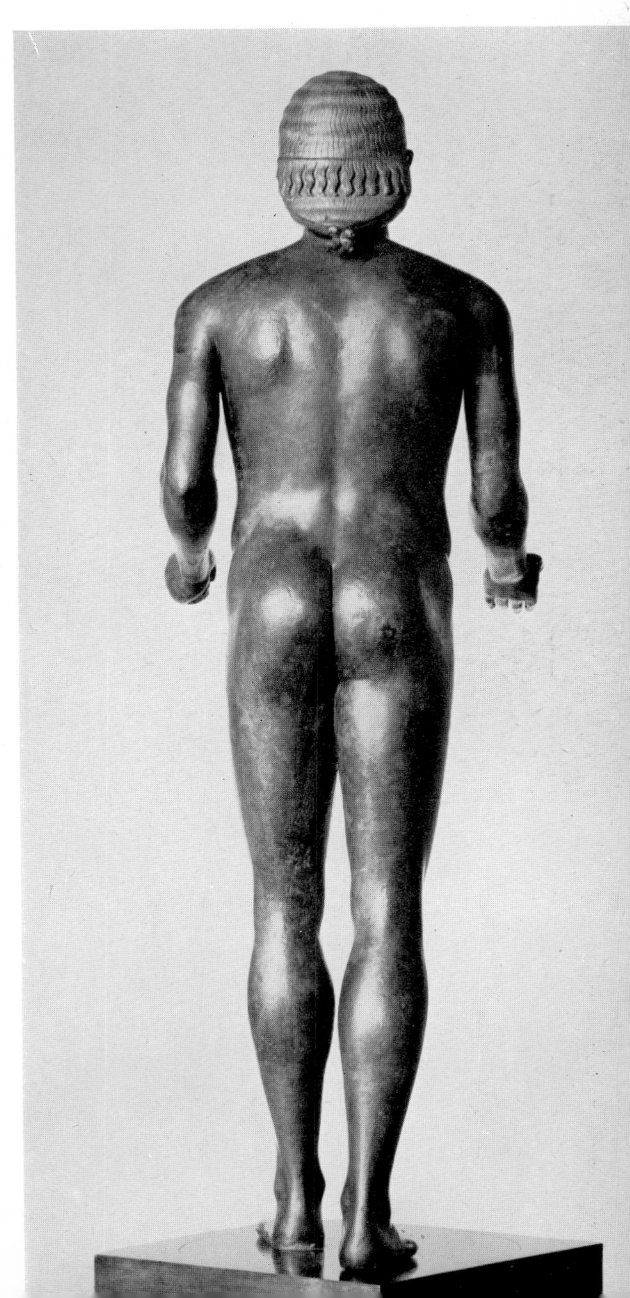

*111 Apollo of Piombino, early 5th century* B.C.

## *The Ionic – Femininity of Form*

Freed from magical forces, the joy of life that already animated the faces in the Cretan paintings blossoms into a smile upon the features of the Greek girls, sets the folds of their clothes quivering and bends the Ionic volutes to delicate inflexions; but the sovereignty of the mind subjects it to a harmonic order, the columns of the temple are, as Valéry called them, 'daughters of the golden number'.

*113 Bust of an antifix from Fuseo, Sicily, late 6th century* B.C.

*112 'La Parisienne', fresco from the palace of Minos, c. 1500* B.C.

*114 Capital from Megara Iblaea, Sicily, c. 500* B.C.

*116 Temple of Athene Nike, Athens, 428–421* B.C.

*115 Girl in sleeved chiton from the Acropolis, Athens, 6th century* B.C.

*117 Old Hebrew man, Roman copy of Greek original*

*118 Crouching Aphrodite from Rhodes, c. 100 B.C.*

*119 Buffoon of Mahdia, Hellenistic*

*120 Detail from the altar of Pergamon, c. 180 B.C.*

## *Soul in Excess*

In the Hellenistic period the aim of power was glory and its instrument was war; monumental sculpture was invaded by the drama of war and death; bodies were betrayed into disordered actions by the passion dominating the soul; power found its embodiment in an excess of physical force, and authority took this as its outward manifestation; the pugilist's display of muscle became something very like an attribute of the monarch.

121 *Hellenistic King, presumed to be Dionysos I Soter*

*122 Three Greek engraved gems*

*123 'Tazza Farnese', period of Ptolemy*

*124 'Harvester's Vase' from Hagia Triada, Crete, c. 1550* B.C.

*125 Seal impression from Uruk, c. 3000* B.C.

# *Carved Gems*

Classical taste was continued in those small objects, the intaglios engraved upon semi-precious stones, and the cameos in relief, inheriting a very ancient tradition that goes back to the origins of the Mesopotamian civilisations—to the seal. One is amazed by the superb rhythm, the perfect proportions and complete definition comprised within this miniature art, when one reflects that so many of these refinements of relief were executed in concave, that is to say, in reverse.

*126 Cameo from the Cross of Ste Chapelle, early 1st century* A.D.

*127 Seal impression from Mohenjo-daro, 3rd millennium* B.C.

*128 Cretan seal-stone, c. 1500* B.C.

*129 Gold stater showing Alexander the Great, mid 4th century* B.C.

In the art of coinage the Greeks will never be surpassed: they were able to combine in it the rhythms of classical harmony and the realism of the portrait. Coins, being used for exchange, carried forms about the world; and it is curious to watch this sovereign style being transformed in Celtic art into fabulous beasts, and at Byzantium into the hieratic—which in due course the Scandinavians imitated.

*132 Greek coin, c. 380* B.C.

*130 Coin of Constantius III, early 5th century* A.D.

*131 Gold stater of the Parisii, 1st century* B.C.

*133 Coin from Gotland, 7th–9th century* A.D.

*134 Coin of Edward the Confessor,* A.D. *1042–1066*

# *Currency*

136 *Decadrachma from Syracuse, c. 400* B.C.

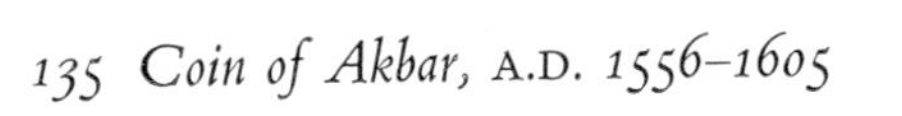

135 *Coin of Akbar,* A.D. 1556–1605

# *Earth of Etruria*

*137 Head of the Hermes of Veii,*
*c.* 500 B.C.

*138 Satyr from an Etruscan funerary urn*

*139* POLLAIUOLO: *Dancing figure*

*140* BOTTICELLI: *Head of Primavera*

A provincial offshoot of Greek art of the fifth century to third century B.C., Etruscan art reproduced its development with a time lag of a century, and kept its autonomy during the Roman period in one kind of popular art. What seems to be an Etruscan spirit comes out in a style that concentrates in contour alone the business of conveying the form, so that the artists are led to galvanise the energy of the line almost to the point of neurosis. This linear energy was reborn in the fifteenth-century Tuscan art, inspired by the Etruscan objects which excavations were then bringing to light.

*141 Head of a girl. Painting from an Etruscan tomb, c. 470* B.C.

*143 Head of an Etruscan from the sarcophagus (left)*

*142 Etruscan sarcophagus, 4th century* B.C.

*144 Head in mosaic, Terme di Caracalla, Rome, 3rd century* A.D.

*145 Portrait in mosaic, Pompeii, 1st century* A.D.

*146 Head of Augustus, 63* B.C.–A.D. *14*

# *Roman Pragmatism*

Greek art satisfies thought, Roman art satisfies life. A whole narrative style in painting, mosaic, and sculpture grew up on the margin of the official style derived from the Greek canons, and made of Roman art an art of expression and illustration that drew its feeling for naturalism from certain Etruscan and Latin sources. But the most original creation of the Romans is in the field of architecture—the invention of Baroque ornamentation, of which nowadays we catch only glimpses from the ruined buildings.

148 *Vestal virgin, Roman, 2nd century* A.D.

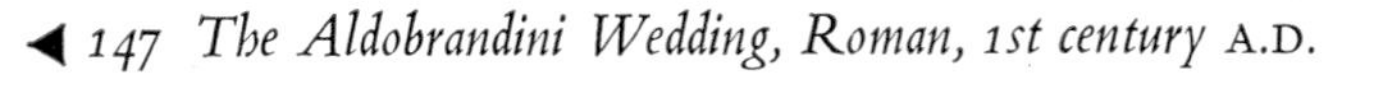

◀ 147 *The Aldobrandini Wedding, Roman, 1st century* A.D.

149 *Pont du Gard, near Nîmes*

150 *Stele of a blacksmith, Roman*

151 *Sabratha Theatre, North Africa, 2nd–3rd century* A.D.

# *Metaphysical Anxiety*

The metaphysical anguish of the Stoic philosophy spread till it permeated the culture of declining Rome. It came from the East along with the religions of salvation; and it transformed portraiture, so that the inner life rose to the surface as an expression of the eyes gazing into the unknown. This is essentially true of the funerary portraits found in Egypt, whither, in the first centuries of Christianity, all the spiritual currents of the dying ancient world returned.

*153 Head of Marcus Aurelius,* A.D. *160–180*

*152 Funeral portrait from Faiyum, 2nd century* A.D.

# NOTES ON THE ILLUSTRATIONS TO CHAPTER III

*106 Statue of Poseidon, found in 1926–8 in the sea off the north coast of the island of Euboea. Bronze. Greek, c. 450* B.C. *National Museum, Athens.*
*Photo: Hirmer.*

*107 Charioteer. Bronze. Found in 1896 at the sanctuary of Apollo at Delphi. c. 470* B.C. *Delphi Museum.*
*Photo: Hirmer.*

*108 Female figure from the Parthenon frieze. Greek, 446–432* B.C. *Musée du Louvre, Paris.*
*Photo: Hirmer*

*109 Temple of Concord, Agrigento, Sicily. Greek, c. 450* B.C.
*Photo: Anderson*

*110 Part of a column from the Temple of Concord at Agrigento.*
*Photo: Germain Bazin*

*111 Statue of Apollo, found in 1832 in the sea off Piombino, Italy. Bronze. Early 5th century* B.C. *Musée du Louvre, Paris.*
*Photo: Hirmer*

*112 'La Parisienne', fresco from palace of Minos, Knossos. Middle Minoan period, 15th century* B.C. *Archaeological Museum, Heraklion.*
*Photo: Josephine Powell*

*113 Bust from an antifix, from Fuseo Necropolis, Sicily. Late 6th century* B.C. *Syracuse Museum.*

*114 Capital from Megara Iblaea, Sicily. c 500* B.C. *Syracuse Museum.*
*Photo: Anderson*

*115 Girl in sleeved* chiton *and cloak, from the Acropolis, Athens. Chios (?) marble. Greek, late 6th century* B.C. *Acropolis Museum, Athens.*
*Photo: Hirmer*

*116 Temple of Athena Nike, Athens. Greek, 428–421* B.C.
*Photo: Dr Helmut Hell*

*117 Old Hebrew man. Roman copy of Greek original. Capitolme Museum, Rome.*
*Photo: Alinari*

*118 Crouching Aphrodite, found on Rhodes. Parian marble. Greek, late 2nd–1st century* B.C. *Museum, Rhodes.*
*Photo: Hirmer*

*119 Buffoon of Mahdia. Hellenistic. Musée Aloui, Le Bardo, Tunisia.*

*120 Alyconeus, Athens and Gaia, the Earth-Goddess. Detail from the Great Frieze of the Altar at Pergamon. Greek, c. 180* B.C. *Staatliche Museen, Berlin.*

*121 Hellenistic king, presumed to be Dionysos I Soter, King of Syria (162–150* B.C.*). Museo Nazionale delle Terme, Rome.*
*Photo: Hirmer*

*122 Three Greek engraved gems. Cabinet des Médailles, Paris.*
*Photo: Eileen Tweedy*

*123 Gorgon head. 'Tazza Farnese.' Sardonyx. Period oj Ptolemy. Museo Nazionale, Naples.*
*Photo: Soprintendenza delle Antichità di Napoli.*

*124 'The Harvesters' Vase' from the Palace of Hagia-Triada, Crete. Black steatite. c. 1550* B.C. *Archaeological Museum, Heraklion.*
*Photo: Hirmer*

*125 Seal impression from Uruk. Jemdet-Nasr period, c. 3000* B.C. *Staatliche Museen, Berlin.*

*126 Large cameo from the Cross of Sainte-Chapelle: Glorification of Germanicus. Agate. Early 1st century* A.D. *Cabinet des Médailles, Paris.*
*Photo: Eileen Tweedy*

*127 Seal impression from Mohenjo-daro. 3rd millennium* B.C. *National Museum, Karachi.*

*128 Cretan seal-stone. Late Minoan I, c. 1500* B.C. *Archaeological Museum, Heraklion.*
*Photo: Hirmer*

*129 Portrait of Alexander the Great on a gold stater oj Lysimachus, King of Thrace (323–281* B.C.*). (Enlargement.) Cabinet des Médailles, Paris.*
*Photo: Jean Roubier.*

*130 Coin of Constantius III.* A.D. *421. (Enlargement.)*
*Photo: Hirmer*

*131 Gold stater of the Parisii. c. 1st century* B.C. *(Enlargement.) Cabinet des Médailles, Paris.*
*Photo: Eileen Tweedy*

*132 Greek coin with the head of Apollo. c. 380* B.C. *(Enlargement.) Obverse signed by Theodorus. Cabinet des Médailles, Paris.*
*Photo: Jean Roubier*

*133 Bracteate of silver-gilt, inspired by Byzantine coins. Gotland, 7th–9th century* A.D. *Statens Historiska Museum, Stockholm.*
*Photo: Antikvarisk-Topografiska Arkivet, Stockholm.*

*134 Coin of Edward the Confessor (*A.D. *1042–66). (Enlargement.) British Museum, London.*
*Photo: Jean Roubier*

*135 Coin of Akbar, Mogul emperor (*A.D. *1556–1605). (Enlargement.) British Museum, London. Photo: Jean Roubier*

*136 Decadrachma from Syracuse, with head of Persephone, crowned with reeds, signed by Evenete. c. 400* B.C. *(Enlargement.) Cabinet des Médailles, Paris. Photo: Eileen Tweedy*

*137 Head of Hermes, from Veii (Portonaccio). Clay. Etruscan, c. 500* B.C. *Villa Giulia, Rome. Photo: Hürlimann*

*138 Satyr. Detail of a relief from a funerary urn. Orvieto. Photo: Donzelli, Milan*

*139* ANTONIO POLLAIUOLO (1433–98): *Dancing figure, detail of fresco from the Villa Galletti, Florence. Photo: Brogi*

*140* BOTTICELLI (*c.* 1445–1510): *Head of Primavera. Uffizi, Florence. Photo: Alinari*

*141 Head of a girl at a banquet, detail from the Tomb of the Leopard, Tarquinia. c. 470* B.C.

*142 Etruscan sarcophagus. 4th century* B.C. *Ny Carlsberg Museum, Copenhagen.*

*143 Head of an Etruscan, from the sarcophagus, plate 142. Ny Carlsberg Museum, Copenhagen.*

*144 Mosaic head, from the pavement of the Terme di Caracalla, Rome. Roman, 3rd century* A.D. *Museo Profano, Lateran. Photo: Alinari*

*145 Portrait of a Roman lady. Mosaic. Pavement in Pompeii. 1st century* A.D. *Museo Nazionale, Naples. Photo: Alinari*

*146 Head of Augustus (63* B.C.–A.D. *14). Marble. Roman. British Museum, London. Photo: Edwin Smith*

*147 The Aldobrandini Wedding. Roman, 1st century* A.D. *The Vatican, Rome. Photo: Eileen Tweedy*

*148 Vestal virgin. Roman, 2nd century* A.D. *Museo Nazionale delle Terme, Rome. Photo: Anderson*

*149 Pont du Gard, Provence. Roman, 1st century* A.D. *Photo: Cichy*

*150 Stele of a blacksmith. Roman. Museum, Aquileia. Photo: Ediz. Assoc. Nazionale per Aquileia*

*151 Sabratha Theatre, Libya. Roman, 2nd–3rd century* A.D. *Photo: J. Ward Perkins*

*152 Funeral portrait, from Faiyum, Egypt. Encaustic on wood. Egypto-Roman, 2nd century* A.D. *Metropolitan Museum of Art, New York.*

*153 Head of Marcus Aurelius (*A.D. *160–80). Bronze medallion. (Enlargement.) Cabinet des Médailles, Paris. Photo: Jean Roubier*

# IV ROME VANQUISHED BY GREECE

## *IV Rome Vanquished by Greece*

The notion of individualism, which Burckhardt showed to have been characteristic of the Renaissance, may easily distort our vision of ancient classicism if applied thoughtlessly. What has been called 'humanism' is, by implication, a resultant, an attitude based on the exploitation of an already existing culture. In the time of Greek classicism there was no humanism in the strict sense: the attitude makes its appearance in the Hellenistic and Roman periods. What the Greek of the fifth or fourth century exalted was not the individual, but man in the individual, and this postulates not so much an effort towards the perfection of the virtues proper to 'the most irreplaceable of creatures' as the fulfilment of an ideal of what man should be. The feeling developed in the small democratic communities where excellence was measured not by a man's intellectual distinction or his noble birth, but by the quality of the services he rendered to the group, of which the man possessed of power or knowledge was merely the delegate. There was already to be found that democratic egalitarianism which chops off the leaders by banishment or even death at the risk of weakening the community: Socrates succumbed to it, as did Pericles. The case of Socrates is especially significant because, at a time when religious fanaticism was on the way to extinction (he was condemned by a majority of only six out of five hundred and fifty-six voters), the charge against him was none the less that his dialectical spirit was dissolving the established beliefs of the Athenians.

The modesty of the private houses of the richest and most important citizens is an image of the strong solidarity that prevailed then—expressed also in the symbol of the temple. But the monarchs of Hellenistic and Roman times dissolved the unity of the small human group into that larger entity, the State, in which the individual had no interest because his status was that of a subject; and so he found himself alone, face to face with himself and delivered over to his own private anxieties. For millions all power was now assumed by one man, and the fact that that man was called 'divine' served to underline the essentially human condition of the others. The Greek of the Hellenistic period was an unemployed citizen and soon found himself tormented by the problems of the soul and its survival, which had left the Greek of the classic period unaffected, satisfied as he was to accomplish his destiny in this life within the city. In the thinking subject who began to make himself the object of his thought, ethics soon followed metaphysics along the same anguished path, and men's minds came to be preoccupied by the outrageous co-existence of good and evil. The individual had the choice of two ways of getting rid of the burden of himself: Stoicism and mysticism. While the disciples of Epicurus and Epictetus withdrew into the fortress of the solitary self, a wave of 'soteriology' (religions of salvation) swept in from the East, offering

*Panel of Duke Hilderic (739–40); altar of the abbey of S. Pietro, Ferentillo*

men the salvation of their souls through redemption by some suffering God or through the revelation of a secret doctrine.

With individual anguish came the portrait, which, during the classic period, had remained impregnated with idealism. It was in the look of the eyes that anguish was to find expression. It is already apparent in the struggling heroes of Scopas, whose gaze, projected beyond them by action, seems to be suddenly struck by a doubt about the use of action and to be drawn by this towards an unknowable end. Coins, which have the advantage of offering us whole series of portraits, show the progress of anxiety in the look of the eyes and also in the sulky set of the mouth: already on the tetradrachma of Clazomenes in Ionia, in the fourth century, the eyes of Apollo are filled with a strange uneasiness. The dynasts who succeeded Alexander created, on their coinage, an Alexandrian iconographic type with a wide gaze greedy for conquest—which grew gradually more melancholy as it was repeated. For philosophic doubt settled on the steps of the throne itself, and Marcus Aurelius, the accomplished emperor, allowed his portraits to express an unanswered appeal to the infinite. The Faiyum portraits, contemporary with the first centuries of Christianity, have crystallised this anguish for us: these funerary effigies (which may, however, have adorned the houses of the living) represent individuals of all races—Greeks, Romans and Egyptians who met in Egypt where all the spiritual currents of the end of

*Plate 146*

*Plate 132*

*Plate 153*

*Plate 152*

Antiquity fetched up. So much inner life wells to the surface in these faces confronting the other world that it overflows through the eyes, those fountains of the soul. Christianity was to calm this torment: it is noteworthy that the figures in the Catacombs have peaceful eyes. Huge, staring eyes are a feature of Oriental morphology that was to pass from the Faiyum portraits into the sixth-century mosaics: the crumbling of a world renewed for men's souls the anguish which had been started by spiritual uncertainty.

It was at the turn of the fifth and sixth centuries A.D. that the metamorphosis from ancient sculpture to the style of the Middle Ages took place.

*A 6th-century capital, like that from the church of Saints Sergius and Bacchus at Constantinople (170), shows the transformation of sculpture into pierced embroidery already completed, while the Ravenna archbishop's chair (160) still has about it a certain plastic feeling, which a 4th-century sarcophagus (157) shows in process of declining*

The transformation of relief into embroidery occurred as early as the sixth century in monumental sculpture, though work in ivory resisted this absorption of relief for a little longer. The phenomenon had for a long time been prepared for by a current from the eternal Orient which, already in the first century of the Christian era, had affected the pagan images at Dura Europos, Palmyra and Baalbek, as well as the extraordinary tombs of the kings of Commagene recently excavated at Nimrud-Dag; it was also favoured by the many forms of provincialism which, within the Roman Empire, made possible an easy transition from Antiquity to Middle Ages, more perhaps in the West than in the East. Roberto Salvini in his study of this phenomenon has shown the existence, in the Empire, of a sort of 'plastic bilingualism'—an official or 'aulic' art applying correctly the principles of the Graeco-Roman aesthetic, side by side with a *sermo rusticus* or provincial language interpreting that aesthetic in popular fashion. These two currents continued throughout the Middle Ages: from the aulic vein issued the Byzantine, Carolingian and Ottonian arts, while from provincial Roman art, promoted from patois to the dignity of literary language, there came Romanesque art, just as the Romance languages emerged from Low Latin. The co-existence of a sophisticated style with a popular one in the Middle Ages is particularly apparent in Italy: the coarse altars of Cividale or Ferentillo stand alongside the stucco-work of Santa Maria in Valle at Cividale, while the ciborium of St Ambrose in Milan upholds Ottonian classicism in the heart of what was barbarian land; and, to take regions more distant from one another, the still Hellenistic style of the Castelseprio frescoes (which may be later than some think) contrast with the rough language of Sant' Angelo in Formis. In the relief arts stone tends to the *sermo rusticus*, while stucco-, bronze- and ivory-work are crafts in which the 'aulic' art is exercised.

*Plate 164*
*Plate 173*

This provincial Roman art was to a considerable extent universal: it appeared wherever the official aesthetic was interpreted by a barbarian community—in Gaul, on the Rhine, in Upper Mesopotamia, in Cisalpine Italy, in Spain, in Etruria (where the native art 'regressed' to primitivism) and even in Campagna; at Pompeii, in the recently excavated Street of the Tombs, sophisticated funerary statues are found cheek-by-jowl with 'popular' tombs, as if the monumental masons had a scale of prices varying in accordance with quality of execution. A study of Roman art in the Danubian provinces, by Ferri, has revealed manifestations of it at Sarajevo, Skoplje and Sofia; and the author noted such similarities between some of the Sarajevo sculptures and the famous Ratchis altar at Cividale that he was almost tempted to believe in some obscure kinship between the two. North Africa offers us an inexhaustible reservoir of this primitivist art of the Roman provinces: if we set aside the statues, obviously imported from Greece or Italy, which have been found in the large cosmopolitan towns, especially at Caesarea (Cherchell) which King Juba II of Mauretania wished to make into a Greek city, North African figurative art in the many garrison towns created by the conquerors to maintain the *pax romana* is everywhere marked by these provincial characteristics. Even official enterprises are sometimes affected by the neo-primitivism: the carvings in relief on the triumphal arch consecrated in A.D. 203 by Septimus Severus at Leptis Magna present us with one of the first Western monuments to display in sculpture the features of the new style, and it has been thought that their spirit may have come from

*Compared with the Ravenna archbishop's chair (160), which retains some elements of the formalism of Antiquity, the Coptic carving (156) is a provincial production; yet they both belong to the same region of the Mediterranean, the Ravenna chair being probably of Alexandrian workmanship*

*Front of the altar offered by Ratchis (c. 740), S. Martino, Cividale*

workmen brought from Asia by this emperor, whose wife was from Syria. But elsewhere the neo-primitivism was native: examples abound, and we need only mention the stelae and low-reliefs of Djemila; the little figures of Pan supporting the tables in the market are like demons from some Burgundian carved capital, and two well-preserved funerary statues in the museum, representing some eminent couple, are so closely related to certain Romanesque works that the statue of the man might serve as a *pons asinorum* to university students of the history of art, so easily could it be taken for a St Peter. Another form of primitivism exists in North Africa, that of the funerary stelae of the Numidian communities which long kept up the Punic cults in spite of many interdicts and whose religion, more spiritual than that of Rome, perhaps explains why Christianity flourished in Africa: it may have won many adherents among these natives driven underground. Should one believe, with Gilbert Charles Picard, who has unravelled the complicated threads of North Africa with such perspicacity, that this spiritual impulse was responsible for the crude carving, flat relief, atrophy of arms and legs, faces with starting eyes, as though the artist were instinctively opposing the pagan materialism of official sculpture? Or should one see in these things a spontaneous primitivism, an example of that 'childhood' of art to be found among segregated peoples like the Bogomils of Yugoslavia, whose stelae, centuries later, are so like those of the Berbers, and who were isolated by their heretical Manichean beliefs in a land where the

*Plate 155*
*Plate 159*

sophisticated forms of Byzantine art were flourishing? The magnificent mausolea of Ghirza in Tripoli are adorned with reliefs that are scarcely less elementary.

Our own time, with its passion for the primitive, jumbles together under this name all sorts of artistic positions, frequently worlds apart from one another. There is a crude primitivism, representing a childhood stage of the form—creative imagination, as yet virgin of any artistic image—a sort of 'pre-formal' stage. Another type of primitivism is that produced when a sophisticated art is interpreted by a popular one, as for example in provincial Roman art: in such a case the primitivism is more of a 'simplification' than, strictly speaking, a stylisation; but the simplification is equivalent to a mutation—it does, in fact, lead to a real change of nature in the forms. This explains the premonition of Christian spirituality which men like André Breton and André Varagnac saw in certain Gallo-Roman sculptured faces—and it is clearer still in our St Peter of Djemila; for the simplification imposed on the human face pares away from it both the marks of individual realism and the characteristics of the prevailing aesthetic and so elevates it to a type: in the particular case of the Roman work, this popular interpretative tendency takes away from the statue the material solidity so essential both to the aesthetics and to the ethics of the ancient world, and, so to speak, disincarnates it, surrounding it with a sort of halo of spiritual dignity.

But there is also a third kind of primitivism, the moment when, after long elaboration, the primitive itself produces a sophisticated style: enriched by the heritage of a thousand years of forms and images, the artist indulges in speculation of his own. It is then that 'stylisation'—which is, strictly speaking, a 'will to style'—comes in, whereas the primitivism that is produced by popular interpretation of a sophisticated form is, on the contrary, a derivative from a given style—one might almost call it 'de-stylisation': and the fact that stylisation and de-stylisation engender various comparable intermediate forms explains many of the strange resemblances to which the history of art bears witness. Romanesque art, the Chinese Buddhist art of the sixth century and Greek archaic art are the most perfect expressions of this developed stage of primitivism. To them one must add Byzantine art. This can, without question, be better understood if one considers it in the perspective of a morphological development and rids oneself of the idea of a 'Golden Age' repeated twice or even three times (a notion scarcely consistent with a Golden Age): this idea has somewhat confused the interpretation of Byzantine art, which has in addition been accused of being static.

The transformation of the forms of Antiquity, one of the most important phenomena in the history of art, to which Aloïs Riegl was the first to draw attention, is usually demonstrated by examples taken from sculpture. But mosaic, which in the later days of the ancient world had become a transposition of the art of painting to the lapidary materials, reveals to us a quite different situation. Mosaic—*opus musivum*—was doubtless applied first to the ceilings of grottoes, sanctuaries of the Muses. Small pictures were also made in it, transposed paintings executed in tiny cubes into which hard and even precious stones were enchased: Caesar used to take some of these with him on his campaigns. Soon the technique was used for decorating floors with a carpet of images, and probably as early as the first century B.C. walls were so covered, but most of the buildings are so ruined that the pavement mosaics are the only ones to survive. It is easy for us, none the less, to appreciate the refinement which this mural art reached in Antiquity by looking at the earliest Christian mosaics—those of the fourth and fifth centuries in Santa Maria Maggiore in Rome, the Baptistery of the Orthodox in Ravenna and the church of St George at Salonica. Working in cubes of marble, with which are blended, as yet, few cubes of smalt, against backgrounds where gold has not yet replaced landscape, the artist of Santa Maria Maggiore transposes the painting of Antiquity, still based on the principles of naturalistic illusionism, into a brilliant material: the varied attitudes and animated compositions are those of life; shadows model the figures and draperies; and the effects of perspective and foreshortening derive from those categories of three-

*Plates 155, 158, 160*

dimensional space which the Romans had conserved at a time when in the Middle East, on the borders of the ancient world, sculpture itself had long been tending towards reabsorption into a surface. The range of colours is of such a prodigious richness, brilliance and variety of shades that it suggests the ideal of the Impressionists: the Crossing of the Red Sea in Santa Maria Maggiore has the tonal richness of Renoir; in the church of St George at Salonica the saints inhabiting the celestial architecture show a breaking-down of chromatic values analogous to the Pointillism of Seurat, the hair and beard of the priest Ananias are 'painted' in violet and blue cubes, and the flesh is realised with the help of pink, violet, and green cubes; the artists of the Baptistery of the Orthodox make form 'turn' in colour without using shadow, as Cézanne tried to do. In their dazzling colour the Apostles of the Baptistery of the Orthodox—note especially the St Bartholomew—retain all the plastic power of Antiquity; and one may say that the painting of antiquity, when it reached this stage, went further than Impressionism by integrating form within colour better than Cézanne himself.

*Bogomil sarcophagus from the necropolis of Radmilia*

Consideration of forms by themselves obliges us to transcend the categories of history. The summit of the art of painting in antiquity is to be found in the earliest Christian mosaics at the very moment when the sculpture of antiquity was already 'regressing' to primitivism.

To go, at Ravenna, from the Baptistery of the Orthodox to Sant' Apollinare Nuovo via San Vitale is to pass from one world to another. The famous imperial scenes in the choir of San Vitale show us the passage from Antiquity to the Middle Ages: of Antiquity these figures retain the Roman feeling for portraiture; the faces are still modelled plastically, but this time in *chiaroscuro* no longer in colour; the bodies come out of the space to the surface and tend to divide frontally. At Sant' Apollinare two stages are to be seen: the scenes from the Life of Christ, which must go back to Theodoric, retain something of the sculpture of Antiquity—a residue; but in the two processions of male and female saints the evolution is complete. There the equal heads and equal bodies, the repetition of stereotyped attitudes in profile and full face, the inexpressive faces with their enormous eyes, the symmetrical compositions and the reduction of background to a few hints, belong to a different system of images, to a new style of which the aim was to break the points of contact between representation and the physical world by doing away with space, volume, weight and the diversity and movement of life. Gold, replacing natural scenery as background, directs the eyes of the spirit towards the supra-sensible—that is to say, the world of the mind, the only valid reality: its brilliance masks the impoverishment of the palette which is now reduced to a few stark colours, without that range of nuance which made of the mosaics of the fourth and fifth centuries a rushing stream of sparkling stones.

The passage from one style to the other appears abrupt, for the capture of Constantinople by the Turks at the beginning of our own era was as destructive as an earthquake to the relics of Antiquity accumulated in that city, and one is reduced to judging a creative centre by dispersed fragments. Certain recent discoveries are, however, greatly helping us to reconstitute what Byzantine art of that great period, the fifth and sixth centuries, must have been like, and they tend to prove that, in the image 'painted' in mosaic, if not in sculptured ornament (which had already been captured by the new style), this imperial art maintained the characteristics of the sculpture of Antiquity. The fifth-century icon of Santa Maria in Trastevere, of which the beautiful traces have been miraculously restored by the *Istituto del Restauro* in Rome, revealing angels of antique beauty alongside a hieratic Theotokos, and the sixth-century Virgin found in the monastery of St Catherine on Sinai, painted in encaustic and so much more alive than the Faiyum portraits—these works of art confirm this first direction taken by Christian imagery. It seems to have been continued at Byzantium until the iconoclast period.

*Plate 182*

The silver work (formerly believed to be Syriac and now restored to Byzantium) and the mosaics of the Great Palace (the finest of Antiquity—they are dated from the beginning of the

*Plate 169*

sixth century), attest that even down to the seventh century (the date of the last of the silver dishes) the court of Byzantium lived surrounded by a pagan décor. Of the mural mosaics few vestiges remain, but they agree with this. The iconoclast crisis destroyed these images at Constantinople. In the church of the Assumption at Nicaea there were still, until they were destroyed in the Graeco-Turkish War of 1921–2, some huge archangels of the sixth or seventh century, whose faces still belonged completely to Antiquity: to these precious works photographs alone now bear witness. As for the art of mosaic on the borders of the Byzantine world, the Transfiguration apse in the Sinai monastery, with the energy and varied attitudes of its Apostles, astonishes us the more since in this remote part of the Middle East one is used to the hieratic primitivism of Coptic art—which may, however, be a 'popular' variant like the art of the Syriac manuscripts. Closer to Byzantium, the church of St Demetrius at Salonica still preserves for us, in spite of the fire which ravaged it, two figures of saints, one with two children and the other with two donors: the small, bad, dark photographs taken some time ago had accustomed us to seeing in them no more than the full-face attitudes and the enormous eyes of the saints, but look at the child and at Leo the Governor in the large-scale coloured reproductions in the U.N.E.S.C.O. book and you will be tempted to apply to them the anecdote about Zeuxis and Apelles.

*Plate 162*

In the same period the medieval style prevailed in the mosaics of Rome and Italy. Is it not possible that the abrupt 'regression' from Antiquity, which makes its appearance at Ravenna in the sixth century, is a phenomenon of 'provincialism' accentuated in consequence of the Barbarian invasions, while Byzantium, preserved from contamination, retained some of the qualities of the ancient world? The modern historian of art has to take account of the monuments that have been destroyed: they may have been much more important than those which have been spared for us by luck from wars, iconoclasm or vandalism.

What is essential is to isolate the spirit of Byzantine art, that spirit which is its 'constant' and was destined, as the constant of Western art, to be subjected to the ebb and flow of forms and civilisations. Instead of speaking of 'renaissances' of Antiquity, renaissances that are too frequent to be the real thing, we should understand Byzantine art better by considering that, in a certain sense, it never repudiated Antiquity but merely subjected it to a change of significance. Byzantine art, in its finality, tended to create a system of images fitted not so much to suggest as to *represent* the world of the mind, which was perceived through Nature by the eyes of the spirit, working back from effect to causes. As André Grabar showed, in an article in which he brought together aesthetic forms and those of philosophy, this concept is related to Neoplatonism and, through it, goes back to Plato himself, who would doubtless have appreciated the static quality of Byzantine art, just as he praised that of Egyptian art. The fundamental thought of the orthodoxy which triumphed after the iconoclast crisis at the Seventh Council was that the divine energy should be present in the image without the image becoming an idol. This energy resides in a *resemblance* between the image and its principle; and, transposed from the magical to the spiritual, this implies a consolidation of the ancient beliefs in the virtue of the copy—of which the East had never entirely let go. But the God of the Christian is a man, and through him human nature has been reclaimed, rendered divine by the Incarnation: the divine image will therefore be a human one, but transcending the singularity of the individual and expressing the archetype which takes it back to the divine principle of all things. How can one fail to see in all this a process of idealisation and generalisation similar to that of Greek art—one that was bound to make Byzantine art develop consciously in the direction of classicism, which has indeed always contributed its forms to the finest images of the divine, whether in the time of Pheidias, of the Chartres sculptor or of the Renaissance? When Byzantine art separates itself from Antiquity it is departing from its own principle under the pressure of the ferments of dissolution, internal or external, Oriental, Roman, barbarian or even Islamic—which enrich it by providing it with obstacles to overcome and, notably in the minor arts, like that of weaving or embroidery, keep a place open for the chimaera.

The morphology of Ravenna is thus an archaism when compared with the classicism of the so-called Macedonian period, which rediscovered the virtue of beauty as the most adequate image of divinity and in its expression of the eternal went back to the serenity of the fifth-century Olympian. In *The Coronation of Romanos and Eudoxia* the Christ has something truly Pheidian in his sovereign grace and ease, though at the same time something less corporeal and therefore Christian: He is more natural than the Emperor and Empress, who are obliged to wear the heavy and elaborate court robes in order to show off to human beings the externals of power; and, being more natural, is more divine, since in His humanity He possesses that fullness of being which the two creatures promoted by His gesture to the imperial dignity can only approach.

*Plate 154*

To understand the essence of Byzantine art and the meaning of its vocation to revive Antiquity, we must avoid regarding this as proceeding only from Hellenistic art. The perpetual effort of Byzantium to get through Alexandrian art and back to Greek classicism has perhaps been obscured for the historians by the illuminated manuscript, whose art is essentially a narrative one and shows many traces of Hellenistic taste transmitted by the copying over and over again of the same prototypes. In mural decoration, and in ivory carving, classified among the 'minor' arts under the narrow categories of the historians when really, for Byzantium, it took the place of sculpture (one need only project the bas-relief of *The Coronation of Romanos and Eudoxia* on to a screen to be able to judge its monumental grandeur), Byzantine art from the ninth to the thirteenth century, in Constantinople itself, strove to pare away from the forms derived from Antiquity the picturesque element characteristic of Hellenistic art: its purpose was to recover that sense of the sacred which had filled the great Greek sculpture of the fifth century B.C., at the very moment when potters were indulging in representing life in all its diversity, just as the Byzantine illuminators would later do. Byzantine art in its plenitude is closer to the Greek than to the Roman, and there is nothing in Roman art to touch the Hellenic quality of the Christ crowning Romanos and Eudoxia.

*A manuscript like the Theriaca of Nicandor (167) is certainly a late imitation of a Greek or Roman original, whereas the Paris Psalter (165) is more likely to be the product of a kind of Renaissance, whose aim was to revive the forms of Antiquity*

Whenever Byzantine art separates itself from Antiquity, it departs from its own line. Luckily it did so, for provincial diversity (Coptic, Syriac, Roman, or Balkan influences), by forcing it to react, preserved it from the static quality—for which it has, none the less, been reproached by short-sighted historians who have judged it according to the criteria of progress in naturalism, which is a Western thing. From the ninth to the thirteenth centuries Byzantine figurative art attained its greatest heights in a classicism that was broad enough to accommodate a certain amount of human feeling, though with a spiritual significance—as in the case of the Apostles fussing over Mary in the Sopočani Dormition, or of the grieving of John at the foot of the Cross in the *deesis* at Daphne, or, in the Vladimir icon, the filial tenderness of the Child Jesus to which Mary in her compassion responds with the infinite sadness which the Western artists were not able to express till a century later. For indeed the 'humanisation' of God, of which the West is proud, was achieved at Byzantium two centuries earlier. The terrible Pantocrator of Daphne, whose frowning hieratic quality is dictated by the demands of iconography, has prevented people from seeing the radiant benevolence of the Gospel Christ, executed a century and a half before the 'Beau Dieu' of Chartres or Amiens. As for the tenth-century ivory Virgin in the Victoria and Albert Museum and the one at Utrecht, dated a century later—what reason have they to envy their French Gothic sisters?

*The Oriental hieratism, which appears very early on in the frescoes at Dura Europos, on the edge of the Roman world (171), was, throughout Byzantine art, a powerful constructive force opposed to the impulse of Antiquity—which, to appear at all, had always to vanquish it. The Chios St Theodore (174) is a sophisticated interpretation of it, while the angel from the church of Sant' Angelo in Formis near Capua (173) is a provincial form, produced in a remote district. It provided the goldsmiths with their inspiration (175), and kept in being the Byzantine formalism which, as one answer to the problem, continued throughout the long history of that art, as is shown by the Ochrid Annunciation (176)—still, in the 14th century, fixed in an immobility which the painter of Our Lady of Vladimir (178) had broken in the 12th*

In the thirteenth century this humanism turned into refinement and elegance, as in the *deesis* of the South Gallery of St Sophia. At the beginning of the fourteenth century the mosaics of the Apostles at Salonica recovered the Impressionist freshness of the fourth and fifth centuries. The same tendency reappears, in a mannered form *à la* Primaticcio, in the church of St Saviour in

*Plate 168* Chora (Kariye Cami) in Constantinople. This is where the art of Mistra comes from, for a long time the only art of this period known, and attributed by historians to some Western influence: it flows straight from the spring and has no need of any such tributary. The movement of feeling just outlined is in perfect accordance with the spirit of an art passing beyond classicism, and the Mistra *Plate 166* 'naturalism', contained as it is within the limits of an elegance that is slightly mannered in comparison with the preceding art, is comparable to the Greek fourth century following upon the severity of the fifth.

Byzantium extended to all the territories it touched, no doubt including Italy, the benefits of *Plate 181* the classicism which it had recovered in the teeth of barbarian primitivism. Vasari praised Cimabue for having broken the Byzantine mould; but who knows if it was not the formal sense acquired from Byzantium that enabled Cimabue to break 'Italiote' primitivism? The Byzantine source is even more apparent in Duccio.

And so, until the fall of Byzantium, its art remained faithful to its vocation as an art of Antiquity Christianised. Dying, it left behind it, in certain marginal areas now deprived of sap, a repertoire of pious images which has done much harm to its reputation. And yet, although Orthodox Russia at first, faithful to the canons of Byzantine art, simply interpreted it in an original *Plate 184* way, it is curious to see how with Andrei Rublev, at the beginning of the fifteenth century, the art of the Russian icon returned, spontaneously, to a classicism whose grace rather suggests the *Plate 183* 'Alexandrian' Duccio succeeding the severe art of Cimabue. Persian influences later turned the *Plate 180* icons towards a sharper stylisation while, as in all the other regions marginal to Byzantine art, the residue of a style which had lost its sap produced an asceticism that was more aesthetic than mystical.

Orthodox Russian art evolved from the imported type of church with a Greek-cross plan, a form conducive to great spiritual elevation: in the penumbra of its small sanctuaries, crowded in on themselves like a beating heart, the believer finds himself at the bottom of a well, aspiring *Plate 177* towards the light that comes from so high up, from the cupolas that spring from their fantastically stretched drums in an upward rush towards the heavens. Is not that precisely the situation of the Christian, living in the half-darkness and catching glimpses of the brightness above? The genius of Le Corbusier has recaptured this symbol in a side chapel to the church at Ronchamp. In Russia this type of sanctuary continued down to the time of Peter the Great, thanks to the Church's resistance to novelties. Through the art of Orthodox Russia something of eternal Byzantium survived until the century of the Enlightenment.

# *Imperial Liturgy*

In the Macedonian period Byzantine art recovered the virtue of beauty, the most fully adequate image of the divine: the Christ in the *Crowning of Romanos and Eudoxia* recovers the certainty of the fifth-century Olympians, and in his superb grace and ease there is something of the quality of Pheidias.

*154 Crowning of Romanos and Eudoxia. Byzantine, c. 950*

# *From Antiquity to the Middle Ages*

The reabsorption of relief carving into the wall surface becomes more and more marked in the last days of the ancient world, and leads on to the 'incorporeal' forms of the Middle Ages. The way was prepared for it by a current from the eternal East, and it was favoured in the Roman world by the many forms of provincial art, which made possible a smooth transition from one artistic civilisation to another. In Africa the carvers of the late Punic stelae practised a real 'disembodiment' of forms, which they brought back to a kind of 'preformal' state, while the provincial interpretation of official art produced statues with a resemblance to those of the Christian Renaissance of the twelfth and thirteenth centuries.

155 *Roman statue from Djemila, late Roman*

156 *Egyptian bas-relief from Daphne, 5th–6th century*

157 *Christ's entry into Jerusalem. Roman sarcophagus, c. 330*

*158 Miracle of the loaves and fishes. Ivory panel from Ravenna throne, c. 550*

*159 'Philosophical argument'. Fragment of a Roman relief, 4th century*

*160 Berber stele from Ain Barchouch*

*161 S. Porfirio. Mosaic from the church of St George, Salonike, c. 400*

*162 Orante from a catacomb; first half of 4th century*

# *Christian Art of Antiquity*

Early Christian art picks up the mosaic art of Antiquity and, in the fourth and fifth centuries, raises it to its finest glory—with effects of perspective, foreshortening and modelling that maintain a contact with the sculpture of Antiquity and its three-dimensional painting, and with a prodigiously rich range of colours which makes one think of Impressionism. Thus the climax of the pictorial art of Antiquity is to be found in the first Christian mosaics—at the very moment when the sculpture of the ancient world had 'regressed' to primitivism. This ancient style managed, in exceptional cases, to survive down to the beginning of the Middle Ages, as is shown by the frescoes of Castelseprio.

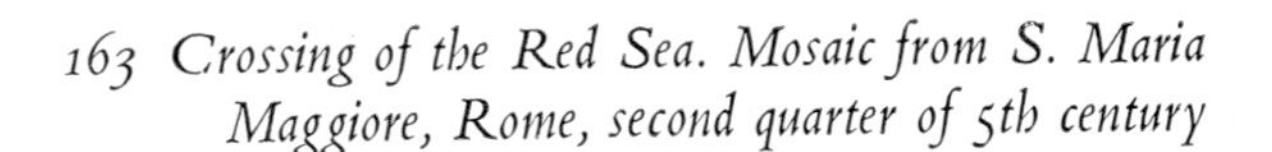

*163 Crossing of the Red Sea. Mosaic from S. Maria Maggiore, Rome, second quarter of 5th century*

*164 Flight into Egypt. Fresco from Castelseprio, 7th century (?)*

# *The Hellenistic Tradition*

Hellenistic grace continues with some constancy in the art of book illustration, where the proto-types are repeated century after century. It is reborn in the mosaics of the twelfth to the fourteenth century, where it succeeds, by a natural development, the fine flowering of classic harmony in those of the ninth to the eleventh century.

*165 Isaiah at prayer, from a Greek Psalter, 9th century*

*166 Nativity. Fresco from Mistra, 14th century*

*167 Illumination from the* Theriaca *of Nicandor, 10th century*

*168 Christ and Mary, mosaic, Constantinople, 14th century*

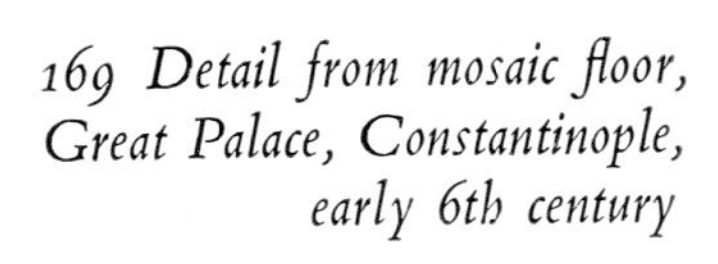

*169 Detail from mosaic floor, Great Palace, Constantinople, early 6th century*

170 *Choir of S. Vitale, Ravenna, consecrated 547*

171 *Capital from SS. Sergius and Bacchus, Constantinople, early 6th century*

172 *Fresco from Dura Europos, 1st century*

## The Hieratic

The new system of forms, later known as the Byzantine style, already makes its appearance, perfectly developed, at Ravenna in the sixth century. Its aim is to break off all points of contact between representation and the natural world, by doing away with space, volume, weight and the diversity and movement of life: everything must contribute to the task of steering the spirit towards the suprasensible world of mind and soul, the only valid reality.

*173 Angel from S. Angelo in Formis, late 11th century*

*175 Archangel Michael, Byzantine book-cover, 11th century*

*174 St Theodore, from Nea Moni, Chios, c. 1050*

# *Icons*

Starting from Byzantine painting, of which very few examples from the best period survive, Russian icons were later enriched by Persian influences, producing an even more marked stylisation. In architecture, meanwhile, the Russian churches, derived from the Greek cross type, expressed, in the rising movement of their domes, a special kind of spiritual elevation.

*176 Annunciation. Icon from Ochrid, 14th century*

*177 Church of St Saviour, near Novgorod, 1198*

*178 'Our Lady of Vladimir', c. 1130*

*180 St George, Russian icon, 14th century*

*179 'Angel with golden hair'. Russian icon, 12th century*

# Recurrences

At the beginning of the fifteenth century Russian icon painting returns spontaneously, with Andrei Rublev, to a classicism whose grace reminds one of Duccio's 'Alexandrine' phase, or of Cimabue's classical Byzantinism and, going farther back, suggests the style of the sixth-century Trastevere Madonna.

181 CIMABUE: *Madonna and Child, c. 1260*

184 RUBLEV: *Archangel Michael, early 15th century*

182 *Icon in S. Maria in Trastavere, 6th century*

183 DUCCIO: *Angel from the Maestà, Siena, 1308*

## NOTES ON THE ILLUSTRATIONS TO CHAPTER IV

154 *The coronation of Romanos and Eudoxia. Ivory. Byzantine, c. 950. Cabinet des Médailles, Paris. Photo: Hirmer*

155 *Statue. Late Roman. Djemila Museum, Algeria. Photo: Germain Bazin*

156 *Fragment of a bas-relief from Daphne. Egyptian, 5th–6th century. Musée du Louvre, Paris.*

157 *Christ's entry into Jerusalem. Detail of the sarcophagus of Adelphia. Roman, c. 330. National Museum, Syracuse. Photo: Hirmer*

158 *The miracle of the bread and fishes. Ivory panel from the chair of Archbishop Maximilian (546–56). National Museum, Ravenna. Photo: Hirmer*

159 *Philosophical argument. Fragment from a relief. Roman, 4th century. Museo Nazionale delle Terme, Rome. Photo: Bulloz*

160 *Berber stele of Ain-Barchouch. Photo: Gilbert Charles-Picard*

161 *S. Porfirio. Mosaic from Hagios Giorgios, Salonica. c. 400. Photo: Hirmer*

162 *Orante from the catacomb of the Vigna Massima, Rome. Wall-painting first half of the 4th century. Photo: Hirmer*

163 *Crossing of the Red Sea. Mosaic. S. Maria Maggiore, Rome. Second quarter of the 5th century. Photo: Hirmer*

164 *The Flight into Egypt. Fresco from Castelseprio, Lombardy. 7th century(?).*

165 *Isaiah at Prayer. From a Greek psalter, 9th century. Bibliothèque Nationale, Paris. Photo: Eileen Tweedy*

166 *Nativity. Fresco. 14th century. Mistra.*

167 *Illumination from the Theriaca of Nicandor. Byzantine, 10th century. Bibliothèque Nationale, Paris.*

168 *Christ and Mary with the Emperor Isaac Porphyrogenitus. Church of St Saviour in Chora (Kariye Cami), Constantinople. 1307–20. Photo: Hirmer*

169 *Detail from the mosaic floor of the Great Palace, Constantinople. Byzantine, early 6th century. Photo: Josephine Powell*

170 *Choir of S. Vitale, Ravenna. Consecrated 547. Photo: Hirmer*

171 *Capital from SS. Sergius and Bacchus, Constantinople. Early 6th century. Photo: Hirmer*

172 *Sacrifice to the Palmyran gods. Detail from the frescoes at Dura Europos. c. 75. Damascus Museum.*

173 *Angel from the church of S. Angelo in Formis, Campania. Late 11th century. Photo: Anderson*

174 *St Theodore from the church of Nea Moni, Chios. c. 1050. Photo: Amilcare Pizzi, Milan*

175 *The Archangel Michael. Byzantine book-cover. 11th century. Treasury of St Mark's, Venice. Photo: Hirmer*

176 *The Annunciation. From the church of St Clement, Ochrid. Painting on panel. Byzantine, 14th century. Macedonian State Collections, Skoplje. Photo: Hirmer*

177 *The church of the Saviour at Nereditsa near Novgorod, Russia. Built in 1198. Photo: Courtauld Institute of Art, London. Copyright A. F. Blunt*

178 *Our Lady of Vladimir. Painting on panel. Byzantine (two heads, c. 1130). Tretiakov Museum, Moscow.*

179 *Angel with golden hair. Icon. Russian, 12th century. Russian Museum, Leningrad.*

180 *St George. Icon. Russian, 14th century. Russian Museum, Leningrad.*

181 CIMABUE: *Madonna and Child. c. 1260. Musée du Louvre, Paris. Photo: Eileen Tweedy*

182 *Angel. Detail of an icon. Painting on encaustic. 6th century. S. Maria in Trastevere, Rome. Photo: Archivio Fotografico, Instituto Centrale del Restauro, Rome*

183 DUCCIO: *Angel from the Maestà. 1308. Opera del Duomo, Siena. Photo: Anderson*

184 ANDREI RUBLEV: *Archangel Michael. Russian, early 15th century. Tretiakov Museum, Moscow.*

# V THE CITY OF GOD

## V *The City of God*

IT WAS THE ARABS who opened the gates of the Middle Ages. The barbarian invasions had severely shaken the world of Antiquity, but not ended it: they had brought into the territories of the Empire peoples who felt themselves inferior and were anxious to be admitted into Roman civilisation. The first of them to be assimilated, once they were settled on the marches of the Empire of which they had become beneficiaries, turned against the newcomers and tried to drive them off.

In the fourth century A.D. the most loyal supporter of the Empire was a Vandal, Stilicho, who opposed Alaric, a Visigoth, and Radagaisus, a German. In the fourth and fifth centuries the Empire, disputed between barbarians, was dismembered, still not destroyed. In 414, at Narbonne, Ataulf, King of the Goths, married Placidia, daughter of Theodosius and sister of Honorius, and gave her as a wedding-present the spoils of Rome. The Emperor Constantius tried to introduce order into this dismemberment of the Empire, which might have become a sort of barbarian confederacy, by means of the bonds of the Roman idea. Genseric himself, once he had conquered Africa, sought to re-enter the Imperial Community and paid tribute to Valentinian III. Theodoric, who was brought up at Constantinople, reigned at Ravenna as a Roman, not as a German, and the policy of his minister Cassiodorus aimed at restoring the Empire through the barbarians. Meanwhile the emperors of the fifth century, mediocre though they were, managed to preserve the eastern nucleus of the Empire at Byzantium. It was a prince of barbarian origin, a Slav, Justinian, who for a moment restored its unity: thanks to Belisarius the Mediterranean became once more *mare nostrum*; and Byzantium maintained, against Persian and Slav enemies, a front which had been that of the Roman Empire. But now, out of prehistory, there arose another people who, this time, in attacking the Empire, had none of the feeling of inferiority the barbarians had had. To Christian orthodoxy Islam opposed an orthodoxy of its own, and the war against Christian Rome was a holy war. In half a century the results of Justinian's efforts were annihilated: half the Mediterranean became an Arab sea, and its waters were forbidden to Christian ships. The hemmed-in Byzantine Empire began to Hellenise, losing its vocation as a universal community; and the West, driven away from the fortunate sea, was cut off from its sources and grew barbarous; the cities withered and became market towns, blood withdrew from the fine circulatory system created by the Romans between the cities of the Empire, and life ebbed from the town into the fields, where it returned to primitive ways.

Recent observations by archaeologists have revealed, in the country life of the West, even in quite late times, an extraordinary resurgence of ancient Indo-European Nature cults. In cemeteries attached to pre-Romanesque and Romanesque churches between the Loire and the Pyrenees

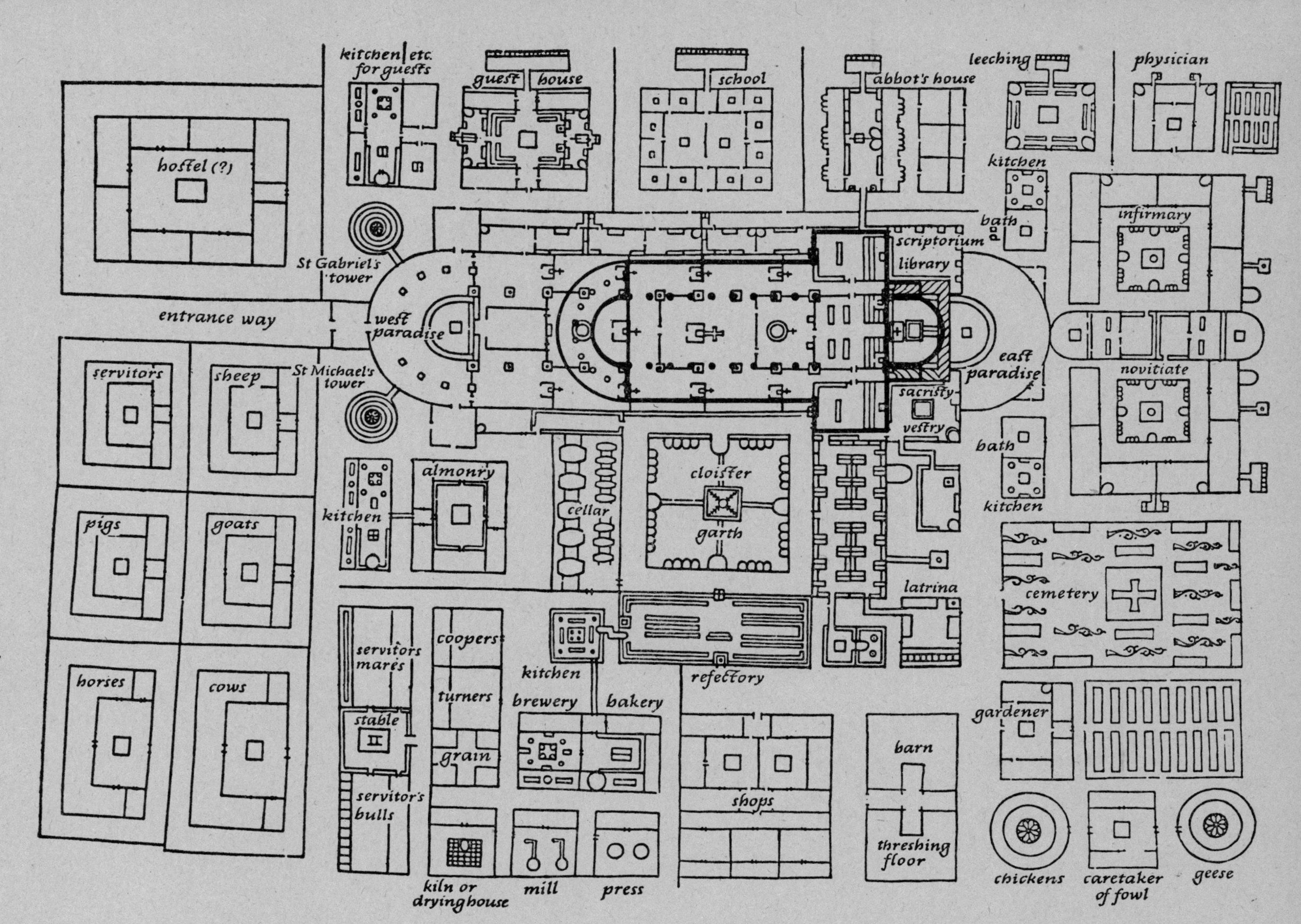


*Ninth-century plan of the projected abbey of St Gall, Switzerland*

there have been found cylindrical or oval ditches filled with votive deposits, vessels broken during *agapes* and anniversary orgies over the tombs of the dead, in the midst of ashes and animal bones which bear witness to ritual holocausts. In Bavaria, Central Europe, Spain, Portugal, and again France, structures that amount to mound-covered vaults with store pits for offerings have been unearthed. In the Bas-Quercy it seems that the cemetery of every church or chapel-of-ease in the twelfth century had its immediately adjacent collective vault. These sites, it has been pointed out, are those where more or less Christianised pagan traditions remained most stubbornly rooted: the Midsummer Fires are kept up there, or were until recently, and so in some cases, in Austria for instance, are the dances celebrating the important dates of the seasonal cycle. Even in the thirteenth century some of the pilgrims who entered the atrium of St Peter's in Rome used to turn towards the east to worship the sun; it was in order to divert their homage to a religious image that, during the papacy of Boniface VIII, Cardinal Stefaneschi commissioned the huge mosaic of the 'Navicella' from Giotto.

These primitive chthonic practices, tenaciously retained by the *pagani* (and confirmed also by a few contemporary texts), help us to a better understanding of what life was like in the West and, incidentally, of the art itself. The monasteries were built in the heart of barbarian and pagan country as fortresses of Christianity, which sometimes had to fight against invasion from within as the mass arrival of lay brothers, who were *pagani*, had the unexpected consequence, in the seventh and eighth centuries, of paganising the monks. Monastic discipline, which had been fierce under St Columban, became mild under St Benedict, who had been impressed with the need for attracting recruits to these Christian militias: 'Nevertheless, let everything,' he wrote, 'be done with moderation on account of the weaker brethren.'

*Figure p. 125* The famous plan of the abbey of St Gall, drawn up for Abbot Gozbert (816–837) is the perfect image of the economic self-sufficiency of these citadels in which the sentinels of the spirit kept watch over the barbarian world. Did not St Benedict teach his monks to sleep in their clothes, 'that they may be always ready'? These agricultural, industrial, and spiritual units revived, *Plate 124* in a way, the spirit of the *polis*, of the small communities that had been the great centres of the civilisation of Antiquity—while congregations like that of Cluny remind one of the confederacies of cities in the ancient world. The monasteries maintained the spirit of the small and highly organised human group, before it developed on a social level into the medieval commune. The City of God prepared the rebirth of the city.

The Middle Ages were so permeated by this idea of a citadel, of a sacred piece of land and of a closed world defended by a wall against the impurity outside, that down to the Renaissance *Plates 189, 190* it governed the way in which the Heavenly Jerusalem, Paradise and the *hortus conclusus* were *Plate 191* represented. In the *Celestial Topography* of Cosmas Indicopleustes, the Kingdom of God is divined as an enclosure within seven ethereal zones, borne upon invisible wings. Before the great invasions, the Roman cities of classic times had been open cities, relay stages in the life of the Empire: now, and for many centuries, the human unit was to be a walled enclosure living a closed life of its own.

And yet in this small world a whole world is seething. The unifying element is supplied by faith, but paradoxically this faith has inherited its means of expression from the pagan world: the Latin language, for a long time the only language of culture in the midst of many patois, helped to maintain throughout the barbarian world an accepted aesthetic with its roots in the rhetoric of Antiquity. The real Greek miracle, as André Varagnac has reminded us, was perhaps the impulse it gave to writing, which made possible the development of logic and of its Roman prolongation, law. It was then that the word emptied itself of individuality, to become the vehicle for a concept. 'The written word also reveals the existence of pure ideas, of which things and living creatures are supposed to be only approximate images. . . . Thus Platonism becomes a meditation on written language.' Writing had encouraged the intellectualisation of culture. With the barbarian invasions this 'scriptural' world found itself suddenly placed in contact with the dumb civilisations which had issued from the depths of prehistory and brought into the West another mentality—an oral civilisation, not fixed, always (so to speak) open and in a state of becoming, one in which forms were not states but stages, provisional stages of a world always in process of transformation yet ceaselessly returning upon itself.

*Plate 185* The Evangelist, dipping his pen in the inkwell, who heads our chapter, is the perfect symbol of that most intimate cell in the monastery, the centre of intellectual life, the *scriptorium*. In the midst of the inarticulate crowd of *pagani*, all those pagans who were to become the 'peasants', the cloister was the citadel in which written thought was concentrated. Writing—writ—acquired there a prestige so great that, spelt with a capital as Writ, it constituted the sacred store of the divine Word. It has certainly been an over-simplification to make of the monks mere copyists, the devoted guardians of classical ideas, but copyists they certainly were, driven on by the need to preserve the masterpieces of that language of culture which was still a living language—Latin; and it was to the Carolingian monasteries that the Renaissance humanists went in search of the oldest texts of the classics. The great Gerbert, later Sylvester II, who was Pope in the year 1000, engaged in the hunt for ancient manuscripts, with which he furnished first the library of the episcopal school at Reims and then that of his Lombard monastery at Bobbio. But there were other monks who condemned the classical authors: St Odilon of Cluny describes them as poisonous creatures; St Mayeul, who denounced the 'lies of Virgil' and banished the Swan of Mantua from the library at Cluny, went so far as to mutilate the manuscript, cutting out the profane passages. Many men of that time regarded the ancient philosophers as magicians, skilful at leading the people astray by

Satanic spells and illusions. In those days, then, there was writing and literary language; and if, in the schools, men had to pass through the dry discipline of the *quinque res*, learning about genus, species, difference, property and accident, the supple minds sometimes formed by this contact with ancient rhetoric might be used to denounce its impostures.

A vestige from this privileged condition of writing has continued almost to our own time: for a very long time the only aesthetics were those of literature, and the fine arts continued to be an empirical, spontaneous, experimental manifestation of the human genius, proper to artisans and with no right to the designation 'art', which was reserved for the liberal arts indispensable to the action of the intellect. It is the writings about the literature in Latin that one must consult if one wishes to see what the art criticism of the Middle Ages was; and we are able to do so, thanks to the accomplished exegeses of Edgar de Bruyn, that great reader of those dusty texts. These reveal very clearly the two deep-flowing currents which at that time coexisted in men's minds—the Classical and the Barbarian. Quintilian had already divided rhetoricians into two categories: the 'Attic', temperamentally inclined to polish and refinement, and the 'Asianic', in love with emphasis and redundance. The 'Asianic' taste, with its swollen verbosity, lack of rules and search for the bizarre, tended to win over the whole of the ancient world, but it was noteworthy that it flourished not only among sixth-century Spanish writers, whose natural bent, it is thought, was towards boasting, but among the Bretons, the Irish and the Celts of the British Isles—all those 'Scots' who seem to have been trying, in response to some deep-down instinct, to escape from the embrace of the Roman world. Using every form of hermetic expression (periphrases, emblematic images, circumlocutions, neologisms, metaphor and hyperbole, in fact literary jargon) to hold the reader at a distance from the concept whenever he thought he was nearly reaching it—the 'Asianic', in love with the elementary forces of Nature, symbolised by the monstrous, created a verbal world that was grandiloquent and confused, making the reader giddy with its jugglery. For those who cannot bear to read this wordy farrago (though many of our contemporaries, if they knew Latin, would enjoy it) the world of Anglo-Irish miniature painting will provide a faithful image of it. The single theme of this painting is interlacement, a tracery of abstract and living forms including even the human figure within a world in gestation where nothing is engendered except to die immediately and be reborn in monstrous and ephemeral creations, which take metaphor as their principle and evoke the immemorial beliefs of the Celts.

*The Book of Kells (202) is the masterpiece of this refined, non-iconic art, of which the Würzburg Bible (200) is a popular interpretation, treating the human form purely as a motif*

Romanesque sculpture gave this infinite play of metamorphoses (whose secret mechanisms have been laid bare by Jurgis Baltrušaitis in a famous book) a vocation—to serve the monumental. The aptitude for passing from one form to another with such ease—for considering every individual form as a transitory state of the universal life that is one and indivisible in every creature it brings to birth—is a heritage from the ancient Celtic mentality. To the Celts, in fact, the world was a world of spirits in perpetual transmigration, manifesting themselves by making use of successive forms within a sort of naturalist continuum where men and animals ceaselessly exchange their bodily appearances. The fairy-story, packed with metamorphoses, has handed down to us the evidence of this mentality. In the same period, in contrast with all this tumult, the Carolingian miniature painters produced their calm and noble images of Evangelists and, in works like the Utrecht Psalter, maintained the classical spirit of an art in harmony with human activity. Thus the Middle Ages were divided, or rather torn, between those two outlooks.

*The juxtaposition of an Early Christian fresco (193) and a detail from the Utrecht Psalter (194) proves how much the artist of the latter drew from ancient sources*

The dividing-line is impossible to establish: it does not seem to have depended merely on territorial or historical factors, but to have concerned the very nature of the different arts. The jewelled arts, those which used bronze or gold and were practised in the monasteries, were influenced more by classical taste. Their great centres of production were in Carolingian or Ottonian Germany, which was in contact with Byzantium just when it was cultivating the tradition of Antiquity, and where the new-born fiction of the Holy Roman Empire kept up the memory of Rome. At

*While, under the Ottonian Dynasty (192), what had been Gaul sank into anarchy, Germany faithfully pursued the 'Attic' taste that had come in with the Carolingian period (199). The craftsmen in metal kept it up, in the Rhineland and the Meuse, until the 12th century (197). In Southern Italy, in the 13th century, under the impulse of Frederick II's humanism, certain sculptors directly imitated works of Antiquity (196); and in Sicily, in churches where the mosaics are Byzantine, the capitals reproduce classical forms with great purity (205)*

*There is no more striking way of bringing out differences of style than to compare interpretations of the same subject. The Cremona Isaiah (204), riveted to the wall, seems not to have come from the same world as the dancing figure at Souillac (212). To depict the Adoration of the Magi, Antelami at Parma (206) places straight statues in line under an arcade, while the Vézelay sculptor gives his people the rhythm of the arch's curve (209). Wiligelmo's funerary genius (207) shows the artist's inability to bend a winged figure into an arabesque, though the anonymous creator of the tympanum of Saint-Michel at Entraigues (210) could draw from that a magnificent rhythm. French Romanesque painting is inspired by the same principles (211)*

Hildesheim, at the foot of the Hartz Mountains, rich in copper, tin, gold, and silver, a bishop of the year 1000, St Bernard of Hildesheim, the teacher of Otto III whose dream was to reconstitute the *imperium mundi* for his own benefit, was not above practising the goldsmith's art himself, and had set up in his cathedral a bronze column inspired by Trajan's Column, though with the story of Christ instead of the expedition against the Dacians; this work is contemporaneous with the golden altar at Bâle, that masterpiece of classic taste—but also with the primitive lintel of St Génis-des-Fontaines at the foot of the Pyrenees. The art of sculpture in stone, long neglected in favour of work in metal (at a time when a church was a large shed providing protection and storage space for this liturgical furniture), was doubtless at first left to more modest artisans; and the stone-carver, when the architect required his assistance, had painfully to carry out all over again the experiments in the conquest of forms which the metal-smith had been spared.

The richness of Romanesque sculpture is the result of the confluence of these two streams, the 'Attic' and the 'Asianic', of their clashing, and of the eddies caused by their meeting. Deep down, it is still dominated by the aesthetic of metamorphosis; at the same time the over-all monumental discipline imposed by the architect canalised this still untamed force, guaranteed it a place but limited that place, obliging it to exercise self-control and to work out the laws capable of reducing that chaos to unity. But in its finest examples, which are in France, Romanesque sculpture tends towards low-relief—that is to say, towards a mural form of the plastic art preserving, in close co-operation with architecture, the full expressive value of movement. The quality of energy is well served by this mural instinct which, rather than filling a frame with dense forms, gives it life by means of a whole system of lines of force. At the dawn of the Western impulse the pilot art-form, the most fruitful one, the one by which the artists controlled their experiments, was in Italy sculpture, in France architecture—and for centuries this was to remain so. Sculpture in France remained an art of low-relief: the statues, even when worked out all round, were really made to have their backs against a wall. This was still the case with Jean Goujon: the way in which the wet draperies of the nymphs of the Fontaine des Innocents send a tremor over the wall surface reminds one of the statues on the *portail royal* at Chartres; and the *Diana of Anet* (due no doubt to a pupil) is a bas-relief transposed into the round. In the seventeenth century the French painters inherited this instinct for composition in low-relief: how many of the pictures of Poussin and of Philippe de Champaigne are arranged full face or in profile like cathedral tympani!

The case is quite different in Italy where sculpture is the pilot art-form. There it tended, by inertia, from the beginning and without hesitation, towards the statue proper. The first attempts appear in Emilia: even though they are still carved in low-relief, the stocky and compact figures of Wiligelmo with their knotty curves, fluted folds, concentrated faces, frank volumes and rude contours, assert a savage determination to stand on their own as forms independent of the wall. At the end of the twelfth century Benedetto Antelami for the first time created important pieces in the round, which jut, almost with violence, out into space: these beings, like the 'monads' later painted by Piero della Francesca, are self-contained, walled up in their matrix of stone, captives of their own volume, prisoners of their weight. It is as if for Antelami, in this genesis of the statue in the West, the material from which the first man was created was not clay but bronze. How Giotto's expressiveness issued from that of Nicolo Pisano in the *dugento* is well known—as also how, in the *Quattrocento*, the statue, conceived as such and apart from its architectonic function, guided the experiments of the painters, even stimulating them to the *tour de force* of making each figure a *trompe-l'œil*. The Florentine experiments in architecture were likewise somewhat independent of those in sculpture; and in reality it needed the Baroque—whose fore-runner in Venice was Sansovino, an architect and sculptor—fully to integrate sculpture and architecture.

*Plate 207*

*Plate 206*

With Antelami there appeared for the first time that *harsh classicism* of which Nanni di Banco, Masaccio and Piero della Francesca were later to create the highest expression—a classicism that

*Plates 251, 254*

encloses its human figures (each of them an individual permeated by his own essence, by the pride and might of his destiny) and forbids them any merely relative life. Like the *Quattro Santi Coronati* of Nanni or the sleep-walking protagonists in Piero della Francesca's *History of the Cross*, Antelami's human beings have haggard eyes and clenched jaws, their faces like their hands are inert—whereas in France, fifty years earlier, on the *portail royal* of Chartres, the bodies still tightly swathed in draperies have faces that smile on the believer entering the church, hands that seem to flutter, and lips that have parted to let pass words of love. Thus in Italy, whose subconscious was still filled with Antiquity, the rebirth of humanism in the twelfth century was achieved through the definition of the body, while in France (where Christian spirituality had few pagan traditions to contend with), the flowering of the soul upon the shank of stone produced an awakening of anthropomorphism.

*Plate 252*

*Plate 214*

The soul of Celtic paganism, penetrating the Romanesque artist through and through, had urged his imagination forwards into a fairy world that was bound to take him away from the corporeal definition towards which the Italian soul, still dominated by Graeco-Roman paganism, spontaneously moved. Chartres was to set a limit to the imaginative excesses reproved by St Bernard: its figures herded the fabulous denizens of Moissac back into the past, and these prophets are already apostles. But Chartres looked towards Gothic and closed an age, while Antelami's Baptistery at Parma opened the way which led to Nicolo Pisano's Baptistery at Pisa.

After the heart-felt effusions of St Augustine, many centuries went by before Christianity once more found the Man-God. The feeling of the humanity of Christ, which was so strong in the Bishop of Hippo because he was a man of the ancient world, was to remain foreign to the Byzantine intellectuals. As for the barbarians, their stage of development made them accessible only to a religion of observances. How moving are the first transports of St Anselm, begging his 'most dear friend' to admit him into the sanctuary of His love—the soul's aspiration to set itself free from its fears and find once more the way of the heart. This divine friendship, still timid in Anselm, became passionate in Bernard, and from that time onwards the soul could feel that it was 'the Bride of the Word'. The sense of the human did not arise in man from deliberate attempts at self-knowledge: it was by deepening his conception of the nature of the Man-God that man succeeded in finding his own way again. The contemplation of Pure Being led the theologian to the discovery of the human being. When the mystics—St Anselm, St Bernard—had sounded the depth of the soul, the philosophers could intervene, and in the thirteenth century St Thomas Aquinas constructed the first psychology of Western man.

This discovery of man in God was not made without meeting obstacles. Many Christians had refused to accept the dogma of the two natures of Christ, and at Byzantium this had led to the Monophysite heresy. As for the barbarian peoples, great numbers of them had adopted Arianism, which denied the divinity of Christ, and this, by isolating them from Catholicism, led them to destruction. Arius thought that, if the Son really proceeded from the Father, then he was not also uncreate: though the first in the hierarchy of the world, he was still a creature.

Backwash from these controversies on the nature of Christ still affected, from the ninth to the thirteenth centuries, beliefs about the Eucharist: a Carolingian thesis regarded the Host as the immortal Body of Christ, of Him Who has risen to Heaven and sits at the right hand of the Father, while on the contrary, in the twelfth century, the theologians of the school of St Victor and the schoolmen of Chartres asserted that the Host was the *corpus verum*, the Body of the living Christ. The whole iconography of the cathedral of Chartres, executed in the twelfth and thirteenth centuries, is visibly inspired by the determination to stress the double nature, human and divine, of the incarnate Christ: the *corpus verum* appears in the Christ of the tympanum of the *portail royal*, the last apocalyptic and the first evangelical Christ, and on the thirteenth-century south transept porch Christ as the teacher of the Apostles and founder of the Church by the Word gives His blessing

*Plate 214*

*Plate 215*

on the central pillar, right underneath the image hovering in the tympanum of Christ in Judgment on the Last Day.

It had taken ten centuries for the teaching Jesus of the Sea of Galilee and the Sermon on the Mount to appear in Christian art—with, in His gaze, that infinite compassion on the part of unlimited divine power, which measures man's misery better than man himself because it is itself measureless. The anonymous creator of the south porch unquestionably gave to Christians the most profound of all the images of the Man-God. A few years later, in the work which popular admiration has christened the 'Beau Dieu d'Amiens', the features are dedicated to the expression of truth alone and are undisturbed by love. By its perfect unity, its unruffled modelling and its abstract gaze, this figure reminds one of the beautiful formal definitions of the *Summa theologica.*

*While the French cathedrals are permeated with the divine serenity, 13th-century Italy introduces drama into art. Even in the 'primitive' paintings the expression of human suffering comes through (233, 234)—through a Byzantinism which Giotto then rejects in order to set man face to face with pain and death (225). Nicolo Pisano imagines even the despair of the damned (222), and his son, Giovanni, the prophetic delirium (220)*

Since the end of the Incarnation is Redemption the humanity of Christ is expressed in the drama of the Passion. Man must suffer something of God's sufferings before he can arrive at some pity for his own griefs. The Passion led to the birth of pathos: this discovery, which escaped the French of the thirteenth century, impregnated as they were with theological serenity, was reserved for the Italians, whose sensibility had been profoundly stirred by the Franciscan preachers. Transposing the divine on to the plane of everyday life, Giotto brought about the rebirth of tragedy. It has been said that he may have been inspired by certain stage spectacles of his time, in particular the *Ecerenis* of Albertino Mussato, who had tried, at Padua itself, to revive ancient tragedy. The theme of Christ come down to earth and living like a human being, gave rise to a whole world of gestures, attitudes, and feelings whose access to art had been barred for centuries; and the theme of His exposure to the power of Evil set in motion a whole new range of expressive devices, reawakening the eternal conflict of human feelings. Of all sufferings the worst is that of the damned: Giotto tried, clumsily, to express it by depicting torture; but the suffering of a despair stubborn in its perversion had already found its true countenance in the carvings of Nicolo Pisano on the Siena pulpit, where the wind of terror troubles the serene figures that came from ancient sarcophagi.

*Plates 214, 215*

The God of Chartres welcomes the faithful to the threshold of a world of mystery. During the last century or so many speculations about the Gothic cathedrals have been put forward. Viollet-le-Duc, who looked at them as an architect only, gave currency to the idea that the master masons had sought to increase their lightness and admit more light. Increase the lightness, certainly; but as regards the amount of light let in, there is room for discussion. A view such as his can only have been deduced from studying those denatured monuments, the cathedrals stripped of their stained glass by the seventeenth-century canons—for example, the cathedral of Amiens, inundated as it is by a glacial light that seems to make the building transparent and led Huysmans to describe it as 'Jansenist'. But when you go into cathedrals that have retained their old glass—Chartres, Bourges or Leon—certainly you cannot say you are entering a world of bright light: as you stumble about in the darkness, what strikes you is not light but colour. Recently Louis Grodecki, a historian whose knowledge includes the art of stained glass as well as that of architecture, has even defended the thesis that the continual increase in the size of the cathedral windows was due to the desire to counteract the darkness caused by the new style of stained glass which, in the thirteenth century, was becoming darker and darker: had not the Abbot Suger, when this art was still at its beginnings, caused abnormally large windows to be made in the ambulatory at Saint-Denis for this purpose? The idea is confirmed by the reabsorption of sculpture within the buildings—sculpture that would be invisible in these circumstances: in Gothic cathedrals the capitals are all much alike and are merely plastic elements entrusted with a simple architectural function; but in a Romanesque church the narration of the Scripture stories—which in the Gothic period is done by the windows—is concentrated on the capitals, and these can only be legible in the clear light let in by the pale window glass most frequently used in the monastic churches. This has not

*Plates 216–219*

prevented the *Monuments Historiques* from installing modern stained-glass windows in the aisles ot Conques, thus burying in incurable darkness one of the finest series of Romanesque capitals.

In the night of the tall nave of Chartres are seen the flaming swords of the archangel who, to make the sublime hymns of the Beyond perceptible to gross men, wears a breast-plate of gold, purple and azure. Here the eye is no longer the visual, it is the visionary organ. From the beginnings of Neoplatonic mysticism the invasion of the spirit by the supreme brightness had been symbolised by an illumination in darkness: the Pseudo-Dionysius, source of all the later mystics, says that 'the secrets of God appear in *a darkness brighter than light*'. Innumerable visionary mystics later sang the praises of this splendour in darkness, down to St John of the Cross who added to this poem of radiant night its last and finest stanzas.

For all, spiritual illumination in the midst of night appears comparable not to bright light but to fire: some speak of live and spurting flames. Is not this precisely the impression given by the nave and aisles of Chartres?

Light, that symbol of the supernatural world, is embodied in those rarest bodies of creation, gold and precious stones—materials so pure that they seem to us a message from the other world, drops of brightness, condensation of light which, kept captive in them, radiates dazzling fires. At first they were used to render homage to God and the Saints; later, from the fourteenth century onwards, when luxury, no longer merely power, was the measure of pre-eminence, they were made to enhance the glory of princes.

As for painting, it was at first an imitation of the goldsmith's work. On the pages of the missals the holy images, preserved from the assaults of time by the darkness of the libraries, bathe in lakes of gold—mirrors into which the light dives as soon as the book is opened. With its backgrounds of burnished gold and its pure flat enamel-like colours set in the cloisonné of draperies picked out by gold, a painting by Duccio is a piece of goldsmith's work reflected in a mirror. The fresco-painter was at a disadvantage in not being able to use gold: he replaced it by another precious colour, worth its weight in gold—ultramarine. Age has scattered its ash over this, tarnishing the lapis lazuli depth which it possessed initially; but the panels of Fra Angelico—and later, in the centuries when night was admitted into pictures, that of the mystic Le Sueur—have preserved for us, undiminished, the supernatural virtue of the colour which Cennino Cennini, in accents trembling with respect, called 'noble, beautiful, and more perfect than any other'.

If the fiery qualities of light blazing in darkness are the image of the divine illumination, its brightness is the symbol of truth and beauty. Medieval poetry made immoderate use of these words 'clear' and 'bright', applying them to everything beautiful and noble—to the purity of springs, the gleam of the sword, the complexion of a woman and her hair. When the painter first looked at Nature he did so with an eye greedy for light. The world of Van Eyck, impregnated with limpid brightness, seems seen by the eye of God in the morning of the world: everything is enveloped in a translucent finery; the most humble object is a precious stone; the fields are enamelled with flowers, and the trees bear apples of gold. Everything, even the distances, is close at hand, everything manifests the equal presence of God in each one of His creatures, everything is radiant with the *splendor veri* which illuminated Adam's soul in the Earthly Paradise.

*Plate 235*

In this definite world everything is in the state of original perfection; even man with his face scored by care, even the ugliness of Arnolfini with his horsey features, is integrated into an incorruptible stuff. It is a world that seems executed by a painter who was a goldsmith, and it is no surprise to find, sometimes, the goldsmith receiving back from the painter what he has given him: the *Little Horse of Altötting* is like an illuminated miniature transposed into gold, pearls and rubies.

*The whole of European art at the end of the 14th and beginning of the 15th centuries is impregnated with the fragrance of Nature: artists strive to discover animal life (226, 228), they enumerate and study plants (227, 229). In the course of the 15th century this naturalism is worked out by the French weavers (230)*

Already before Van Eyck, in the secrecy of the illuminated manuscripts, the Lombard school had expressed its wonder at the discovery of that enchanted world, a field in the month of

*Fragmentary stone head from Heidelberg, showing ornaments in the form of* mouchettes.

*Plates 230, 231*

May. The fifteenth-century weavers created whole series of tapestries that turned the rooms of princes into an eternal springtime. Flowers, surrounded by a whole miniature world that lives in their neighbourhood—butterflies, dragonflies, beetles, birds and small animals—made their entry into painting, a source of inspiration which has never been exhausted.

*The walls of the châteaux are covered with sumptuous tapestries (231); the princes wear crowns of gold studded with pearls and precious stones (233). The finest object that has come down to us from this period is an ex voto to the Virgin, which Queen Isabelle of Bavaria gave to Charles VI on their marriage (234)*

Civilisations nearing their end, as Huinziga has shown, do not abandon their ideals: when they cease to put them into practice they 'irrealise' them—projecting them into an imaginary world. So it was that the fifteenth century made itself drunk on the poetry of courtesy, chivalry and even of mystical reverie; but it was only a game, indeed a fashionable game, designed to divert a princely society that was filling the void in its soul by an excess of display. The dukes of Burgundy, dazzling the crowd and their guests by extravagant pageantry and display of wealth, seem to have administered their estates as though they were life-tenants, in a hurry to get the most out of them as if they knew they had no future.

*Plates 240, 245*

The fever spread over a Europe that was suspended between two worlds. It was expressed by that last Gothic style, known as *flamboyant* because of the form of its window traceries. This style is the full-blown expression of what we have already called the 'Asianic' taste for sensuous and interlacing curves and counter-curves: is not the *mouchette* to be found in Siberian gold jewellery? This instinct, which came from remote ages and had inspired so many barbarian and Romanesque forms, was repressed by the rationalism of French Gothic, but in the fifteenth century it invaded the whole of Europe in the shape of a luxuriant vegetation. Even Italy succumbed to it—and not only in architecture (*flamboyant* architecture prevailed at Naples as at Milan), but even in painting: a resurgence of the Germanism that was buried in this classic land produced the thorny forms of Cosimo Tura, which are so like those of Bernt Notke at the other end of Europe.

*Plate 246*

Religious art found inspiration in suffering with all its train of evils. The Passion of Christ was the pretext for this display of physical and moral pain. Each people showed its nature by the suffering it chose to emphasise: Italy remained faithful to its tradition of making it a drama; in the Flemish painters one can almost hear the pure cry of the natural human being who is hurt; Germany revelled in cruelty, tortures and deformity; and France withdrew into a reserved, compassionate meditation, and sometimes attained a sublime utterance. At the cross-roads between south and north the *Pietà d'Avignon* stands in its isolation above all schools, as though Europe had united to produce the masterpiece of the century, the spirit of which is yet so profoundly French. This single castaway from a whole art that has vanished remains the highest spiritual expression of the Middle Ages.

*Both sculptor (248) and painter (249) have shown the grief of Mary as she withdraws beneath the shelter of her veil*

## *Writing*

The Evangelist dipping his pen in the ink, who introduces this chapter, is symbolic of that most intimate cell in the monastery, centre of intellectual life, the *scriptorium*. There, in the silence, what remained of the culture of Antiquity and of Biblical study was transmitted through the Dark Ages and the new philosophy and theology elaborated.

185 *St John from the Gospels of Godesalc, 781–5*

*186 St Benedict and St Desiderius, from an 11th-century life of St Benedict*

# *The City of God*

St Augustine's *City of God* made current the concept of an ideal city, a sacred territory, an enclosed world defended against the impurity of the outer world and living in self-sufficiency. In this concept the monastic life, codified in the rules of St Columbanus, and, above all, of St Benedict, found inspiration; and it so permeated the Middle Ages that even in the Renaissance it affected the manner of representing the world, the Heavenly Jerusalem, Paradise, and the *Hortus conclusus* which symbolised the purity of the Virgin.

*188 St Martin blessing a tree. Capital from Vézelay, c. 1130*

*190* LIMBOURG BROTHERS: *Temptation, Fall and Expulsion* ▶ *from the* Trés Riches Heures, *1411–16*

*187 Fountains Abbey, Yorkshire, 11th–15th century*

*189* UPPER RHENISH MASTER: *Paradise Garden, early 15th century*

*191 'I Cori Musicali', from MS of Cosmas Indicopleustes*

# *Atticism*

'Attic' taste, as defined by Quintilian in the first century in his discussion of oratory, continued well into the Middle Ages and, during the Carolingian Renaissance and its continuation, Ottonian art, maintained the harmony, refinement, and nobility of the art of Antiquity—and even its sense of the picturesque.

*192 Otto III, from a Gospel manuscript, c. 1000*

*195 St Matthew, early 9th century*

*196 Bust from Acerenza Cathedral, Apulia, 13th century*

*193 'Love Gathering Flowers'. Palaeochristian fresco*

*194 'The Harvesters' from the* Utrecht Psalter, *c. 830*

*197 Baptism, from the font of St Bartholomew, Liège, c. 1120*

*199 Angel. Gold relief from the Bâle altar, 11th century* ▶

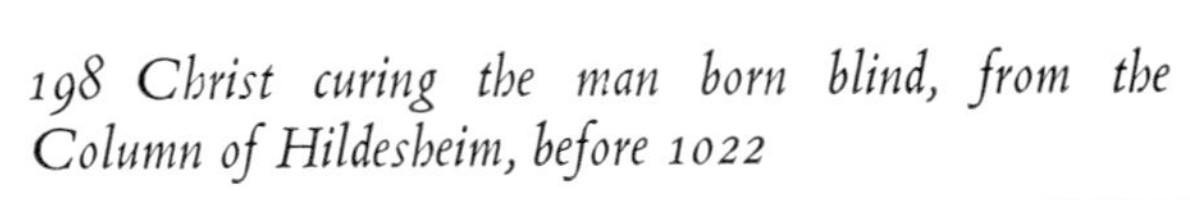

*198 Christ curing the man born blind, from the Column of Hildesheim, before 1022*

## *Asianism*

The second type of oratory, as defined by Quintilian, is 'Asianism', with its tendency towards a tumid verbosity without rules, a search for strangeness and the use of metaphor and hyperbole. In the realm of visual forms its closest equivalent is Anglo-Irish miniature painting, that world of metamorphosis, in which nothing comes into being unless it is immediately reborn in the form of monstrous and transitory creations whose very principle is metaphor. Another manifestation of 'Asianism' is the complication of the sculpture of this period.

*200 Page from the Würzburg Bible, 8th century*

202 *Initial from* The Book of Kells, *Celtic, c. 760–820*

201 *Figure from the lintel of S. Genis-des-Fontanes, c. 1020*

# *The Two Romanesque Styles*

205 *Capital from Monreale Cathedral, c. 1175*

203 ANTELAMI: *'July' from the Baptistery, Parma*

204 *Isaiah, Cremona Cathedral, early 12th century*

206 ANTELAMI: *Adoration of the Kings, from the Baptistery, Parma, early 13th century*

207 WILIGELMO: *Funerary genius, Modena Cathedral, early 12th century*

The richness of the Romanesque style comes from the confluence of those two streams, 'Attic' and 'Asianic'—from the conflicts between them and the eddies produced by their collisions. In France the monumental discipline imposed by architecture upon the sculptor kept the untamed energy of 'Asianism' under control on the wall surfaces. In Italy sculpture was the pilot art: it descended directly from the forms of Antiquity, and from the start asserted its fierce determination to exist independently of the wall.

*208 Capital from Autun, c. 1130*

*209 Adoration of the Kings, Vézelay, c. 1130*

*210 St Michael conquering the Dragon, from S. Michel d'Etraigues, c. 1140*

*211 'Lust', fresco from Tavant, first half of 12th century*

*212 Isaiah from Souillac, c. 1130–40*

## *The Man-God*

The feeling of the humanity of Christ emerged in the last days of the ancient world, especially through St Augustine: it disappeared in the Early Middle Ages, that dark age when men could be reached only by a religion of observances. In the twelfth and thirteenth centuries it was reborn. It had taken more than ten centuries for the teaching Christ of the Sea of Galilee and the Sermon on the Mount to make His appearance in Christian art, with His eyes full of that infinite compassion on the part of divine omnipotence which had already filled the faces of the Bodhisattva of Hadda, Gandhara, and Lung-Men.

*213 Christ in Majesty. Book-cover, last quarter of 12th century*

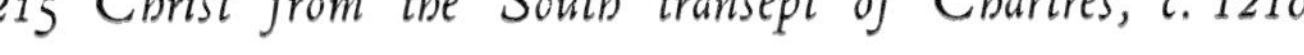

*215 Christ from the South transept of Chartres, c. 1210*

*214 Christ from the West front of Chartres, c. 1150*

*216 Northern rose window of Chalons-sur-Marne, late 13th century*

From the beginning of neo-platonism mysticism, the flooding of the spirit by the supreme brightness, had been symbolised by a light in darkness. The meagre light which the narrow windows let in to the Byzantine churches is enriched by the gold and brilliant colours of the mosaics. In the Gothic cathedral the windows are made very large, but are adorned with deep-hued glass that transforms the light into fire. To the medieval mystics spiritual illumination seemed more like fire than like light.

*217 South tower of Chartres, begun 1145*

*218 Annunciation to the Shepherds. English, late 14th century*

*219 Border detail. Canterbury, 13th century*

221 MAGDALEN MASTER: *head of Madonna, mid-13th century*

220 GIOVANNI PISANO: *head of Miriam, Siena, early 14th century*

222 NICOLO PISANO: *a damned soul. Siena pulpit, 1261–8*

# *Rebirth of Tragedy*

Through the Man-God, man discovered himself. He shared the sufferings of God before he conceived a certain pity for his own griefs. The Passion aroused pathos, expressed so strongly from the thirteenth century onwards by the Italians, whose sensibility had been deeply disturbed by the Franciscan preachers. Giotto, transposing the divine on to the plane of daily life, achieved a rebirth of tragedy. Before him, Nicolo Pisano had treated the subject of the ultimate suffering—the irredeemable despair of the damned.

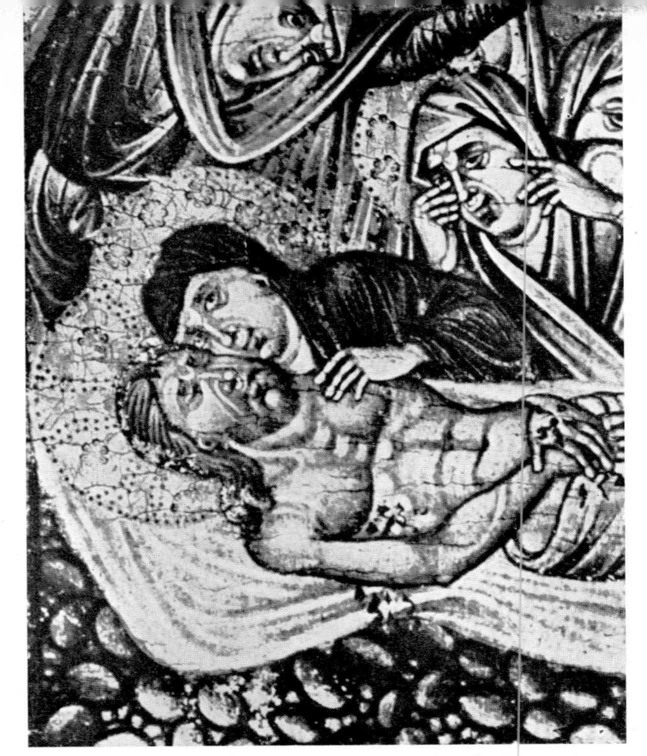

223 MASTER OF ST FRANCIS: *detail from the Lamentation, c. 1270*

224 GIUNTA PISANO: *St John, from a Crucifix, c. 1350*

225 GIOTTO: *detail from the Lamentation, Padua, 1304–8*

# *Discovery of Nature*

At the end of the fourteenth century, in the secrecy of the illuminated books, the miniaturists discovered the marvels of Nature. An unceasing series of tapestries produced by the fifteenth century weavers turned the halls of the princes into an eternal Spring. At the same moment the love of the chase stimulated the painters to a more attentive observation of animals.

*226 Page from the Holkham Bible. English, second quarter of 14th century*

*227 Egerton Manuscript: detail of illumination, 13th century*

228 PISANELLO: *study of a ram, early 15th century*

*229 'Tacuinum Sanitatis', c. 1380–90*

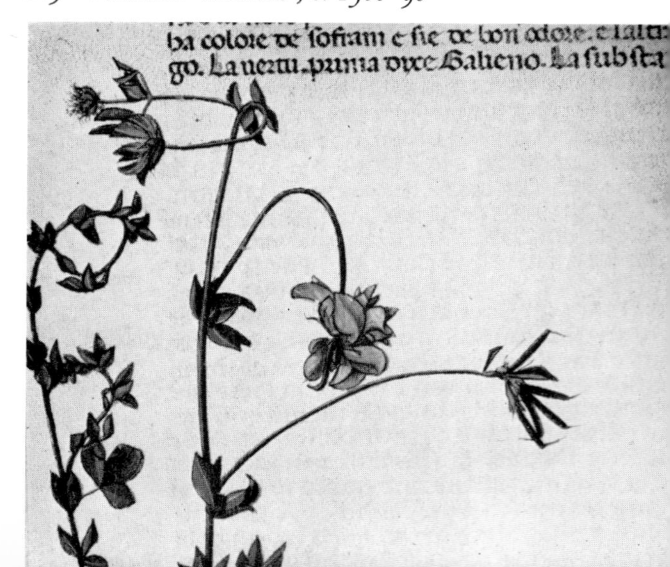

*230 'The Hunt of the Unicorn', tapestry, c. 1500*

# The Europe of the Princes

At the end of the Middle Ages a princely society seeks to fill the deepening void in its soul by an excess of splendour. Display becomes the measure of power. The gold and jewels that served as symbols for the other world now enhance the brilliancy of the life of the feudal aristocracy.

*231 King Arthur. Wool tapestry. French, late 14th century*

*232 Seal of Edward III (1340–72)*

*233 Crown of Princess Blanca, before 1399*

*234 The 'Little Horse of Altötting', before 1404* ▶

# *Mirror of Truth*

Van Eyck's world is filled with limpid brightness: it seems to be the world seen by the eye of God in the morning of the Creation—clear-cut in its original perfection. Everything, even Man with his face scored by care, even the ugliness of Arnolfini with his horsey features, is absorbed into an incorruptible medium. This Flemish way of painting was to conquer Italy through Antonello da Messina.

235 JAN VAN EYCK: *detail of the Madonna of Chancellor Rollin, about 1435*

236 MAÎTRE DE FLÉMALLE: *detail of Virgin and Child before a fire-screen, 2nd quarter of 15th century*

*238* ANTONELLO: *Portrait of a man, about 1470*

*237* JAN VAN EYCK: *detail from the Arnolfini marriage portrait, 1434.*

*239* Bernt Notke: *St George defeating the dragon, 1448*

*240 Chinese sign of the 'Yang'—male—(red) and 'Yin'—female—(black)*

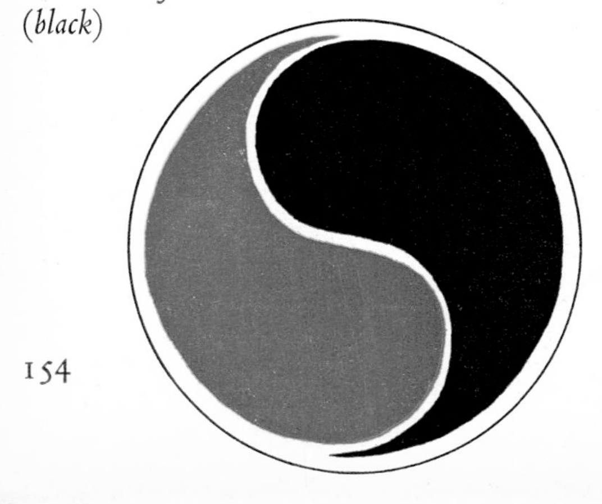

*241 Stucco decoration from Samarra, late 9th century*

*242 Panel from Nishapur, late 10th century*

# *Flamboyant style*

The fever that invaded Europe at the end of the Middle Ages expressed itself in the Gothic style known as 'flamboyant' from the shape of its window traceries. This style, with its sinuous and complicated curves and counter-curves, is another flowering of the Oriental and barbaric taste which Quintilian called 'Asianic'. The same bristling style influenced sculpture from one end of Europe to the other. Flamboyant ornamentation, in particular the 'mouchette', has an antecedent in the Siberian and Celtic jewellery and in certain Moslem motifs. Two 'mouchettes' together in a circle were a Chinese symbol for the cosmos, in which *yin* and *yang* are indissolubly united.

243 *Beverley Minster: detail of a window, 14th century*

244 *La Tène style gold disk, 4th century*

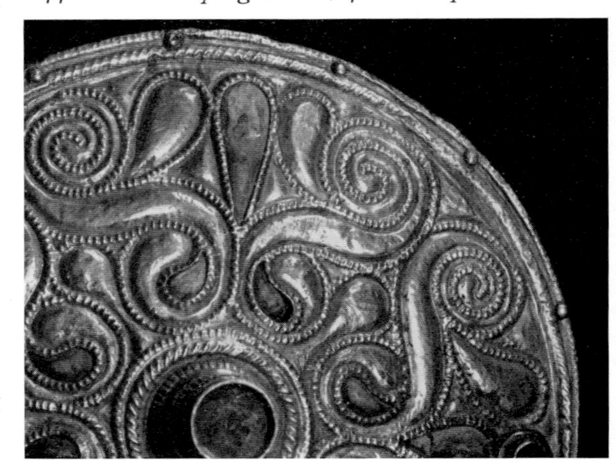

245 *Celtic tankard handle, 2nd century* A.D.

246 COSIMO TURA: *Allegorical Figure*

247 *Iberian stele, 2nd century* B.C.

# On the Peak of the Sublime

Alone at the meeting-place of North and South, the Avignon *Pietà* stands above all schools, as though Europe had united to produce this masterpiece, the highest spiritual expression of the Middle Ages at their pathetic, disrupted end.

*248* JEAN MICHEL *and* GEORGES DE LA SONNETTE: *head of the Virgin, 1451–3*

*249* SCHOOL OF AVIGNON: *Notre Dame de Pitié, mid-15th century*

# NOTES ON THE ILLUSTRATIONS TO CHAPTER V

185 *St John. Illumination from the Gospels written and illuminated between 781 and 785 by the scribe Godescalc for Charlemagne. Bibliothèque Nationale, Paris.*
*Photo: Eileen Tweedy*

186 *St Benedict and St Desiderius. From an 11th-century MS. of the life of St Benedict. Desiderius, abbot and benefactor of the monastery of Monte Cassino, receives the blessing of its founder. (c. 480–c. 543.) Vat. Lat. 1202 f.2.r.*
*Photo: Direzione della Biblioteca Vaticana, Rome*

187 *Cistercian abbey of Fountains, Yorkshire, England. 11th–15th century.*
*Photo: Aerofilms Ltd, London*

188 *St Martin and the tree sacred to the pagans, which is about to crush him. Capital from Vézelay, Burgundy. c. 1130.*
*Photo: Archives Photographiques, Paris*

189 UPPER RHENISH MASTER: *Paradise Garden. Early 15th century. Städelsches Kunstinstitut, Frankfurt.*

190 LIMBOURG BROTHERS: *Temptation, Fall, and Expulsion from Paradise. From the Très Riches Heures du Duc de Berry. 1411–16. Musée Condé, Chantilly.*
*Photo: Archives Photographiques, Paris*

191 *I Cori Musicali, from the 'Topographia Christiana' of Cosmas Indicopleustes, after a prototype of the 6th century. Vatican Library, Rome.*

192 *Otto III. Gospels of Otto III. Painted at Reichenar, c. 1000. Staatsbibliothek, Munich.*

193 *Love Gathering Flowers. Palaeochristian. From the Cimitero di Domitilla, Rome.*
*Photo: Pontificia Commissione di Archeologia Sacra, Rome*

194 *The Harvesters, from the Utrecht Psalter. c. 830. University Library, Utrecht.*
*Photo: Arthaud*

195 *St Matthew. MS. illumination. Early 9th century. Schatzkammer, Vienna.*
*Photo: Bildarchiv Foto Marburg*

196 *Bust from Acerenza Cathedral, Apulia. 13th century.*
*Photo: Professor Willemsen, Bonn*

197 *St John baptizing, from the font, St Bartholomew, Liége. c. 1120.*
*Photo: A.C.I. Brussels*

198 *Christ curing the man born blind. Column of Hildesheim. Before 1022.*
*Photo: Bildarchiv Foto Marburg*

199 *Angel. Detail from an altar, gold relief over a wooden core, given c. 1020 by the Emperor Henry II to the cathedral of Bâle. Musée de Cluny, Paris.*
*Photo: Eileen Tweedy*

200 *Würzburg Bible, Epistle of St Paul. Anglo-German style, 8th century. (Mp. theol. F. 69, fo. 7v.) University Library, Würzburg.*
*Photo: Bildarchiv Foto Marburg*

201 *Figure from marble lintel of St Génis-des-Fontaines, Rousillon, France, c. 1020.*
*Photo: Yan. Reportage: Zodiaque*

202 *The Book of Kells, initial letter. Celtic, c. 760–820. Trinity College, Dublin. By permission of the Board of Trinity College.*
*Photo: Urs Graf-Verlag GmbH., Lausanne.*

203 *Workshop of* BENEDETTO ANTELAMI: *July. From the Baptistery, Parma. Early 13th century.*
*Photo: Tosi*

204 *Isaiah, from the façade of Cremona Cathedral, Italy. Early 12th century.*
*Photo: Alinari*

205 *Capital from Monreale Cathedral Sicily. Begun 1175.*
*Photo: Anderson*

206 BENEDETTO ANTELAMI: *Adoration of the Kings. Baptistery, Parma. Early 13th century.*
*Photo: Alinari*

207 WILIGELMO: *Funerary genius. Modena Cathedral. Early 12th century.*
*Photo: Courtauld Institute of Art, London*

208 *The Temptation. Capital from Autun, Burgundy. c. 1130.*
*Photo: Jean Roubier*

209 *Adoration of the Kings. Tympanum of south door, Vézelay, Burgundy. c. 1130.*
*Photo: Jean Roubier*

210 *St Michael conquering the Dragon. Tympanum of St Michael d'Etraigues, Angoulême, France. c. 1140.*
*Photo: Archives Photographiques, Paris*

211 *Lust. Fresco at Tavant, Touraine, France. First half of the 12th century.*
*Photo: Giraudon*

212 *Isaiah, from doorway of Souillac, Quercy, France. c. 1130–40.*
*Photo: Jean Roubier*

213 *Christ in Majesty. Book-cover. Limoges enamel. Last quarter of the 12th century. Musée de Cluny, Paris.*
*Photo: Eileen Tweedy*

214 *Christ, from the Tympanum of the* portail royal, *Chartres Cathedral. French, c. 1150.*
*Photo: Courtauld Institute of Art, London*

215 *Head of Christ. Sculptural detail from the south transept porch, Chartres Cathedral. French, c. 1210.*
*Photo: Houvet*

216 *Northern rose window of the cathedral of Chalons-sur-Marne. French, late 13th century.*
*Photo: Hurault*

217 *South tower of Chartres Cathedral. French, begun in 1145.*
*Photo: Bulloz*

218 *Annunciation to the Shepherds. Stained-glass roundel. English, late 14th century. Victoria and Albert Museum, London.*
*Photo: Alfred Lammer*

219 *Border detail of stained glass from the north side of the Trinity Chapel, Canterbury Cathedral. English, 13th century.*
*Photo: Alfred Lammer*

220 GIOVANNI PISANO (*c.* 1245–1318): *Detail of Miriam, sister of Moses. Early 14th century. Cathedral, Siena.*
*Photo: Grassi, Siena*

221 MAGDALEN MASTER: *Detail of Madonna's head from the Madonna Enthroned. Mid 13th century. Yale University Art Gallery, New Haven.*
*Photo: Anna Wachsmann*

222 NICOLO PISANO (*c.* 1210–*before* 1284): *A damned soul. Detail from the pulpit of Siena Cathedral. 1261–8.*
*Photo: Grassi, Siena*

223 MASTER OF ST FRANCIS (*mentioned in Umbria between 1265 and 1275*): *Detail from The Lamentation. c. 1270. Pinacoteca Vannucci, Perugia.*

224 GIUNTA PISANO (*mentioned between* 1236 *and* 1284): *St John, from the S. Ramerino Crucifix, Museo S. Matteo, Pisa.*
*Photo: Grumm, Provence*

225 GIOTTO (1266/7–1337): *Detail from The Lamentation, fresco in the Arena Chapel, Padua. 1304–8.*
*Photo: Josephine Powell*

226 *Page from the Holkham Bible Picture Book. English, probably second quarter of the 14th century. British Museum, London.*

227 *Detail of an illumination from Egerton Manuscript. Late 14th century. British Museum, London.*

228 PISANELLO (1395–1455): *Study of a Ram. Drawing. Early 15th century. Cabinet des Dessins, Musée du Louvre, Paris.*
*Photo: Archives Photographiques, Paris*

229 *Tacuinum Sanitatis. Lombard, c. 1380–90. Bibliothèque Nationale, Paris.*

230 *Detail from a set of tapestries: The Hunt of the Unicorn. Wool and silk with metal threads. French or Flemish, c. 1500. Metropolitan Museum of Art, New York.*

231 *King Arthur. Detail from a set of wool tapestries: The Nine Heroes. Late 14th century. Metropolitan Museum of Art, New York.*

232 *The sixth seal of Edward III (1340–72). British Museum, London.*

233 *The Crown of Princess Blanca, daughter of Henry IV of England; in 1402 she married Ludwig III, Elector Palatine. Solid gold, with enamel, emeralds, pearls, and diamonds. It is mentioned in an English inventory of 1399 as 'an older jewel'. Residenzmuseum, Munich.*
*Photo: Permission of the Department of Castles, Gardens, and Lakes, Munich*

234 *The Little Horse of Altötting given by Queen Isabelle of Bavaria to Charles VI of France on their marriage, January 1st, 1404. Charles VI is shown kneeling before the Virgin under a rose hedge. Pawned in 1405 by the King to his brother-in-law Ludwig of Bavaria, to whom he owed money. Given by him to the church of Altötting in Bavaria. Parisian workmanship, solid gold with pearls and enamel.*
*Photo: Hirmer*

235 JAN VAN EYCK (*died* 1441): *Detail from the Madonna of Chancellor Rollin. c. 1435. Musée du Louvre, Paris.*

236 MAÎTRE DE FLÉMALLE: *Detail from Virgin and Child before a Fire-screen. Second quarter of the 15th century. National Gallery, London.*
*Photo: Zoltan Wegner*

237 JAN VAN EYCK (*died* 1441): *Detail from Marriage of Giovanni Arnolfini and Giovanna Cenami. 1434. National Gallery, London.*
*Photo: Zoltan Wegner*

238 ANTONELLO DA MESSINA (*mentioned in* 1456, *died in* 1479): *Portrait of a Man. c. 1470. National Gallery, London.*
*Photo: Zoltan Wegner*

239 BERNT NOTKE (1440–1509): *St George defeating the dragon. 1488. Storkyrkan, Stockholm.*
*Photo: Antikvarisk-Topografiska Arkivet, Stockholm*

240 *Chinese sign of the* Yang (*red*) *and* Yin (*black*), *male and female principle of the Universe, united in a circle like two Gothic* mouchettes.

241 *Stucco decoration from Samarra. Late 9th century.*
*Photo: Courtauld Institute of Art, London*

242 *Panel from Nishapur. Iranian, late 10th century. Metropolitan Museum of Art, New York.*

243 *Detail of a window in Beverley Minster, Yorkshire. 14th century.*
*Photo: Courtauld Institute of Art, London*

244 *Gold disk. Auvers. 'Waldalgeheim' style (La Tène, 4th century* B.C.*). Cabinet des Médailles, Paris.*

245 *Tankard handle. Celtic, 2nd century* A.D. *Liverpool Libraries Museums and Arts Committee.*

246 COSIMO TURA (1430–95): *An Allegorical Figure. Panel. National Gallery, London.*
*Photo: Eileen Tweedy*

247 *Iberian stele. 2nd century* B.C. *Prehistoric Museum, Berlin.*

248 JEAN MICHEL *and* GEORGES DE LA SONNETTE: *Head of the Virgin from an Entombment. French, 1451–3. Hospital, Tonnerre.*
*Photo: Giraudon*

249 *School of Avignon, probably Enguerand Querton: Notre Dame de la Pitié. French, mid 15th century. Musée du Louvre, Paris.*
*Photo: Eileen Tweedy*

# VI RENAISSANCE MAN

# VI Renaissance Man

'IT IS CERTAIN,' says Alberti, 'that temples which give men's souls a sovereign pleasure and hold them by charm and wonder are wholly fitted to direct men towards piety. Therefore I would wish that the temple should really include all imaginable beauty, such as cannot anywhere be surpassed, and that it should be so laid out that those who enter it are stupefied and that it causes them to thrill with wonder at the dignity and excellence of the objects before them, so that they can hardly prevent themselves from exclaiming aloud: "This place is worthy of God!" ' A place charged with *mana* and communicating to the believer the feeling of the 'altogether other' is still, in our day, the definition given by historians of religion to the consecrated space.

The words of Alberti echo those of the Abbot Suger, the builder of Saint-Denis, who, three centuries earlier, thought of a church as 'a strange region of the world, existing neither wholly in the mud of the earth nor wholly in the purity of the sky'. Again, he says, 'It seems to me that from enjoyment of material beauty, with the help of God, we can feel ourselves transported, by analogy, to the spiritual heights of the sublime beauty.' The thought that animated the builder of Saint-Denis in the conception of his revolutionary basilica was already contained in the *De Cœlesti Hierarchia* of the Pseudo-Dionysius. In order to 'capture' the believer, the church from its early days mobilised art in its service.

Artistic sensation is essentially an intuitive knowledge, the capture of an unintelligible reality through and in the sensible—*mediantibus sensibus*, as the schoolmen put it; tending towards science, towards the *splendor veri*, it nevertheless opposes itself to intellectual abstraction. The aim of the artistic act is enjoyment or delectation, produced by the irradiation of an intelligible light intuitively perceived; this delectation is all the greater since the intellect is incapable of explaining its basis. The spectator has the feeling of approaching a mystery which he will never be able to reach and this approach fills his heart with a joy that is ceaselessly renewed by desire. Through this dark brightness he thinks he can see a few rays of the essential brightness: from deep down in his nature as a being 'exiled in imperfection' he can hear the murmur of the call to perfection. It is easy to understand that the Church should have wished to make this artistic trance serve the purpose of raising souls upwards, and should have closely associated with the mysteries of the liturgy those of art, which intensified them and, so to speak, materialised their presence. In several periods the place of worship has been conceived as a world *charged with art* and so fitted to act upon the senses of the faithful, in order to arouse in them an impulse towards the sublime realms of light. Music, the plastic arts, and even incense helped to make of the church another world, in which the believer felt himself, as it were, possessed by a power that forced him to his knees, with his eyes

*Bramante's plan for St Peter's, Rome*

raised towards the celestial spaces ringing with angelic melodies and shining with a supernatural light.

In the Early Christian, Byzantine, and Gothic periods the Church had sought this '*effet sacré*' in an orgy of art—chiefly in a prodigal stream of colours and gold and an accumulation of images, altars, furniture, and goldsmith's work. Alberti, in opposition to this tradition, desired that 'on the walls and floors of the church there should be nothing that is not philosophical'. As for the light, it must be white, with that candid clearness that is pleasing to God. 'Cicero,' he said, 'is of the opinion—and in this he follows Plato—that it is good to keep all the delicacies of ornament out of the temple, in order that it may be the purest [*candidissimus*] thing of all.' And he adds, 'I am easily persuaded that the thing most agreeable to God will be purity and simplicity of colour, just as purity of life is, and certainly it is not suitable that in temples there should be things that distract men from thoughts of religion.'

This is how Bernardo Rosellino, imbued with his master's way of thinking, conceived the tribune of St Peter's, where later Julius II wanted his tomb by Michelangelo to be placed: round windows were to 'distribute the rays of the sun in such a way as to give the worshippers a definite idea of divine glory'—a crown of light like the one over which already the dome of St Sophia was suspended.

The ideal church according to Alberti was realised by Bernardo Rossellino in the city to which Pope Pius II gave his name: Pienza in Tuscany. In the act decreeing the foundation of the cathedral, which dates from 1462, it is said that: 'In this temple, which we are building to the glory of the Blessed Virgin Mary, Mother of God, nothing is to tarnish the purity of the walls and columns, there must be no painting there, nobody is to bring any picture there, nor to add chapels; nobody is to modify its form.' Thus the soul rises to the Intelligible in a direct intuition, without recourse to the senses, by means of pure spacial speculation; and this is achieved through knowledge of numbers and through a simple, almost abstract lighting that brings out, in its recovered purity, the behaviour of volumes and the harmony of proportion. It is a supreme art, obtained by the purification of art, from Alberti to Bramante, and in it a church becomes an ideal place, essentially 'philosophical', reaching the divine through the Platonic sense of beauty, open to the delectation of refined minds—but the believer no longer feels any 'warmth of soul' there.

The medieval cathedral was indeed the city of God, an all-mothering organism, capable of infinite development, changing constantly in accordance with men and times and drawing from

*Plan of the cathedral of Pavia*

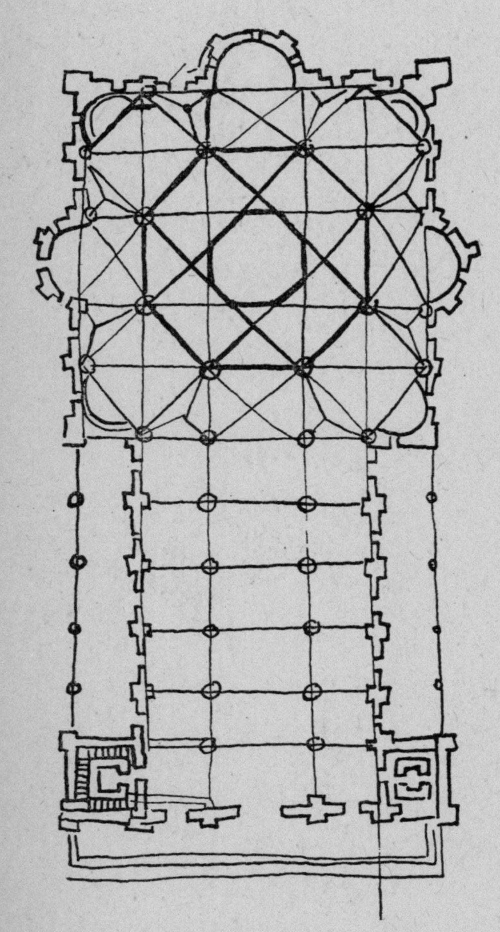

*Leonardo da Vinci: church showing combination of the basilican and central plan*

Nature an energy comparable to that of the proliferation of species. In the Renaissance church, on the contrary, nothing was supposed to trouble its harmony, once this had been established by geometrical relations; and this harmony could not be better realised than by the centralised plan, in which the tension between forces was resolved at one point, an ideal symbol for Infinity. But this point, where the altar was, and from which everything was to be judged, called for the presence of man, who thus placed himself at the very centre of Pure Being—whereas in the cathedral the believer, as he came in through the door, perceived the sacred point at the end of the vista, a symbol of the human condition which aspires to God without being able to reach him.

In the Renaissance church, man, raised up from this condition of subjection, is an ideal creature, 'the measure of all things'. While the centralised plan is the most adequate image of God, the basilical plan is that of man. The basilica opening out into a centralised plan appears in the drawings of Leonardo da Vinci who perhaps adopted the idea from the cathedral of Florence: it formed the original project for the cathedral of Pavia, then for that of Pienza, and was later realised by Diego de Siloe in the cathedral of Granada. Some thought it the ideal plan for a church consecrated to the Man-God; and there is a famous drawing by Francesco di Giorgio representing the man-church—the ground plan of a church coinciding with Christ on the Cross.

While Renaissance man tried to concentrate his thought upon God through supreme beauty, he at the same time, contradictorily, pursued that projection beyond himself, that quest for a beyond, that cult of progress which is part of the essential nature of Western man and will, no doubt, lead him to destruction. It was through the vistas of nave and aisle that Western man had already expressed this deep need to *tend* towards some aim, at a time when this aim was a future life: how is it possible to doubt that this feeling for 'perspective' was intentional when one sees a thirteenth-century architect, like the architect of the cathedral at Poitiers, strengthening this effect by accelerating the convergence of the lines at the cost of making the bays no longer square? But now this element of 'tending' or striving was to seek satisfaction outside the ways of God. God, once apprehended by Renaissance man through beauty, no longer had to do with *tendency*: it was the world that now called forth his ardour and offered its mirages to his thirst for knowledge. The painters gave expression to the passion for itemising each thing or being (the Florentines by formal texture, the Venetians by adding materiality to it), but in their attempts to situate everything in its place in a universe imagined as governed by strict laws, they succeeded only in projecting outside man, always a little further, his essential aim: and so man renewed the desire that goaded him on, and what he was seeking fled before him just as he thought he was reaching it. Without yet realising what he was doing, he was arousing the tragic problem of a consciousness that can only define itself by taking itself as object.

Through this unwearying quest for the object the painter, together with the architect, discovered a world—or rather a universe. Meditating on the statics of domes and on the dizzy vistas of perspective, these artists, emerging from the dark naves of the medieval churches, were dazzled by so much light and by all that space lying open before them. In the second half of the *Quattrocento* Mantegna played hide-and-seek with the vanishing point and laid hands on the convexity of the globe, flattening it so as to see the world over it, while Piero della Francesca, Baldovinetti and Pollaiuolo took their places, at one bound, on Olympus and from it, like gods, took in the world at a glance. Leonardo gathered up all these researches, and ransacked this space in all its dimensions: enchanted by the harmony of domes, which reduces movement to a divine immobility, he took also to climbing the Alps in order to contemplate from one and the same pinnacle the structure of the world's mountains and the formation of the clouds. But Leonardo's intellectualism dried up these springs as soon as captured: it was the men of the North, more attentive to the reality of things, who gathered the fruits of these efforts. With great patience Patinir prepared the way, making a laborious study of natural forms which, with a mind that had still remained

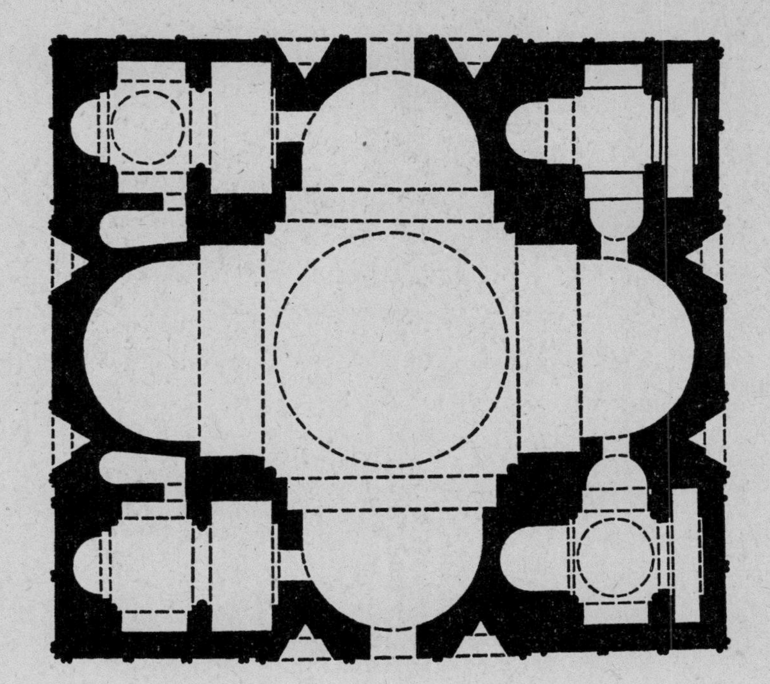

*Byzantine central plan: church of the Holy Apostles at Ani*

primitive, he set side by side like items in an inventory, spread out over the surface of his paintings. It was Brueghel who created the picture that is also the world—pictures that contain within their few square inches a whole seething world and offer to the mind and senses something like an attempt, though vain, to reduce the multiplicity of things to the unity which is nevertheless their soul, arousing in us both a feeling of gusto and a kind of despair. In these pictures the drama of history, till then subdued in the flatness of frescoes or cramped within the engulfing vistas of the paintings that explored perspective, is seen at last on a world scale: at last human activity is deployed in all its complexity and expands into a vast field. One painter of genius had already, in the first third of that century, made the world converge into a single picture that contains in itself all that the art is capable of: in the *Battle of the Issus* Albrecht Altdorfer raises the collision of two armies and the crumbling of an empire to a cosmic scale, in the setting of a tremendous meteorological phenomenon. Here *mimesis* achieves its masterpiece, for the spectacle, which is as complex as that of Nature, forces the eye to make a choice and leaves the mind bitter at not understanding all.

*With Isenbrandt (276), as with Patinir, this instinctive feeling for space is still expressed in an artificial and conventional manner. Then Brueghel took in at a glance all the disparate elements of the world and gave them the unity of his thought (282)*

*Plate 278*

All these works belong to or keep contact with the earth. But in the last third of the sixteenth century the links are broken. Tintoretto, setting the spectator free from the notions of high and low, launches him out into pure space—a space into which Veronese's figures were even then ready to take off from the ceilings of Venice. The woman pointing upwards on the swirling stairway in the *Presentation in the Temple* in the Madonna dell' Orto (1552) shows the way. The *Origin of the Milky Way* in the London National Gallery is an oscillating picture, carrying us from the mythological or humanist stage to the sidereal or cosmic. In 1548 Copernicus had published the work that put an end to the Ptolemeic geocentric cosmology—the *De Revolutionibus Orbium Coelestium Libri VI*: Tintoretto's *Paradise* in the Sala del Gran' Consiglio in Venice seems a reflection of this astronomical revolution. A long road had been covered since the time of Orcagna's *Paradise* in Santa Maria Novella—that theological world in which the blessed, incorporeal and flattened out against the wall, are arranged in rows like those of school photographs, while God, who is crowning the Virgin, is shown on a far larger scale in accordance with medieval ideas of the divine hierarchy. The first to have the courage to depict Paradise in three-dimensional space was Fra Angelico, that little-understood artist whom people still obstinately treat as a survival of the Middle Ages, whereas he was a pioneer of the Renaissance which was still, in his time, permeated with religion. In his pictures the choirs of angels move in the circular orbits described by the Pseudo-Dionysius: these he sees as rings arranged in space at an angle of forty-five degrees to the spectator. After him Lippi—that profaner and pure pagan (in the Christian, not the ancient,

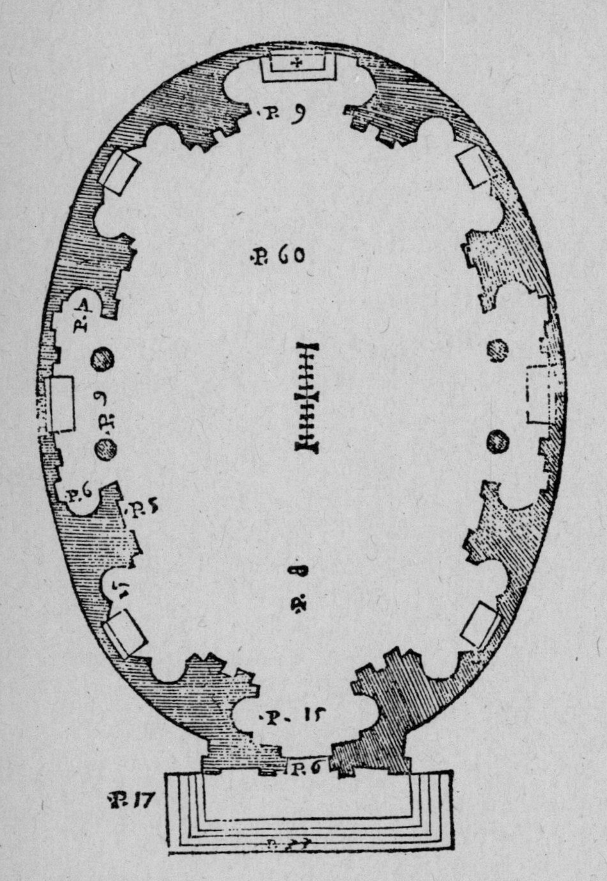

*Elliptical church plan by Sebastiano Serlio*

sense of the word)—turned Paradise into a fashionable diversion; but Raphael, in the *Disputà*, spreads the celestial assembly in a half-circle that hangs in supra-terrestrial space, where the Saints conduct their controversy; in this he is more than a century in advance of the scenery devised for opera. The Virgin and Jesus, placed in the foreground by Orcagna for theological reasons, withdraw, in the paintings of Fra Angelico and Raphael, into the background assigned to them by perspective. At the end of the century Tintoretto in his *Paradise* (which should be judged by the sketch in the Louvre rather than by the colossal painting in Venice, weighed down as this is by the heavy hand of Palma Giovane) achieved what amounts to a cosmogony: in it all the figures which he had hurled into the chaos of his *Last Judgment* in Santa Maria del Orto (later than 1570) are launched into orbits and gravitate about the central luminary, the radiant head of Jesus. But are these curves ellipses, or are they circles seen in perspective? In astronomy the circle was not demoted from its royal station till the seventeenth century, when Kepler relegated to the scrap-heap the old system's apparatus of eccentric and epicyclic circles and spheres that had satisfied so many minds from Aristotle to Copernicus; but often in history the sensibility of artists has created forms in advance of the intuition of the scientists. In painting, as in architecture, the circle attained its finest expressions in the early years of the sixteenth century, but in about 1530 Mannerism rejected it substituting the ellipse, and pictures became full of oval forms. It made its appearance in architecture rather later: the first oval plan seems to have been put forward by Serlio in the Fifth Book of his *Architettura* (1547); and the idea was taken up by Vignola in the dome of Sant Andrea in Via Flaminia in Rome (1550) and in the church of Santa Anna dei Palafrenieri (1572). While the circle, that image of repose, is the perfect symbol of contemplation, the ellipse, a curve in a state of tension (a circumference, as it were, distorted by the breaking of its centre into two), is a dynamic figure governing the rotation of worlds. In art the movement from the circle to the ellipse expresses that *warping of space* which became evident round about 1530 and was to inspire Tintoretto with his cosmic speculations at the end of the century.

*Hieronymus Bosch (279, 281), to show the weakness of man, had had recourse, fifty years earlier, to the manifestations of madness, to which men of the 16th century attributed a philosophical significance*

In the *Battle of the Issus*, in the midst of all that eddying of different worlds and men, there is a dog, a millimetre or two high, lying curled up asleep in front of a tent: all those great people and events are nothing to this creature, which is alive but preserved from thinking. The vanity of heroism! The futility of history, viewed on the scale of the universal! When the man who is in love with height comes down again alone from the peaks, he cannot help finding ridiculous all those people of the plains, busying themselves with such insignificant labours. This rejection of man by man, expressed by Brueghel with such incisiveness, is simply another part of the humanist attitude, one that implies a philosophical distancing: certain minds from the North of Europe were alone capable of expressing it fully, for there man was thought of as one element in the universe and not as a statue casting on the world a shadow of its profile. And yet the Germans themselves, with their tendency to sentimentality, took a more indulgent view of the creation than has sometimes been thought: their *naïveté* is as ineradicable as their cruelty. Dürer always sets Mary in the midst of the enchanted world of the *Paradisgärtlein*; and decidedly Paradise haunts the German imagination. Cranach, in his *Golden Age* and his *Fountain of Youth* shows us humanity at play, naked, in the midst of animals and flowers; and during the Second World War the *Frontbuchhandelsausgabe der Wehrmacht* published the *Jungbrunnen* with seductive detail, that the German footslogger might go to his death dreaming of the Germanic Eve—who was no innocent.

*Plate 275*
*Plate 274*

* * *

Gothic had infiltrated into Italian art like a virus, sapping its internal energy, and one of its worst effects had been to make these artists give second place to the statue, whose primacy in the Romanesque period had guided them towards the recreation of a figurative art. The real rebel against the flat Byzantine images had been Nicolo Pisano, who in 1260 had carved the Pisa pulpit with its athletes jutting from the marble, and so restored that corporeal tradition of Antiquity which an unknown artist of the time of Frederick II had tried to recover on the Capua gateway in an awkward, excessively direct imitation. At the end of the thirteenth century, Giotto brought this art of statuary into painting, and at that time Boniface VIII made so much use of sculptured portraits that he was accused of idolatry. But the fusion of the Giottesque with the Gothic diluted this powerful style, and Andrea Pisano completed the process by assimilating, a century after its creation, the elegant classicism of the low-relief carvings of the French cathedrals. Then, in the first years of the *Quattrocento*, Nanni di Banco—with more success than Donatello, who was somewhat distracted by Nature—fixed his gaze resolutely on Antiquity, establishing in his *Quattro Santi Coronati* a college of *togati* who burst the ridiculous Gothic niche in which they were intended to be confined. This was the real example from which Masaccio drew his inspiration. The impulse lasted for fifty years: to both sculptors and painters the statue came to seem the ideal form, embodying within the limits of its strict volumes the fierce independence of a human being determined to be 'himself alone'—soon indeed to be ready to assert his rights as a *prince* by sword and poison. To break the stiffness, those inflections of line became necessary which, in the time of Lorenzo de Medici, led artists to seek the expressive quality of the figure no longer in volumes but in contour: the motionless colossi of Paolo Uccello, Andrea del Castagno and Piero della Francesca are changed, in Antonio Pollaiuolo, in Botticelli, and in Piero di Cosimo, into dancing figures, mannered and tortuous, who seem trying to offer and to share with us a soul which the figures of the preceding generation had kept secret, shut up in their bronze or marble. No doubt the influence of Etruscan art, seen in glimpses by Alberti but seriously excavated in the time of Lorenzo, who collected its vases, cists, statues and funerary urns, also helped to define this really 'Tuscan' style, which was soon consciously opposed to the Roman style.

*The constant practice, throughout the 15th century, of imitating a certain Graeco-Roman type emerges plainly in the affinity of Michelangelo's David (253), Nanni di Banco's Isaiah (252) and Masaccio's Saint John (251)*

*Plate 254*

There is no better example of the passage from the one to the other than Raphael. Both at Perugia and at Florence—that is to say, when he was in Etruscan country—Raphael learnt all the resources of the arabesque, carrying it to an inimitable grace, a grace that was truly the messenger of sublime beauty, in which the bodies are so subtle that they are now no more than the phases of a wave.

*This tendency to harmony leads Raphael quite naturally to paint compositions on the circular theme (264) which, before him, had preoccupied the architects (262) whom he sometimes imitates (260). Later Primaticcio, when his problem was to paint the Dance of the Hours upon a ceiling (261), conceived it as a circling movement of forms*

Michelangelo, himself a Tuscan, was no stranger to such suppleness, but he imposed it on the volumes themselves, and the movement he tried to infuse into the bodies was not strong enough to carry with it the mass, whose prisoner it remained. Raphael lost his flexibility of line partly, no doubt, through contact with Michelangelo, but partly also because of the atmosphere of Rome, for it always imposed on the artist who came to the Eternal City—it hardly produced any artists of its own—a certain rhetorical grandeur (to be found already in Pietro Cavallini) and led to an exaggeration that deprived volume of its density and style of its expressiveness. Although the *togati* in the *School of Athens* still recall the noble draped figures of the *Ara Pacis Augustae*, those in the *Transfiguration*, the *Sistine Madonna* and the cartoons of the *Acts of the Apostles* offer us nothing better than the empty forms of the Marcus Aurelius bas-reliefs in the Capitol Museum.

*Proud Brutus (250) seems unable to move his head, which is ossified in the marble it is made of*

In Italy the ancient world gushed out through several springs: while Chiusi and Tarquinia had their 'renaissance' in Florence, Rome was always Rome, and Venice remained the Alexandrian city she had never ceased to be. Legend is always right, as against history. Did a Venetian fleet in 829 really bring back as a trophy the body of the Apostle St Mark, stolen from Alexandria? True or unfounded, that legend contains a profound symbol: the ancient capital of the Ptolemies did indeed transmit a treasure to Venice—the civilisation which bears its name. Venice is a Hellenistic city that has miraculously survived into our time. In the crude Middle Ages, with their turmoil of dogmas and fanaticism, the city on the lagoon inherited that mission for universal syncretism which had constituted the grandeur and glory of Alexandria at the ending of the ancient world. In her the extremes united: the West and Byzantium melted together, and a marriage took place on the lagoon between Christian civilisation and its mortal enemy Islam. Jews and Moslems had citizens' rights in a town so little subject to Christian principles that usury was admitted there. And Venice even supplied a harmonious conclusion to the antinomy which divided the Middle Ages—that between the pursuit of the absolute (given a spiritual form by Byzantium and conceived by Florence as the ideal Beauty) and the quest for expressiveness which harrassed the Gothic artists (those called *tedeschi* by the contemptuous Italians but welcomed by Venice, just as she welcomed everything that was alive, and held her commerce with equal readiness under the tropical sun or in the mists of the North). The real eternal city is Venice, not Rome. Rome, before its 'renaissance', had fallen to the rank of a medieval market town; but the Republic of Venice, in the pride of its extraordinary longevity had taken the name 'Most Serene'. The inviolate city sustained the glory of its name splendidly until 1797 when, after thirteen centuries, the soldiers of Bonaparte undid her girdle for the first time in history. Protected against invasion by her rampart of water, she is the only one of the Western cities to have come down to us straight from the ancient world: the few families of Venice who placed the water between them and the cavalry of the Huns saved the heritage of Antiquity from wreck. On the confines of the two empires (colossi with feet of clay) and surrounded on all sides except that of the sea, which was the doorway of liberty, by the anarchy of barons, communes, princes and princelings, Venice in her wisdom, like a Greek city, united the advantages of monarchy and of the democratic régime in that compromise, a tyranny elected by an oligarchy. The people of the Middle Ages marvelled at it, and in the eleventh century Pope Hildebrand declared: 'The spirit and liberty of ancient Rome are still alive in Venice.' For Venetian society, like that of the ancient city state, was made up of free citizens—free but served by slaves. Circassians, Georgians, and Ethiopians supplied the most thriving slave market in the world. The tranquil insolence of Venice, insensible to time and fashion, maintained slavery, that reproach of the ancient world almost to our own day!

Venice was no city of chivalry: the wife there did not play the eminent and dignified part allotted by the Gothic communities to the feudal princesses; her role was restricted, domestic. As in Athens or Alexandria, it was the courtesan who set the tone and received in her alcove the homage of poets and philosophers. The fame of some of these *femmes d'amour*—as for example Veronica Franco, to whom the Grand Council assigned the honour of sharing the bed of Henri III, King of France, when he visited Venice—spread through Europe: Montaigne mentions Veronica in his *Essays*. In the civilisations where Christianity had gone deep, the *femme d'amour* was an outcast; confined in a sort of ghetto, she led a despised life. But in Venice, a pagan city, the State considered her as indispensable to a balanced life and to the refinement of manners. At the beginning of the sixteenth century, in order to counteract sodomy, which the taste for manly beauty was making widespread in Italy, an edict of the Grand Council ordered the courtesans to sit at their windows with their bosoms displayed, so as to attract men and to turn them by natural means from the sin against Nature! Perhaps it was in obedience to the orders of the Grand Council, perhaps to please himself that Palma Vecchio, the most voluptuous of the Venetian artists, painted the courtesans with their hair down and the pearly opulence of their bosoms impudently uncovered.

*Plate 266*

Botticelli had painted Venus, but standing. Giorgione was the first to show her lying down, ready for love; but the pure body with the closed eyes is still that of a goddess. Giorgione was, indeed, only transforming into an image the sleeping nymph described in Chapter 8 (folio CC) of the *Dream of Poliphilus*—who herself was certainly inspired by some sleeping Ariadne of Antiquity: such is the way in which forms pass from sculpture to literature, then from literature to painting, in an unbroken chain—until we arrive at Titian's Urbino *Venus*, wide awake and, what is more, lying on the bed in her own room. No more ambiguity here; this is a mortal woman.

In this endless chain lies the secret of Venice. Long before Florence the great Venetian emporium had started a new trading, that in *anticaglie*; and in 1204 the finest trophy brought back from the pillage of Byzantium was the four Corinthian horses with which Venice adorned the basilica of San Marco. At about the same time, Villard de Honnecourt, the architect from Picardy, was drawing an ancient tomb: he was not very sure of what it was and called it '*sarrazinois*', meaning 'pagan'—a term of contempt, just as the word '*tedesco*' was for the Italians of the Renaissance. Venice did not, like Florence or Rome, experience any real artistic 'revolutions': the Renaissance, introduced by the Florentines, seeped into Venice so subtly that it seems a prolongation of Byzantium. The charm of a monument like Santa Maria degli Miracoli, that marble church which has issued from Lombard bad taste purified by Byzantium and Antiquity, is that it is at the meeting-point of so many tendencies as to seem quite outside time. Venice was the place that escaped from time, from that abyss of time in which the Middle Ages buried Antiquity: for her the words 'ancient and modern' have no meaning, any more than have the terms Gothic or Renaissance—and this because the spirit of Venice was so open, so relatively free from the hatreds that seem, alas, indispensable to self-knowledge both in individuals and in societies. Both constant and perpetually changing, Venetian civilisation achieved its great brilliancy because, alone in a tormented world, it lived the passing moment fully. The passing moment cannot be pinned down, neither can Venice: over the web of time the history of Florentine art is traced in clear outline like the figures on an Etruscan vase; but in the mirror of the ages Venice, like the sparkling reflections of its palaces in its waters, quivers with innumerable gleams.

Certain Venetians took issue vigorously against the Neoplatonism which, elaborated in Florence in the *Quattrocento*, was dominant in Rome in the sixteenth century. In his *De Pulchro et Amore* (written in 1529 and published in Rome in 1531) Agostino Nifo, a philosopher of the naturalist school of the University of Padua, where he had been a pupil of the Averroist Nicoletto Vernia, violently denied that beauty was situated in the soul of the artist and not in the object to be painted; in opposition to Marsilio Ficino, he rejected the idea that it was transcendent—to him it appeared to be 'in the nature of things'. Raphael, writing to Baldassare Castiglione at a time when he was working at the Farnesina, claimed that in order to paint a beautiful woman it was essential actually to see the most beautiful ones—failing which, he would make use of a certain idea he had in his head. Giorgione's *Venus* is still clinging to this conception, governed by an 'Idea' borrowed from Antiquity but perhaps elaborated through the imitation of several models—as Zeuxis had done with the most beautiful girls of Crotona. But Titian's Urbino *Venus* is the imitation of a single model, to which the painter submits, thus subjecting art to Nature which—as the humanist Pietro Bembo, librarian of San Marco, said in reply to Pico della Mirandola, representative of Florentine Neoplatonism—contains beauties 'unknown to Antiquity'.

*Plate 266*

*Plate 267*

The ideal, like a refracting prism, had for more than half a century guided the naturalistic researches of the *Quattrocento* towards a classical balance, ending in Raphael's soaring flight into pure beauty. When Raphael died the crystal clouded, and the Idea turned into Ideism. Mannerism, that neurosis of the imagination, is an intellectual game, in which one may see a resurgence of the old 'Asianism'—which the artist of the time of Paul III set up in opposition to the 'Atticism' of the pontificates of Julius II and Leo X. In through the breach, up from their depths, came all the old demons imperfectly repressed by classicism—especially the Gothicism which, not having been either assimilated or expelled by Italy, remained a tenacious virus. In the very place where, by the light of the idea, Apollo, Venus and Jesus had for a moment been reconciled, the hordes of the chimaeras and monsters were let loose, while from a corrupted Neoplatonism there issued a taste for artificiality and refinement that changed art from a creation to a mirage. This escapism showed in an unbridled passion for adornment: man hid his real identity under an armour of brocade, gold, enamels, pearls, rubies

*Mannerism, in its passion for experimenting with forms, returns to the complexities of Gothic (284), revels in the monstrous (285) and even invents Cubism (286), or goes for an extreme refinement of elegance, which often issues in an elongation of human proportions (287)*

*The passion for ornament, which, in the Elizabethan Age (298) and later, turned women into walking reliquaries, is served by the talents of the Mannerist goldsmiths (299) and jewellers (300), who attained at that time a preciosity and refinement that have never been excelled*

*A generation later than Berruguete, Juan de Juni (289) instilled into the older painter's tormented art a vitalism that already fore-runs the Baroque*

*The most 'pagan' of the Renaissance* grotteschi, *unquestionably, are those in the Castel S. Angelo: they are full of eroticism (292). In the second half of the 16th century the* grotteschi *provide the inspiration for decorative artists who excel in developing their delicate fantasies over the curved surfaces of vases (297) or the expanses of tapestries (296)*

and diamonds. Only El Greco—and before him Berruguete—pushed the game so far that it attained tragedy, carried along as they were by the genius of Spain, which sees no value in man except through his relation to God.

The most exquisite form of this game is that of the *grotteschi*. Inspired by ancient paintings discovered at Rome in what were thought to be grottoes (nearly all of them have now disappeared, but Pompeii has given us others like them), the *grotteschi* are a sort of plastic variation on that literary game, the *Metamorphoses* of Ovid. Such 'sophisticated play', the delight of artists in love with Antiquity, lasted—with various fresh starts—down to the end of the eighteenth century and had its parallels in the humanist game of *emblemata* and the literary diversion of *concetti*. Raphael in his grotesque designs for Cardinal Bibbiena's bathroom and the *loggetta* of the Vatican re-awakened all the winged enchantment of ancient fable; but after him the *grotteschi* became 'mannerised' and by about 1560 the startling interchanges between the different realms of nature under the deceptive mask of symmetrical composition almost suggest that the free fantasy of the Anglo-Irish miniatures has been reborn. Did the Renaissance end by producing its contrary?

250 MICHELANGELO: *Brutus, c.* 1539

252 NANNI DI BANCO: *head of Isaiah, Florence Cathedral, 1408*

253 MICHELANGELO: *head of David, 1501–4*

251 MASACCIO: *head of St John from the Brancacci Chapel, Florence, 1425–8*

# *Humanism*

To the Italian artist of the *Quattrocento*, who drew inspiration from Antiquity yet at the same time followed a tradition that came to him from the twelfth century, the statue was the ideal form, for it embodied within the limits of its strict volume the fierce independence of a creature determined to be 'himself alone'. The painters took from the sculptors this feeling of working in the round.

Piero della Francesca, Andrea del Castagno and Paolo Uccello paint human beings as closed circles, walled up in their matrix of stone, captives of their own volume, prisoners of their weight. Even in Michelangelo, the action which he stamps upon a body cannot carry its mass along but remains prisoner to it: his Brutus, in trying to turn his head, contracts a goitre.

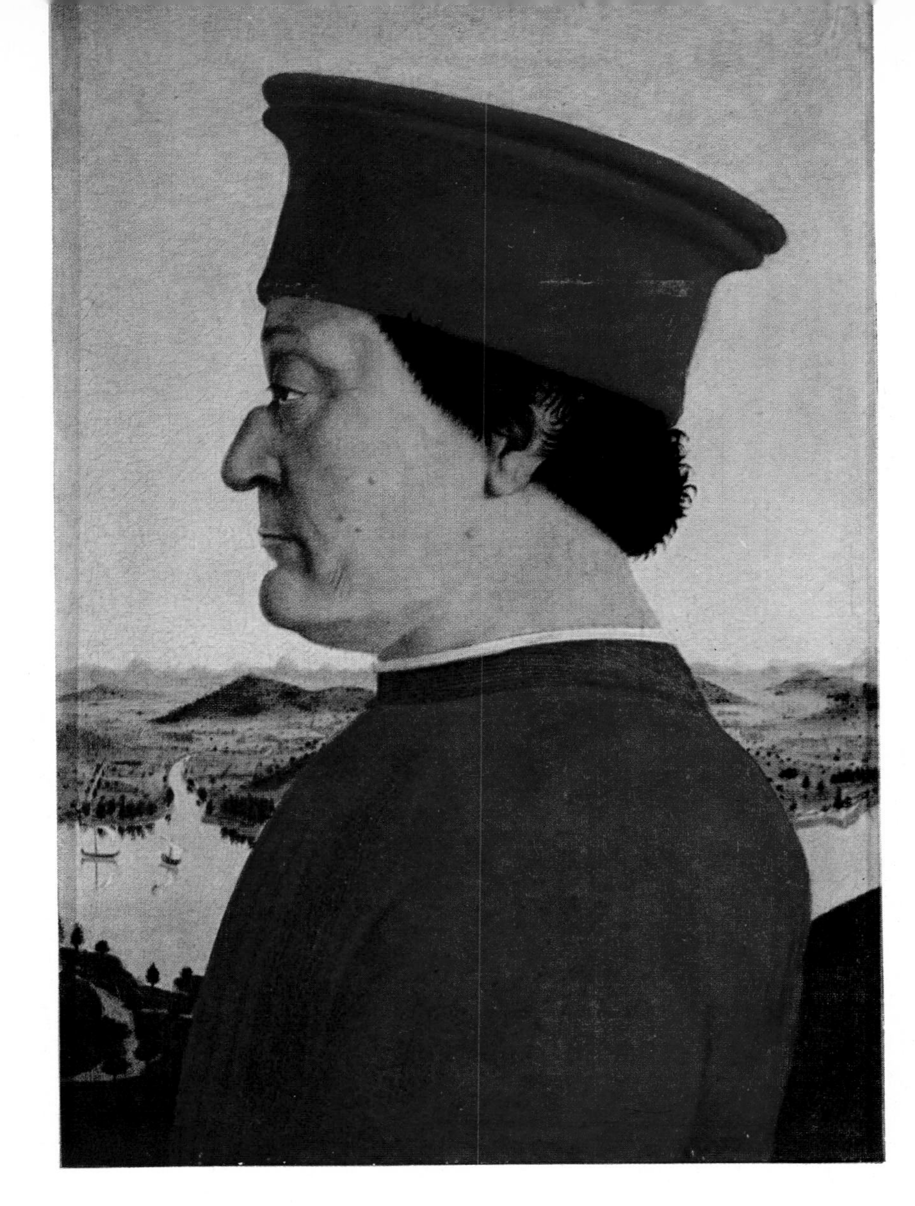

254 PIERO DELLA FRANCESCA: *Federigo da Montefeltro, c. 1465*

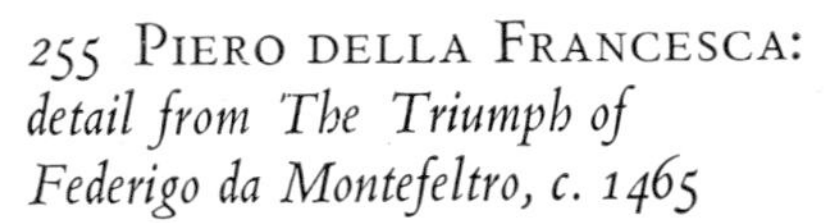

255 PIERO DELLA FRANCESCA: *detail from The Triumph of Federigo da Montefeltro, c. 1465*

# New Perspectives

The need to *tend* towards some aim is essential to Western man. In the Middle Ages it was expressed by the vista of the nave—at a time when life on earth was subordinated to the life to come. But now this need to tend or strive will seek satisfaction outside the ways of God: the painter, in obedience to this passion, itemises objects and living creatures and tries to give each its place within a strict world, from which the only opening for the spirit is into the distance, through the accelerating suction of perspective.

257 UCCELLO: *design for a chalice*

256 CARLO CRIVELLI: *Annunciation, 1486*

258 JACOPO BELLINI: *Banquet of Herod and beheading of John the Baptist*

259 PIERO DI COSIMO: *Mythological subject*

To Alberti and to Bramante a church comes to be an ideal place with an essentially 'philosophical' character: it attains the divine through beauty in the Platonic sense. This harmony, established by means of geometrical proportions, is best achieved by the 'central plan', in which the tension of all the forces is resolved at the ideal point, the symbol of infinity. Several artists combined the central and basilical plans, their dream being to make a church in the image of man, that masterpiece of creation.

260 RAPHAEL: *detail from Lo Sposalizio, 1504*

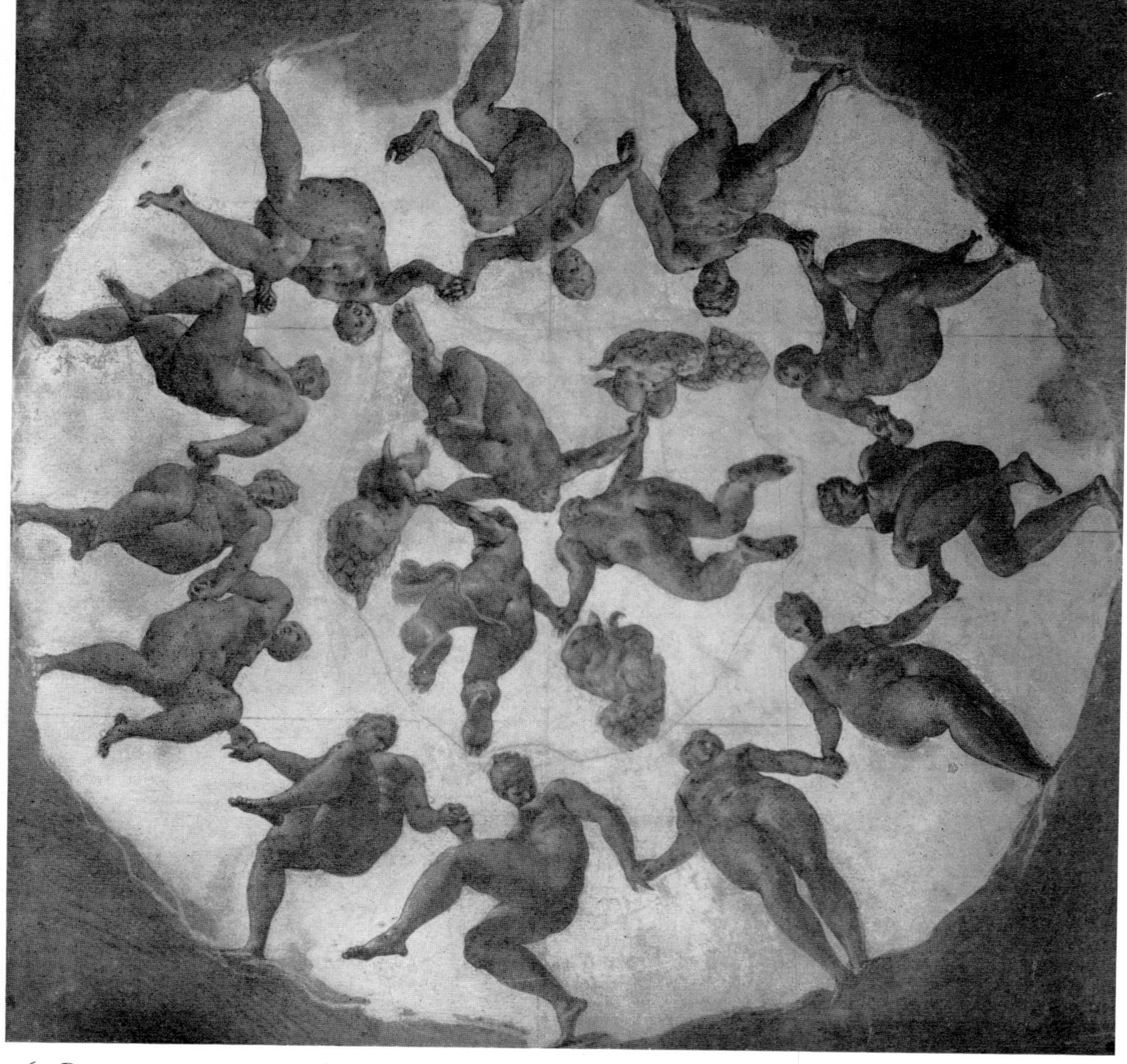

261 PRIMATICCIO: *Dance of the Hours*

262 BRAMANTE: *Tempietto of S. Pietro in Montorio*

263 FRANCESCO DI GIORGIO: *Church plan to human proportions*

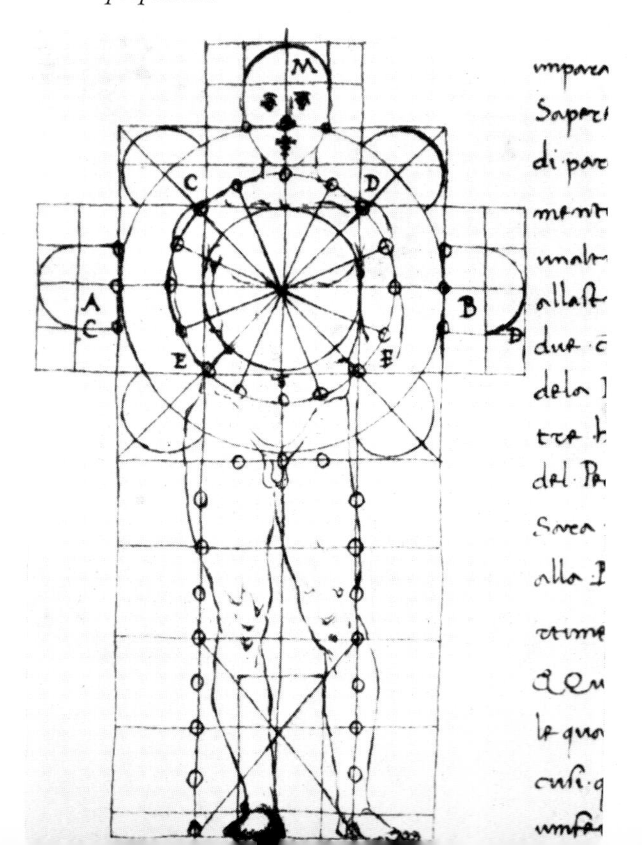

# *Meditations on the Circle*

*264* RAPHAEL: *The Alba Madonna, c. 1510*

*265* BRAMANTE: *plan for the dome of St Peter's*

*266* GIORGIONE: *The Dresden Venus*

*267* TITIAN: *The Venus of Urbino, 1538*

## *The Venetian Goddess*

Renaissance Venice, so it seems, restored the cult of Venus. Giorgione, inspired by some image of the sleeping Ariadne, shows the pure body of the goddess with eyes closed, asleep in an ideal landscape. In contrast, Titian's *Venus of Urbino* lies awake in a room of her palace and has become a mortal. Inspired by this picture, centuries later, Manet will paint his *Olympia,* that Venus of the streets, lying on the first couch that comes to hand.

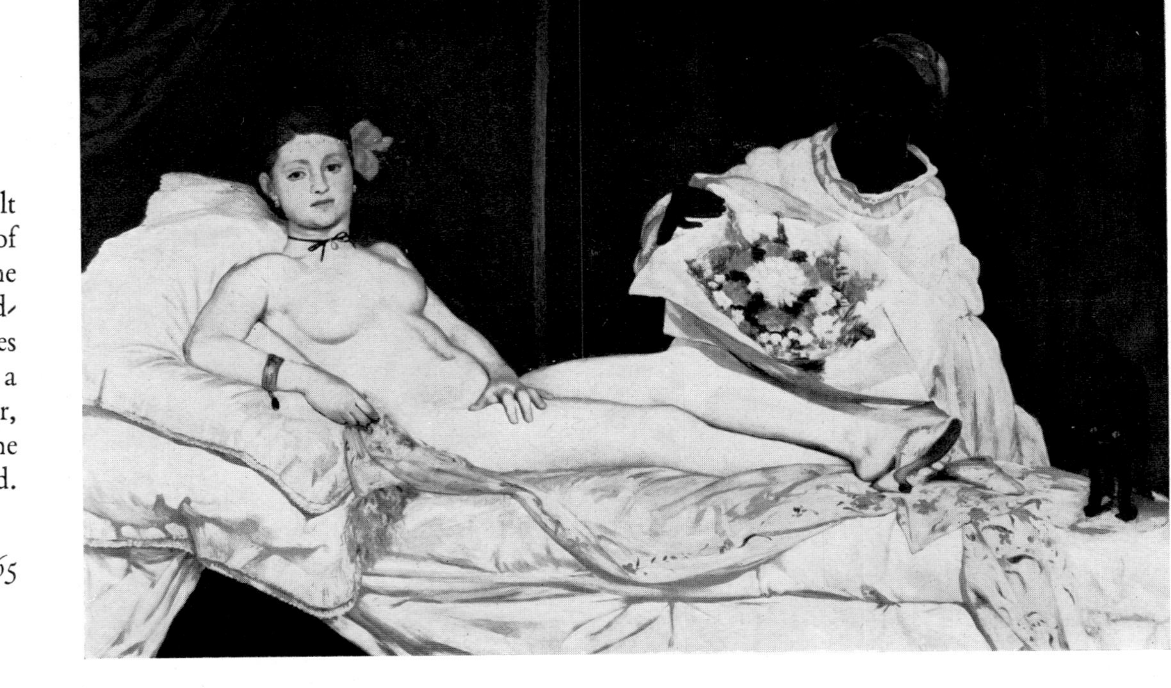

268 MANET: *Olympia, 1865*

269 TITIAN: *detail from Venus and Adonis*

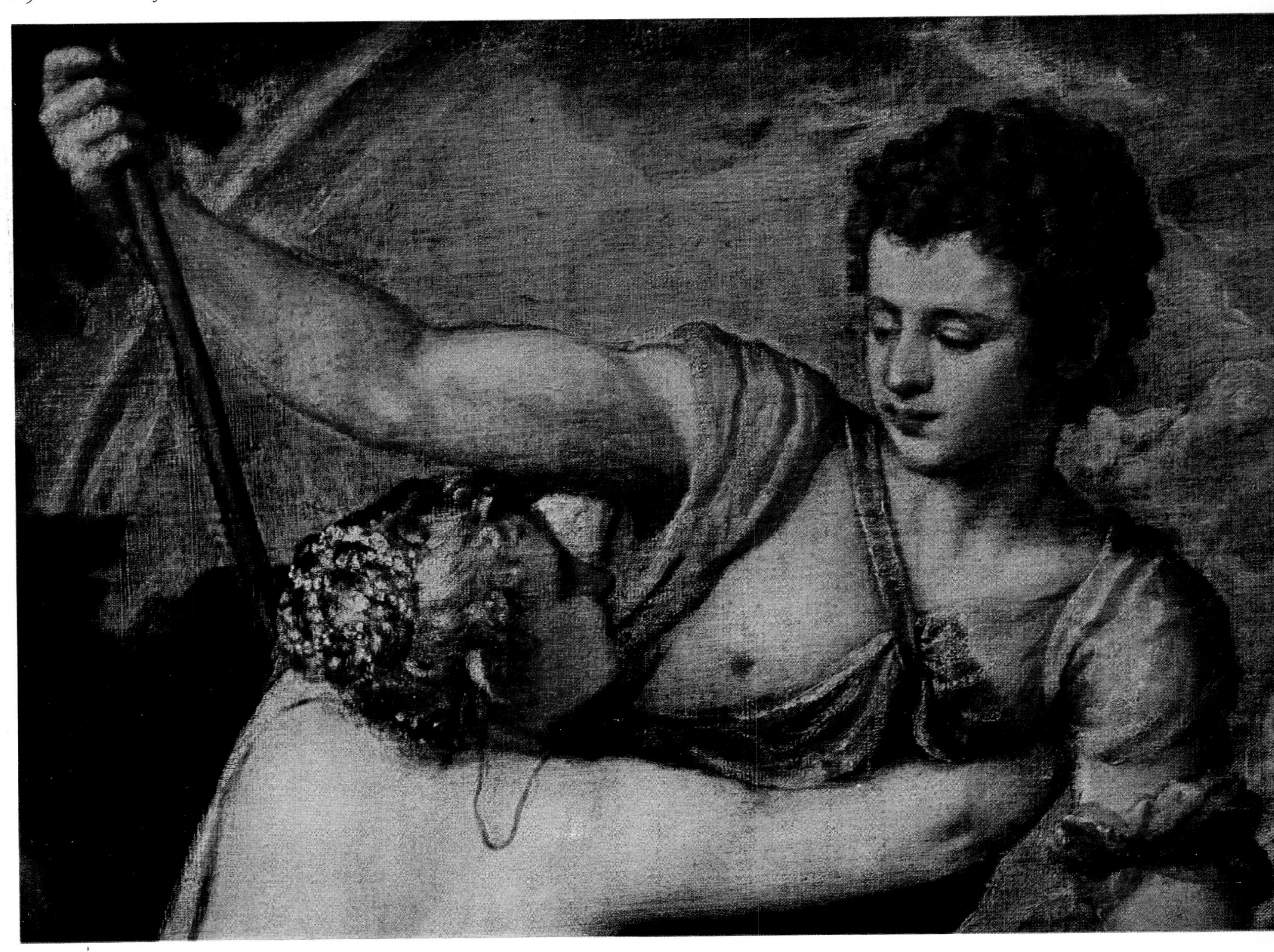

# *A Boundless Universe*

Tintoretto sets the onlooker free from the ideas of above and below, and launches him into pure space. *The Milky Way* sways, released from all feeling of gravity; and the *Paradise* in the Sala del Gran' Consiglio seems to reflect the revolutions of the Heavens—whereas at the beginning of the century Raphael's was spread out in a semicircle, still keeping faithful to a theological concept.

*270* TINTORETTO: *The Origin of the Milky Way, c. 1575*

271 TINTORETTO: *study for oil-painting of Paradise, c. 1588*

272 RAPHAEL: *La Disputà, c. 1510*

# *German Sentimentality*

Naïveté is as firmly rooted as cruelty in the Germanic spirit. Dürer always places his pure proud Virgin in the midst of the enchanted world of the 'little Paradise garden' which has always haunted the German imagination; and Cranach, in his '*Golden Age*', sets nude men and women of dubious innocence gambolling among animals and flowers.

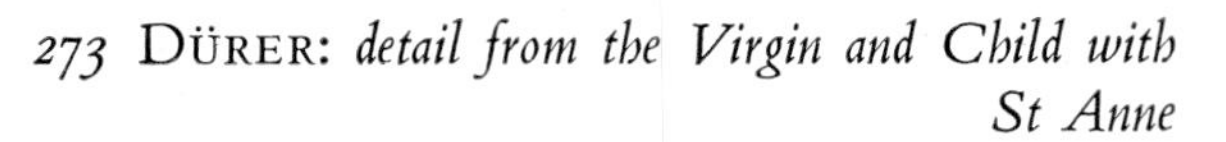

*273* DÜRER: *detail from the Virgin and Child with St Anne*

*274* CRANACH THE ELDER: *The Golden Age*

275 DÜRER, *Madonna of the Animals*

# *Dizzy Heights*

The humanist, a familiar of the heights, gazes down into the immense distances and takes his pleasure in contemplating from a peak the world's mountains and valleys and the formation of the clouds. He sees history itself by the scale of the universe; and Altdorfer, in a picture that is unique, brings together everything that the art of painting can comprehend, celebrating the crumbling of an Empire at the collision of two armies in the midst of a storm on the grand scale.

276 ISENBRANDT: *detail from Rest on the Flight to Egypt*

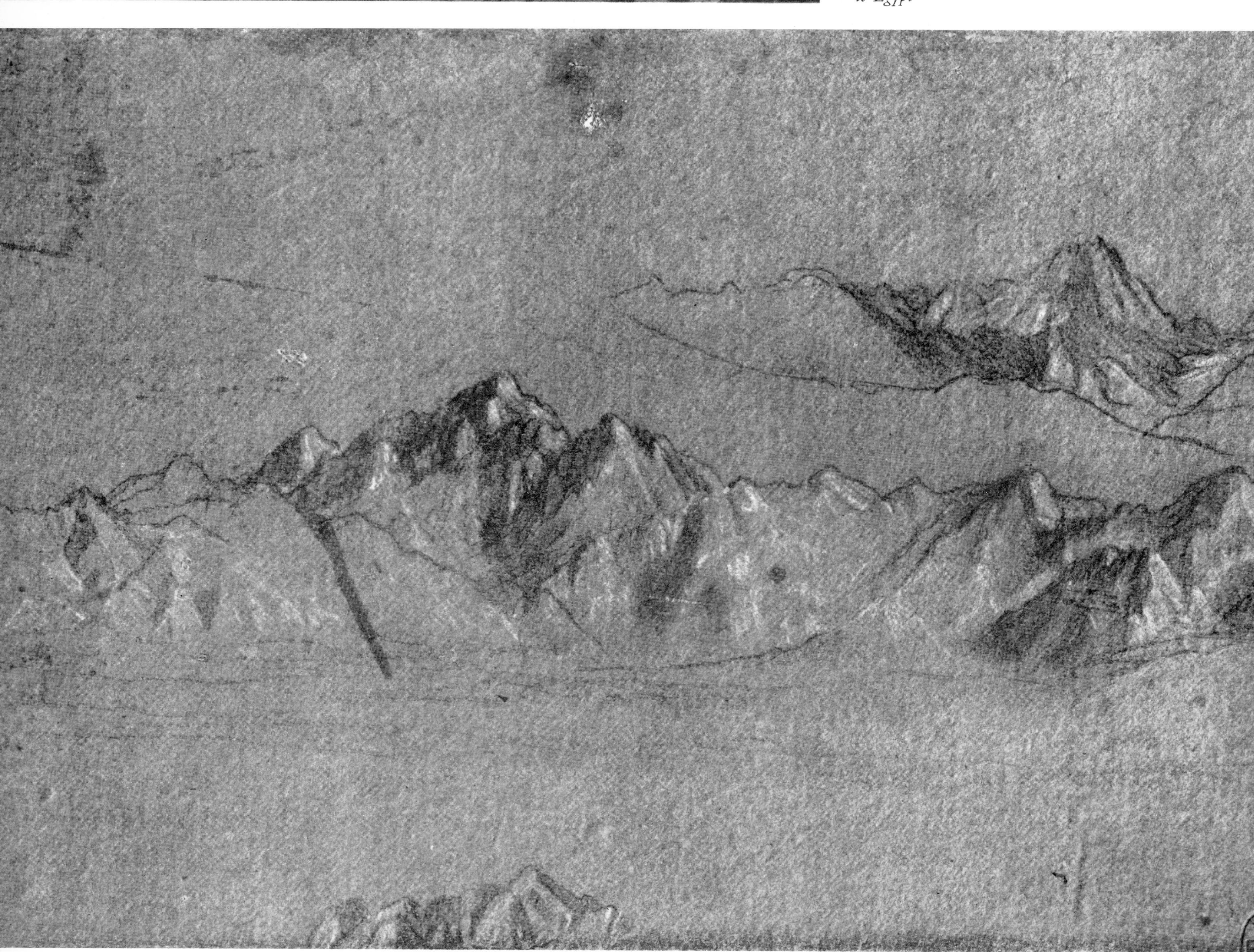

277 LEONARDO: *Mountain Landscape*

278 ALTDORFER: *detail from Battle of Alexander on the Issus river, 1529*

# *Man the Absurd*

When the man in love with height comes down alone from the peaks, he cannot help finding absurd the men and women of the plains toiling at their puny labours. This rejection of man by man, which implies a philosophical 'distancing', is still a humanist attitude; but it could only be brought out fully by Nordic minds, inclined to look on man as one element in the universe.

*279* BOSCH: *detail from The Haywain*

*280* BRUEGHEL THE ELDER: *Everyman, drawing*

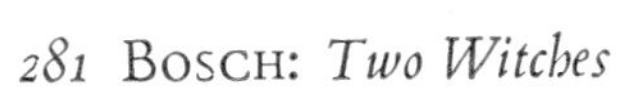

281 Bosch: *Two Witches*

282 Brueghel the Elder: *detail from the Fall of Icarus, c. 1555*

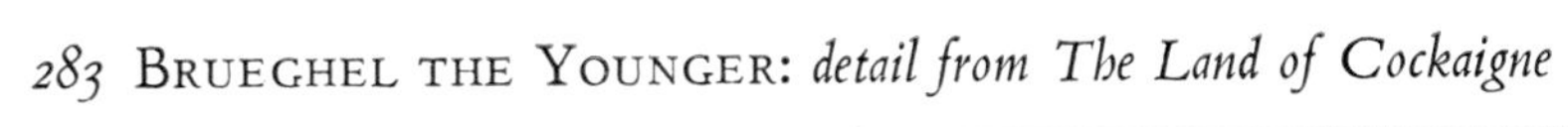

283 Brueghel the Younger: *detail from The Land of Cockaigne*

285 Pietro Tacca: *Bronze fountain, 1627*

284 Dietterlin: *Fountain of the Composite Order, 1598*

# *Mannerism*

That neurosis of the imagination, Mannerism, is an intellectual game in which one can recognise a resurgence of ancient 'Asianism'—which the artists from the time of Paul III onwards upheld against the 'Atticism' that prevailed during the pontificates of Julius II and Leo X. It lets loose the hordes of the chimaeras and monsters, inspires speculations, refinements and artifices that turn art into a mirage, and corrupts with a revived Gothicism the Classicism which the artists still claim to take as their model.

*286* Lucas Cambiaso: *Study of figures*

*287* Parmigianino: *Madonna with the long neck, c. 1535*

*288* BERRUGUETE: *detail from Abraham sacrificing Isaac, 1527–32*

Supported by the genius of Spain, which sees in man no value except in relation to God, El Greco—like his predecessors Alonso Berruguete and Juan de Juni—forces the Mannerist game till it attains tragedy. By breaking the bounds, these painters transform the Mannerist impotence into that of Man in his desperate aspiration towards the sublime.

*289* JUAN DE JUNI: *Meeting of Joachim and Anne, 1557*

*290* BERRUGUETE: *St John, 1527–32*

*291* El Greco: *Burial of Count Orgaz, 1586*

292 PIERINO DEL VAGA: *detail of a ceiling in the Castel S. Angelo, Rome, 1542–5*

293 RAPHAEL: *putto pulled by a snake, 1516*

294 *Fresco from Pompeii, 1st century* A.D.

# *Learning at Play*

The most exquisite form taken by the Mannerist game is the '*grottesche*'. Raphael was its inventor, and was inspired by examples from Antiquity. It is a kind of plastic exercise based on Ovid's literary game in his *Metamorphoses*—which consists in associating the various realms of Nature and the forms derived from Antiquity together in graceful arabesques, governed by the freest fancy.

296 *Tapestry. Fountainbleau factory, second half of 16th century*

295 GIULIANO DA SAN GALLO: *page of a sketch-book, c. 1515*

297 STUDIO OF FONTANA: *Wine cooler, 1565–71*

## *Personal Splendour*

The men of the Mannerist period, in their passion for splendour and profusion in clothes and in table ornaments, concealed their real identity under an armour of brocades, gold, enamel, pearls, rubies and diamonds.

*298* MARC GHEERAERTS: *Queen Elizabeth I*

*300 Jewel from the treasure of the Grand Duke of Tuscany, 2nd half of 16th century*

*299* CELLINI: *Salt-cellar, 1570*

# NOTES ON THE ILLUSTRATIONS TO CHAPTER VI

250 MICHELANGELO (1475–1564): *Brutus (unfinished). c. 1539. National Museum (Bargello), Florence. Photo: Sansaini, Courtesy of Professor Tolnay*

251 MASACCIO (1401–28): *Head of St John. Detail from the frescoes in the Brancacci Chapel, Sta Maria del Carmine, Florence. 1425–8. Photo: Josephine Powell*

252 NANNI DI BANCO (*c.* 1384–1421): *Head of the Prophet Isaiah. Marble. Florence Cathedral. 1408. Photo: Brogi*

253 MICHELANGELO (1475–1564): *Head of David. 1501–4. Galleria dell' Accademia, Florence. Photo: Alinari*

254 PIERO DELLA FRANCESCA (1410/20–92): *Federigo da Montefeltro. c. 1465. Uffizi, Florence.*

255 PIERO DELLA FRANCESCA (1410/20–92): *Detail from The Triumph of Federigo da Montefeltro (on the back of the portrait above). c. 1465. Uffizi, Florence. Photo: Anderson*

256 CARLO CRIVELLI (*active* 1456–93): *The Annunciation with St Emidius. 1486. National Gallery, London. Photo: Zoltan Wegner*

257 PAOLO UCCELLO (*c.* 1397–1475): *Design for a chalice. Drawing. Uffizi, Florence. Photo: Soprintendenza alle Gallerie di Firenze*

258 JACOPO BELLINI (1429/30–1507): *Palace courtyard with the banquet of Herod and the beheading of John the Baptist. Drawing. MNLP 3814 f. 17. Cabinet des Dessins, Musée du Louvre, Paris. Photo: Archives Photographiques, Paris*

259 PIERO DI COSIMO (*c.* 1462–*after* 1515): *A Mythological subject. National Gallery, London. Photo: Zoltan Wegner*

260 RAPHAEL (1483–1520): *Detail from Lo Sposalizio. 1504. Pinacoteca di Brera, Milan. Photo: Anderson*

261 PRIMATICCIO (1504–70): *Dance of the Hours. Design for the ceiling of the Galerie d'Ulysse, Fontainebleau. Städelsches Kunstinstitut, Frankfurt.*

262 DONATO BRAMANTE (*c.* 1444–1514): *The Tempietto of S. Pietro in Montorio, Rome. 1503. Photo: Georgina Masson*

263 FRANCESCO DI GIORGIO (1439–1502): *Church plan to human proportions. Codice Magliabecchiano (42.v.). National Library, Florence.*

264 RAPHAEL (1483–1520): *The Alba Madonna. c. 1510. National Gallery, Washington. Photo: Anna Wachsmann*

265 DONATO BRAMANTE (*c.* 1444–1514): *Plan for the dome of St Peter's. From Serlio: 'Tutte l'opera dell'architettura', Book III.*

266 GIORGIONE (1477–1510): *Sleeping Venus. Gemäldegalerie, Dresden. Photo: Alinari*

267 TITIAN (*active before* 1511; *died* 1576): *The Urbino Venus. Painted in 1538 for Guidobaldo II, Duke of Urbino. Uffizi, Florence.*

268 EDOUARD MANET (1833–83): *Olympia. 1865. (Inspired by the Urbino Venus.) Musée du Louvre, Paris. Photo: Giraudon*

269 TITIAN (*active before* 1511; *died* 1576): *Detail from Venus and Adonis. Metropolitan Museum of Art, New York. Photo: Anna Wachsmann*

270 TINTORETTO (*c.* 1518–94): *The Origin of the Milky Way. c. 1575. National Gallery, London.*

271 TINTORETTO (*c.* 1518–94): *Paradise. c. 1588. Study in the Louvre for the picture in the Sala del Gran' Consiglio, Palazzo Ducale, Venice.*

272 RAPHAEL (1483–1520): *La Disputà (Disputation concerning the Blessed Sacrament). c. 1510. Stanze, Vatican. Photo: Alinari*

273 ALBRECHT DÜRER (1471–1528): *Detail from The Virgin and Child with St Anne. 1519. Metropolitan Museum of Art, New York.*

274 LUCAS CRANACH THE ELDER (1472–1553): *The Golden Age. Nasjongalleriet, Oslo. Photo: O. Vaering*

275 ALBRECHT DÜRER (1471–1528): *Madonna of the Animals. Water-colour. Albertina, Vienna. Photo: Karl Meyer*

276 ADRIAEN ISENBRANDT (*active* 1510–51): *Detail from Rest on the Flight from Egypt. Alte Pinakothek, Munich. Photo: Hirmer*

277 LEONARDO DA VINCI (1452–1519): *Mountain Landscape. Royal Library, Windsor Castle. By gracious permission of Her Majesty the Queen.*

278 ALBRECHT ALTDORFER (*before* 1480–1538): *Detail from the Battle of Alexander on the Issus River. 1529. Alte Pinakothek, Munich. Photo: Hirmer*

279 HIERONYMUS BOSCH (1450–1516): *Detail from The Haywain. The Prado, Madrid.*

280 PIETER BRUEGHEL THE ELDER (*active* 1525–69): *Everyman. Drawing for an engraving of Jerome Cock. British Museum, London.*

281 HIERONYMUS BOSCH (1450–1516): *Two Witches. Drawing. Boymans-van Beuningen Museum, Rotterdam. Photo: A. Frequin, The Hague*

282 PIETER BRUEGHEL THE ELDER (*active* 1525–69): *Detail from the Fall of Icarus. c. 1555. Musée des Beaux-Arts, Brussels.*

283 PIETER BRUEGHEL THE ELDER (*active* 1525–69): *Detail from the Land of Cockaigne. 1567. Alte Pinakothek, Munich. Photo: Hirmer*

284 WENDEL DIETTERLIN (*c.* 1550–99): *Fountain of the Composite Order. Engraving. 1598. Photo: R.I.B.A., London*

285 PIETRO TACCA (1577–1640): *Bronze fountain. 1627. Piazza della SS. Annunziata, Florence. Photo: Alinari*

286 LUCA CAMBIASO (1527–85): *Study of figures. Drawing. Uffizi, Florence.*

287 PARMIGIANINO (1503–40): *Madonna with the long neck. c. 1535. Uffizi, Florence.*

288 ALONSO BERRUGUETE (1486–1561): *Detail from Abraham sacrificing Isaac. From the altar of S. Benito. 1527–32. Valladolid Museum. Photo: Germain Bazin*

289 JUAN DE JUNI (*died* 1579): *Detail from the Meeting of Joachim and Anne. Capella de los Benavente, S. Maria. 1557. Medina de Rioseco. Photo: Garasi, Santiago*

290 ALONSO BERRUGUETE (1486–1561): *St John. From the altar of S. Benito. 1527–32. Valladolid Museum.*

291 EL GRECO (1541–1614): *The Burial of Count Orgaz. 1586. Church of S. Tomé, Toledo.*

292 *Detail from the ceiling of the Sala dell'Apollo, Castel S. Angelo, Rome. Decoration carried out under the direction of* PIERINO DEL VAGA. *c. 1542–5. Photo: Anderson*

293 RAPHAEL (1483–1520): *Putto pulled by a snake; detail of decoration of a small stove, belonging to Cardinal Bibbiena. 1516. Mus. Vaticani. Photo: Renato Sansaini, Rome*

294 *Putto riding on a crab. Detail of fresco from Casa dei Vettii, Pompeii. 1st century* A.D. *Photo: Alinari*

295 GIULIANO DA SAN GALLO (1445–1516): *Page from a sketchbook. Towards the end of the artist's life. Bibliotheca Communale, Siena. Photo: Bonnoli, Siena*

296 *Tapestry. Fontainebleau factory. Second half of 16th century. Photo: Eileen Tweedy*

297 *Studio of* ORAZIO FONTANA *at Urbino*: *Wine cooler for the service of the Duke of Urbino (1565–71). Museo Nazionale, Florence. Photo: Electa Editrice, Milan*

298 *Attributed to* MARC GHEERAERTS (*c.* 1547–1619): *Queen Elizabeth I of England. The 'Armada Portrait'. Duke of Bedford Collection, Woburn Abbey. Photo: Eileen Tweedy*

299 BENVENUTO CELLINI (1500–71): *Salt-cellar commissioned in 1540 by Cardinal Ippolito d'Este, bought by François I of France, and given by Charles IX to his brother-in-law Ferdinand of Austria as a wedding gift in 1570. Kunsthistorisches Museum, Vienna.*

300 *Jewel from the treasure of the Grand Duke of Tuscany. Second half of the 16th century. Museo degli Argenti, Florence. Photo: F. Pineider, Florence*

# VII THE GOLDEN CENTURY OF PAINTING

# VII The Golden Century of Painting

THE HORSE THAT STAMPS with his stupid hoof upon the fallen body of St Paul is trampling the whole world. Poussin, whose anathema has weighed upon Caravaggio until our own day, was not wrong: that Michelangelo in reverse, breaking into the temple newly built by Lomazzo to the glory of painting, had thrown down its idols; and in this sense—the sense intended by Poussin—he did indeed destroy painting, at least the ideal world of painting inherited from the Renaissance. The efforts of the Carracci were directed towards renewing the Idea by subjecting it to a discipline capable of tempering its Mannerist extravagances and, still more, by injecting into it a new sap of naturalism. Their innumerable drawings, which are perhaps the finest part of their work, bear witness both to their indefatigable attention to the model and to their intellectual working out of form in an art whose essence is probity. With Caravaggio there are no drawings, no design: he inaugurated the modern method of art in the raw. The ninety-seven sensational X-ray photographs taken by the Rome *Instituto del Restauro* of the *Martyrdom of St Matthew* in San Luigi dei Francesi have revealed the way in which he worked, which was that of an empiricist. He dispensed with the series of sketches which painters had hitherto made on paper before starting the painting, in order to get its essential idea clear: like a workman he went straight at it, attacking the canvas without knowing where he was going, and the first version of the *St Matthew*, composed by mere juxtaposition, is singularly poor; he fights the picture as one fights a battle, and, having lost it, joins battle again, is defeated again and finally, at the third engagement (I nearly said the third round) wins. Caravaggio replaced creation by action. All that expense of effort was required so that in the end, having got inside the skin of his people, he should not merely have thought out the drama but lived it. And yet, in this struggle with a theme of murder, this painter of equivocal figures and genre scenes did achieve self-mastery: he overcame the Mannerist in him and, by this purely sensory, almost manual method, rediscovered that feeling for dramatic action which makes him—across a gap of three centuries of conscious 'composition'—really the direct successor of Giotto. And this destroyer of painting was to prove the true restorer of form, of genuine Italian form, which is always sculptural and suggests the density of bodies. He used light like a chisel: his slanting rays, economically distributed, carve out huge folds of night, polish the foreheads, build arms, busts, feet and hands in full strength and give the force of violent relief to the transient depth of a world defined by shadow. He calls forth on the canvas a colossal humanity that puts to flight the puppets of the Mannerists and disperses the whole false world of gods, Venuses and gigolos. He could indeed make nothing of the fine gentlemen, refined ladies and *cavalieri serventi* who then inhabited the Roman palaces: only the *popolo minuto* of the

*Plate 301*

suburbs could supply him with the authentic models for his restoration of man in his whole strength. What grandeur he achieves! Beside his colossi the tailor's dummies of Courbet seem the work of some painter of inn signs; and indeed there was in Courbet too much literature, and bad literature at that; this man who had so little gift for thinking made the mistake of imagining himself a thinker. Nothing deflected Caravaggio from his path; he was a 'populist' painter with the luck to be born before Socialism; he was a pure instinct.

These colossi are set in motion by the elementary activities in which their life is involved—their life including their death, a death that is the irrevocable end of existence. At the beginning of the century in which the great controversy upon Grace arose, Caravaggio brought out in all its starkness the loneliness of the human being cut off from God, and cut off from the world, which the night in which he is plunged annihilates, or rather '*néantise*', to use a term from the materialist Existentialism of Jean-Paul Sartre. In a penetrating analysis that is obviously, though not avowedly, inspired by this philosopher's theories, Giulio Carlo Argan has powerfully described the poignant loneliness which forms a bond between the humanity of the second Michelangelo and that of the first; but to Buonarroti a man is a divine creature that has fallen, while to Merisi he is a being without God.

'Caravaggio's painting,' says Argan, 'represents the breaking-point between reality and a this-side and a beyond, both of them problematic—the instant when the fury of being falls into the absolute immobility of non-being.' Caravaggio, the painter of night, introduced into Western art a new metaphysical value, nothingness. In his period of maturity the darkness still has a positive value, it is the hollow from which the artist draws his Titanesque forms; but in his last works—the Syracuse *Martyrdom of St Lucy* or the Valetta *Torture of St John the Baptist*—this density of shadow dissolves into a kind of ash, the value of nothingness is itself '*néantisé*', and in this smoking dust there lives and dies a sickly humanity—one that has lost even the physical solidity that gave their resistant strength to the figures in his *Story of St Matthew*, his *Conversion of St Paul*, his *Crucifixion of St Peter* or his *Death of the Virgin*.

The challenge of night was to be taken up by others after Caravaggio. In Georges de la Tour and Zurbaran it was the blessed night of the mystics with its annunciation of the divine presence, and in Rembrandt the shadow is all palpitating with the soul's passion and the heart's impulses. The Neapolitans and Genoese of the seventeenth century blended this value of night with all their colours and inaugurated pictorial romanticism. Velasquez alone scattered around his figures the grey ash that cuts them off from the world so that they brood in a closed circle on their human nothingness.

*Plate 323*
*Plate 310*
*Plates 308, 309*
*Plate 304*

* * *

For a long time Caravaggio—who received more honour in his lifetime than has often been realised—was considered as a side road of painting, an original, or even a misfit. (This was Berenson's view; for the whole of his long life he maintained the sanctity of the Ideal against all comers.) The rehabilitation of Caravaggio, which goes back some thirty years, has led modern criticism to regard the influence of Caravaggism as determining all that was greatest in seventeenth-century painting. There seems to be now a certain reaction, and the question is being asked whether Caravaggism was not in fact an international tendency to which the painter of the *St Matthew* lent both his name and his power. In fact Caravaggism, whether it worked directly or indirectly or by encouraging spontaneous tendencies, was the essential impulse that drove seventeenth-century painting forward: all the painters except Poussin and Claude were in its debt—Rubens, Frans Hals, Rembrandt, Velasquez, Zurbaran (though this is sometimes denied) and Vermeer himself. Meditation upon man, his condition, his nature, his grandeur and his misery, his exceptional excellence and his humble status in the sight of God, together with the slightest facts of his daily life, even including the objects with which he is surrounded, which were now promoted to the dignity of subjects for pictures—became the great poetical and philosophical theme of seventeenth-century painting. But for these psychological and metaphysical speculations to be possible at all and for the painter to plunge deep into the soul, it was first necessary that man should be restored, established and defined in his bodily existence, his physical, organic reality—natural man, even *troppo naturale*—and this is what painting owes to Caravaggio.

*Plate 307*

The revolution made by him was so fertile that it even permitted its extreme contrary—the refinement of a Vermeer. The 'plastic education' of the Northern peoples came from Italy on two occasions: in the sixteenth century through the influence of Roman Baroque and in the seventeenth through Caravaggism. But the Roman style, with its abstract character, had little correspondence with the innate tendencies of the Northern peoples, who always kept a deep feeling for the material world. Except in France, therefore, it ended in bankruptcy, whereas in the Low Countries Caravaggism was destined to throw out deep roots and to make possible, after the sixteenth-century struggles to cope with a Roman influence that proved sterile, that emancipation from primitivism which led to the great seventeenth-century masters. The pure, indeed literal, Caravaggists—those of Utrecht, Van Baburen, Terbrugghen and, to a lesser extent, Honthorst who succumbed to academicism—led on to Vermeer: the luminous principle in these artists makes the bridge from Caravaggio's *chiaroscuro* to the luminism of the master of Delft; it is the lateral, slanting and transient light—that is to say, the real light—of the Caravaggists that sets the form in relief and, in the work of the Utrecht painters (who, as pure imitators of Italian style, retained something of the *ostinato rigore* from beyond the Alps), twists the volumes with a crude vigour. This 'realistic' light replaced the abstract brightness of the Roman style, which was a geometrical light with its source at the zenith, born of form and creating none. Where did Vermeer get that purity of volume which helped to give his works such formal perfection? Partly from the Caravaggian light, but by subtly combining with it atmospheric values.

Whether its source was diurnal or nocturnal the light of the Caravaggists was crude, designed to set in relief unevenesses of volume; but that of Vermeer is subdued, either (in the interiors) by a window or (in the case of a landscape) by the cloudy sky of Holland. The sensibility of this Northern painter knew all there was to be known about the attenuations or softenings or, on the contrary, the increases in intensity—the vibrant quality—that the atmosphere adds to light. In his work the sharp contour of the Utrecht Caravaggists is transformed into a vibrant, indefinite region, in which the last modulations of the volume gently die away—a region not delimited by an outline; and this method of expression is already to be found in the works of Terbrugghen's last period, which are the link between Caravaggio and Vermeer. In Vermeer, that most objective of painters, all the internal and external elements of the object—volume, material, atmosphere—depend upon the light, which is considered as the very condition of the visual, that is to say human, existence of things. In him are blended the contradictory tendencies which usually attract artists in alternation—according to whether they respond more naturally to the permanence of the world or to the fugitiveness of things: the static, that which delimits motionless and discontinuous forms conceived by the mind; or movement, an indefinite passage of forms into one another. All this is contained in Vermeer, and indeed in a single picture by Vermeer. It might well be said that he was the most perfect painter of all, if Van Eyck had not existed before him; but is he not even more profound than the painter of Arnolfini—is he not the Van Eyck of the soul?

* * *

Already with Titian the field of painting included, in d'Annunzio's phrase, 'everything that trembles, weeps, hopes, gasps and raves in the immense landscape of life'. To the Venetian painter nothing was now foreign—neither fabulous dreams of the pagan Golden Age, nor the mysteries of Christianity, nor the tragic liturgies of death, nor the tender caresses of love: nothing, except perhaps thought.

Under Titian's brush painting had learned to obey the expressive demands of every human feeling. The delicate technique of the Van Eycks had been right for the imagery of Flanders, but its use on a monumental scale by Giovanni Bellini give his compositions a certain looseness, almost as if they were enlargements, for on this scale the fluid seems to spread diluted over the surface. Giorgione invented and Titian inherited from him the modern method, and after this a painting was always a sketch—a sketch renewed again and again, sometimes even months later but always with a manual liveliness that kept the spontaneity of the impression intact. The predilection of seventeenth-century painters for painting hands is almost a confession of the important part which the hand now played in painting.

*Plate 269*
*Plate 235*
*Plates 302–306*

The hand, from having been servant, became master: the movements it imparted to the brush produced a handwriting which the painters of earlier times had taken pains to conceal. Now painting became the art of the brush, and the light, formerly reflected limpidly from the enamelled surfaces of the primitive and classical painters, now went through innumerable adventures on surfaces of a bristling roughness, diving into the translucency of the shadows, gliding over the passages of thick paint, colliding with the strong brush-strokes and rebounding from the jutting *impasto*—for in this coloured relief work the highlights were apt to coincide with the most powerful accents of the material: the light became literally salient, it jumped out at the eye, and the canvas was swollen where the sky's brightness became visible through trees and pierced the foliage with its arrows. It is surprising that graphologists have not yet tried interpreting these hand-writings as such: the sword-play style of Frans Hals, the wonderful nonchalance of Velasquez (letting the image come to him without haste from the tip of a lightly held brush that laid on the colour, pricked it or glazed it with superb bravura), Rembrandt's passionate grinding of gilded muds (laying them on thick, as if the brush were a kind of trowel), and Vermeer's patient accumulation of dots, opaque streams, droplets and gleaming pearls, making the light scintillate over his infinity of exact touches. As for Rubens, he was certainly the greatest virtuoso of painting: he adapted the fluid technique inherited from Van Eyck to the modern method, the sketch method working without correction by superposing transparent layers laid on with soft brushes, and making only the luminous accents stand out from the canvas. It is a marvellous skill, this skill in painting thinly: it gives the spectator the feeling that it contains unfathomable depths; and it has enabled the paintings of the Antwerp master—when they have not been spoilt by the interference of other men—to keep a lasting freshness. While most of Rembrandt's pictures have sunk into shadow, and while little more remains of most of Titian's works than half-effaced images, the *Hélène Fourment and her Children* in the Louvre is still just as it was left by the painter's hand, just before the finish that would have glazed the liveliness of these beings in flower.

*Plates 302, 306*
*Plate 303*
*Plate 305*

As for the French painters, they were divided between an impersonal middle-of-the-road manner practised by the court painters and the technique which suited the national temperament and was started, more or less in parallel, by Poussin, Claude Lorrain and the Le Nain brothers. The Frenchman is not much drawn to the transparent technique which requires so much skill: most frequently he paints like a modeller, accumulating *impasto* and *demi-impasto*, well bound together, by dabbing them on with the brush; and in order to obtain an easily handled material, he mixes very little oil with the paint—which has unfortunately not helped the conservation of the paintings. Such was the method used by Chardin, and also by Corot when he was not doing hack-work for the *Salon* or for customers but was working for himself; Courbet and Claude

*Plates 316–319*

Monet carried it on, developing it in the direction of increased opacity. It is a technique that suits the timid approach to the work that was natural in Frenchmen who had not had an academic training and were slow to acquire manual virtuosity—that '*tour de main*' which, preserving all the power of the artist's emotion at the moment of execution, will lead him perhaps to some failures but also to felicities of touch that have all the poetry of improvisation.

The Dutch seventeenth-century painters took up again the true technique of Van Eyck, which had been interrupted by the Roman Baroque influence in Flanders; and at the same time, encouraged by Protestantism, they returned to the taste for the image-picture or mirror-picture, which had been a part of the taste of the merchant class. People today, with the exception of a few real art lovers, are prevented by their prejudice against realism and against a painting having a subject from fully appreciating those marvels of painting, the works of the Dutch *petits maîtres*.

To the lover of museums there is something peculiarly enchanting about those of Holland. Here a museum does not ask its visitor to cut himself off from the world: the pictures on the walls, like so many mirrors, offer a series of reflections of the world, prolonging, within the sacred precincts, the mirage of sky and waters. All their liquid play seems to have been arrested by the painter's eye: the lived instant loses its ephemeral quality, to become immutable, and nowhere has the act of thought (the human act, *par excellence*, the act which imposes form on formlessness and moves freely through time and space), been caught so well as it is in these works by artists so humble and free from intellectual ambitions. The spectator is led without a jolt along the path of the world to that of art, he is not importuned by those deep doubts that the great Italian or Spanish works of art force upon us; and by this harmony between the work of a man's hands and that of Nature he feels purified. And yet, if we look at one of these works for too long, we feel this 'light of common day', which was the one thing the painter sought, vanishing: beyond the picture the mirage begins to show, and now we are anxious to experience in ourselves the delicate perception of a time without duration and space without dimension. But the mirage dissolves and the picture imposes itself again—the expression of that-which-was-and-is-no-more, of something that was unique because ephemeral—although a moment ago we had seemed to feel in ourselves the unity of that-which-is. And in this oscillation of our feelings, in this double and fugitive appearance, we experience what it is to be a man—the full strangeness of the fate that makes each one of us an ant and a giant, puny and greater than the universe.

Something of the soul of Pascal is contained in these mirror-pictures painted by the Dutch of the *Grand Siècle*. Our contemporaries, though not much inclined to admire landscapes, have recovered the true meaning of the image picture in the still-life. The seventeenth century was its great period. That deep-searching century cross-questioned the mystery of objects—even expected it to explain destiny; and even if that is not its subject, every seventeenth-century still-life—except the Flemish ones—is always more or less a 'vanity'.

*The Dutchman whose still-lifes best express this quality of silence is Claesz Heda (311); a similar feeling of solitude hovers over the landscapes of Jacob van Ruisdael (312)*

*The most beautiful of Spanish still-lifes is by Zurbaran, who seems here to have succeeded in expressing a unique experience (310)*

This tendency was instinctive in the Dutch, subject as they were to the Calvinistic pessimism: it is not surprising that it should have been conscious in the Spanish, those virtuosi of speculation on nothingness. What can be more troubling than that picture by Coorte in which, against a background of night, a butterfly—a fragile being vowed to an early death—flutters for a moment above fruits that are on the threshold of decay, fruits chosen from among those which attain their full savour only when over-ripe? Or than that other picture by Sanchez Cotán, in which a quince, a cauliflower, a slice of melon, a whole melon and a cucumber are inexplicably bound together in a curve that strives unendingly towards a straight line which it will never quite meet? The philosophical speculations of our time have taught us to look for a secret truth beyond these appearances: does not every object, when our mind tries to pin down its nature and being, vanish, as Jean-Paul Sartre has shown, into smoke? And, to the more profound seventeenth-century painters is not all that solidity of appearance merely a decoy, a message from that which cannot be grasped?

The modern historians' division of seventeenth-century Europe into two aesthetic positions, the classical and the Baroque, did not exist in the consciousness of the men of that time. How indeed can the realism of the Low Countries be made to fit into it? Those whom we nowadays place in one category or the other lived together on good terms and in mutual esteem. Bernini had a great admiration for Poussin, which he expressed in Chantelou's hearing during his visit to Paris. He had come to Paris because the King wanted a fine façade for his palace of the Louvre and wished to induce all the great architects of that time to submit designs; and although the 'Baroque' plans were not adopted, Bernini was none the less treated most honourably, as one of the lords of art, and the King, enchanted by the bust which the sculptor sent him, gave it a good place at Versailles. In Rome classical and Baroque artists rubbed shoulders; Andrea Sacchi worked side by side with Pietro de Cortona; and it was in that somewhat artificial circle that Poussin and Claude lived, the pictures of both eagerly sought after by Roman princes and cardinals. Discussions on aesthetics led to no violent polemics: they were more a sort of social pastime and were centred on the opposition between *Idea* and *Natura*. Never, indeed, was art in Italy more free or less governed by concepts: it was the heyday of temperament, whose various expressions were displayed both in individuals and in the rise of regional schools. If Rome was Baroque the imaginative fantasy of the Neapolitans, Genoese and Venetians made them pave the way for all the later caprices of romanticism. Goya was strongly foreshadowed in Venice by Sebastiano Mazzoni, as he was at Genoa by Magnasco in his scenes of fantasy and Carbone in his portraits. Indeed, eclecticism favoured every sort of extravagance. At Genoa Bernardo Strozzi, having learned the lessons of Venice where he had lived, turned to pillaging Rubens and Van Dyck, who had been in the Ligurian city and left profound traces there. Sometimes Strozzi even displays a kinship to Rembrandt. In spite of their virtuosities, and perhaps because of this excess of facility, the Italians of the *Seicento* never achieved mastery of the technique of painting: they were divided between a sort of middle-of-the-road method derived from the Academy of Bologna and a Genoese or Neapolitan '*cuisine*', too heavily loaded with intentions to attain expressiveness. It is not really surprising that the finest painter of that period should have been a Venetian, Francesco Maffei of Verona, who rises to Velasquin felicities of palette—for it was Venice that, in the next century, was to recover the highest skill.

Classicist and the Baroque are united in the words uttered by Bernini in Chantelou's hearing in front of Poussin's *Bacchanales*: '*Veramento quel uomo è stato un grande istoriatore e grande favoleggiatore!*' A great narrator and creator of myths—that is what, outside Protestant Holland, busy as it was with the portraiture of common reality, a painter was expected to be. Painting was a *divertissement*: almost the whole of seventeenth-century art illustrates that astonishing flight from oneself, sought by a society through literature as well as the fine arts. The pictures of Poussin, like those of Pietro de Cortona, like the statues of Bernini, were to the Romans and French of that time illustrations of the imaginary world on which their spirits fed, in a period when the soul perhaps found consolation in Fable for the terrors caused in it by the uncertainties of Grace. Certainly nothing is as sharply opposed to Poussin's *Rape of the Sabines* as Pietro de Cortona's rendering of the same subject; but their contemporaries were not sensible of this difference: it mattered little to them whether the forms were airborne or weighed heavily on the ground (to use Wölfflin's fundamental distinction)—what charmed them in both pictures was their *mythic* value. They were painted for men saturated in the culture of Antiquity by artists who were themselves imbued with ancient and modern literature of fable—artists who moved at ease in a world of myths that has become difficult for many of us to enter or has lost, for those who still frequent it, the gift it had of carrying a man outside himself, through imagination. The two ways of escape

*Plates 316–319*

in the *Seicento* were History and Fable: History pointing back into the past, Fable freeing a man from his mortal condition by dreams of a Golden Age or of a Paradise regained. The two ways indeed converged, for History meant Antiquity—now considered as a blessed period for humanity; it was not now the custom to oppose Christianity to it, as was attempted for a moment after the Council of Trent. On the contrary, by a movement parallel to the one that had turned the Reformation towards the sources of Christianity, men took an interest in the Apostles, the Church Fathers and the Old Testament—in fact, in what constituted the 'Antiquity' of religion. By a sort of intellectual reconciliation, it became almost at one with that of paganism.

It was the French, however, who began to cast doubt on the value of the Roman ethic and aesthetic: Pascal's fury against the Jesuits was turned against Ultramontane casuistry. The arguments between Bernini and Colbert were not merely those between a sumptuous architect and an economic Minister of Finance: they were the signs of deep-seated divergences in the aesthetic field; and the future to some extent vindicated Bernini, when Versailles was built on a colossal scale worthy of the Cavaliere's sense of the grandeur that befitted royalty. Later the amazement felt by Président de Brosses in Italy, especially face to face with Italian religious art, was evidence of a certain attitude of mind that came of Jansenism and was automatically opposed to the externals of Catholicism in Rome. It is in their respective attitudes to religion that the gulf between Frenchmen and Italians becomes most clearly apparent.

*Plates 320–323*

The significance of French spirituality in the seventeenth century must be sought for quite as much in the school of spiritual life that sprang from Cardinal de Bérulle, as in Jansenism, which was a heresy. That school was hostile to the excesses of ecstatic mysticism as practised by the Italian and Spanish schools. St Vincent de Paul, who was so close in spirit to the Oratory, even addressed to some seminarists a serious warning '*à propos d'excès à éviter dans l'amour de Dieu*'. It was the moment when Bossuet called good sense 'the master of human life'. St Vincent de Paul, according to Maynard's biography, 'possessed this good sense to a supreme degree . . . this good sense that is perhaps, in the measure in which he practised it, rarer than what is called genius, because it implies, in a soul, an assemblage and a balance of faculties that are more numerous and harder to reconcile'. That is a pretty good definition of the classical spirit.

*Plate 321*

Salomon de Brosses tried to judge Italy, that country of passion, by the light of cold reason. It was natural that he should display incomprehension before Bernini's *Ecstasy of St Theresa*, in which the French magistrate saw nothing but the atmosphere of an ambivalent madrigal.

Seventeenth-century French spirituality owes its gravity and asceticism partly to an extremely acute consciousness of fallen human nature (which it took up afresh from St Augustine in reaction against Renaissance humanism, and which is reflected even in the Stoicism of Poussin), but also partly to its own mystical sense, which proceeds not by passionate impulses, as in the case of St Theresa, but by a thoughtful ascent of mind and heart within a great inner silence. The spirituality of Cardinal de Bérulle is wholly based on the contemplation of Christ and of the Mysteries of His life; but what touches the Oratorians in the life of Christ is not so much its facts as the inner dispositions of the Saviour, his '*états d'âme*', to which the Christian must associate himself. 'Each event in the life of Christ,' says the Cardinal, 'has about it something unique, *non seulement dans son effet, mais aussi en son état.*'

*The nun, Catherine de Montholon (320), is so hunched in on herself that her face, emaciated by asceticism, seems already to belong to another world*

The Italians illustrated the *effet* of the supernatural, the French painted its *état*. To the Italians the supernatural was an exceptional manifestation, to the French it was the inner life, a disposition on the part of the soul to go back into itself rather than to escape from itself—and no conception could be more directly opposed to Italian or Spanish ecstasy. The religious pictures of Philippe de Champaigne and those of Georges de la Tour illustrate this interpretation of mysticism.

*Plate 322*

Philippe de Champaigne's *Ex Voto* in the Louvre, offered by the painter in gratitude for a miraculous cure of his daughter, Sister Catherine of St Suzanna, which was attributed to the prayers of Mother Agnès Arnauld, shows the two women praying. An Italian artist would have 'depicted' the divine intervention, he would have made the bodies act out the feelings of the souls: what Philippe de Champaigne conveys is not any such passionate impulse and aspiration to the divine, but the intimate disposition of two souls to receive the visitation of the Spirit. Between the two human beings there is a tacit harmony of thoughts, which bears witness to a life in common and to a strength of cohesion resulting from a whole complex of dogmas, beliefs, moral values and knowledge accepted and shared. This picture is not the representation of a miracle, nor the portrait of two nuns: it is the expression of the *état contemplatif*. It is a perfect example of the French seventeenth century in its tendency always to see the intellectual or moral idea behind a particular act—behind a landscape Nature, behind a man or woman the human, behind the individual his *état*.

The researches of modern historians have brought out the importance, in the seventeenth century, of a social class that arose from the *bourgeoisie* and constituted a new nobility—the *noblesse de robe*: this, alongside the old nobility (the *noblesse d'épée*), which was now shut up in idleness and idle imaginings, acquired a growing influence both in State affairs and in matters of morality and general outlook.

Lucien Goldmann has shown that it was due to this class that Jansenist thinking proved so lasting, and he considers that the form of some of Racine's plays was influenced by the moral demands of this nobility. Others have noticed that the Stoicism of Poussin in the second half of his life was actually practised by this upper *bourgeoisie*, for whom he painted his pictures. This ruling class certainly, more than any other elements of society, helped to elaborate the ethical attitude which has been called that of the '*honnête homme*'. A picture by Le Brun in the Louvre shows Séguier, the Chancellor, as he was when he took part, in full dress, in the processional entry of Louis XIV and Maria-Theresa into Paris in 1660. What a perfect illustration of the life of the nobility this equestrian figure is—what a perfect image of the '*honnête homme*', whose greatness does not consist in externals but is drawn from the balance of the soul's forces! Philippe de Champaigne, when painting a portrait, gives us the person stripped of the public personage—whereas the man of quality who sat for Rigaud was left with no other excellence than that of his rank, so that he makes one think of a saying of the Spanish Jesuit, Baltazar Gracian, the author of a treatise on the Courtier, which in its translation by Amelot de la Houssaye had perhaps even more influence in France than in Spain, when he compares shallow natures to houses 'whose entrance suggests the palace and whose living quarters the hovel'. How did Séguier, in spite of the almost royal apparel in which he dared to have himself painted, manage to keep his dignity within the limits of the natural and retain in the midst of pomp so much wisdom and simplicity? 'Discontent with oneself is weakness, contentment with oneself is folly', said Gracian: this man knows what he is worth, but is in no danger of its making him lose his head, as did the ambitious Fouquet, whose pride offended the King's dignity. In Séguier the vigour of his *bourgeois* blood cools his aristocratic vanity, and in that nobleman's face, in the straight gaze of that 'protector of the *Académie française*', there is a definite touch of sententiousness—who could fail to recognise there the austere frankness of the peasants of Le Nain? This equestrian figure celebrates more than the Chancellor's own rise to eminence, it celebrates the triumph of the *noblesse de robe* which laboriously and silently, behind the stage of operatic Versailles, was busy building France.

*Plate 324*

*Plate 325*

*301* CARAVAGGIO: *The Conversion of St Paul,* *1600–1*

# *The Golden Age of Painting*

In the fifteenth century painting required the artist to conceal his means. It is, in contrast, by displaying them that Giorgione and Titian open the way to modern painting, which spreads throughout Europe in the seventeenth century. Painting becomes sketch: it allows the vivacity of the hand to show, keeping intact spontaneity of impression. The fondness of seventeenth-century artists for depicting hands seems almost a confession of the part the hand will now always play in painting.

*302* VELASQUEZ: *detail from the portrait of Philip IV*

*304* VELASQUEZ: *The Toilet of Venus* ▸

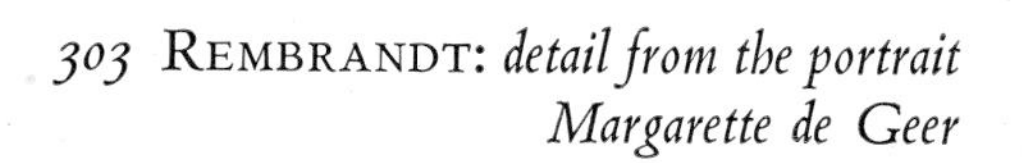

*303* REMBRANDT: *detail from the portrait Margarette de Geer*

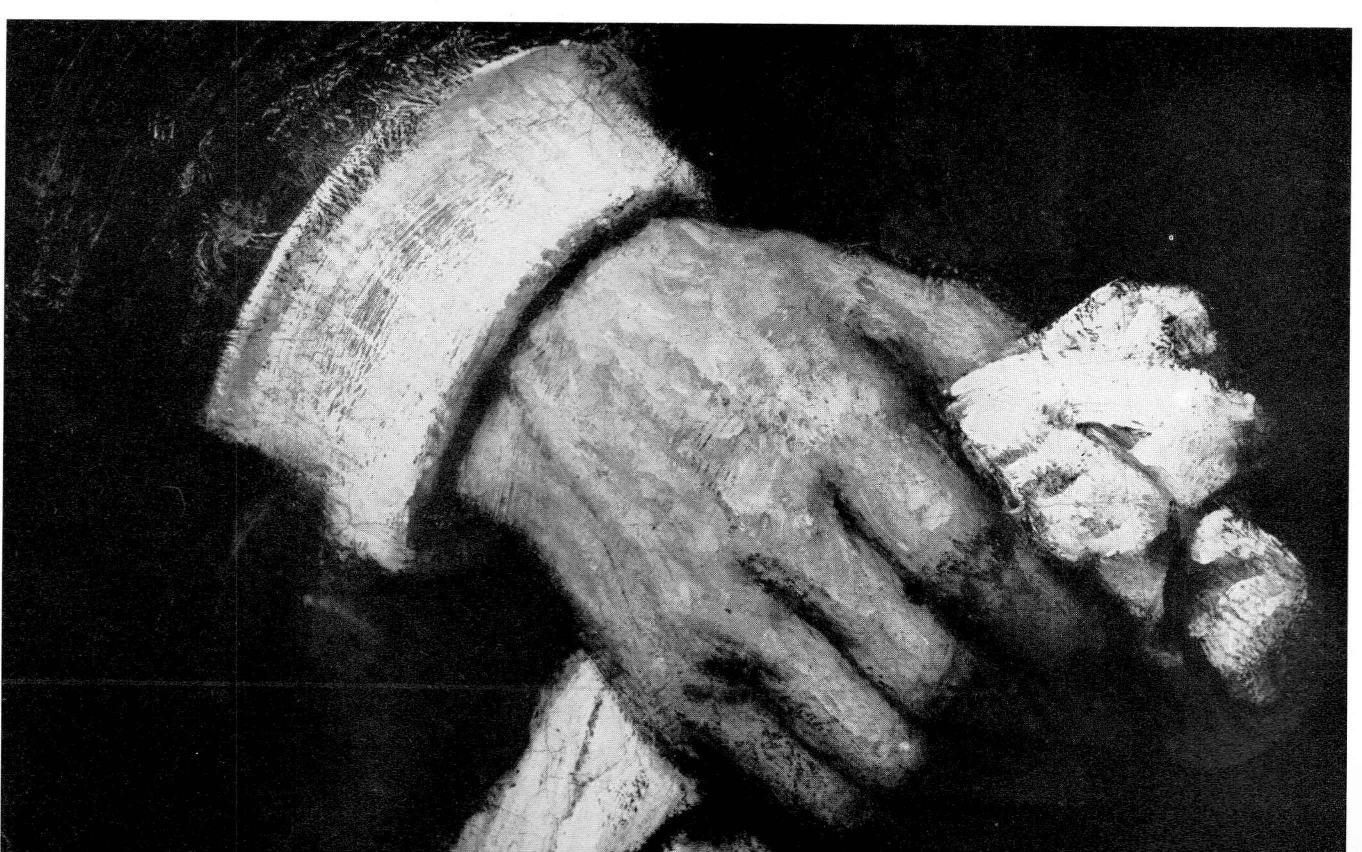

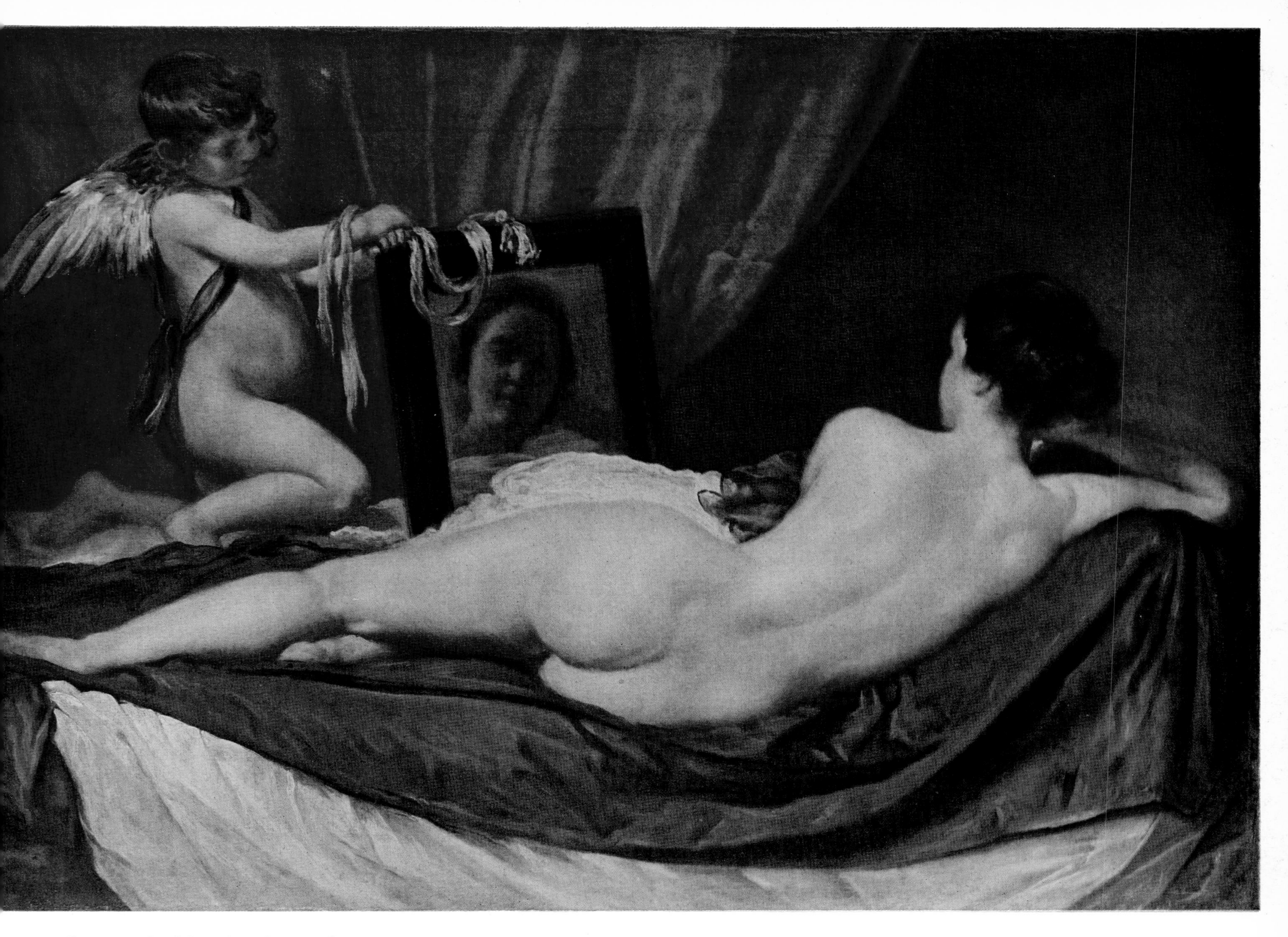

305 RUBENS: *detail from the Judgement of Paris*

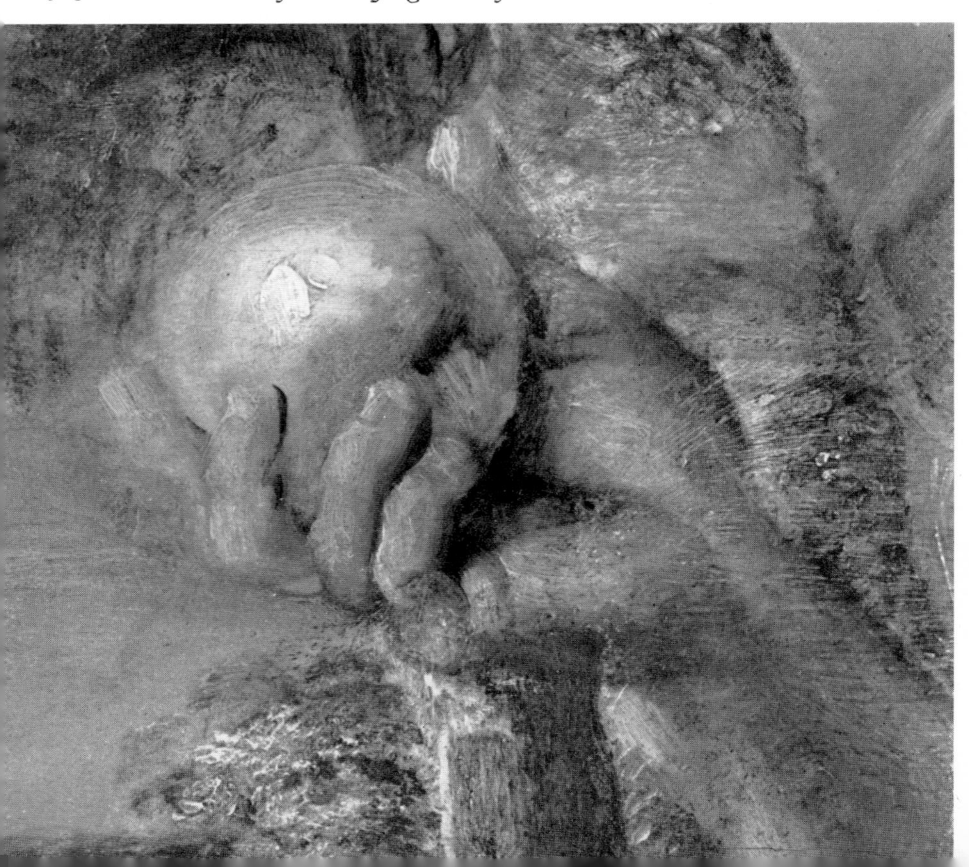

306 HALS: *detail from the Repast of St Jorisdoelen in Haarlem, 1616*

307 VERMEER: *Young Woman at the Virginals*

# *The Inner Life*

Rembrandt's passionate, romantic technique, and Vermeer's meticulous yet quivering handling, alike express the virtues of the inner life—ardent in the former, reflective in the latter, but in both cases dominating the life of the senses and subordinating it to the soul's aspirations.

*308* REMBRANDT: *Jeremias de Decker, 1660*

*309* REMBRANDT: *detail from Jacob blessing the sons of Joseph, 1656*

## *The Silent Life*

A large part of seventeenth-century painting, especially from the Dutch school, with its faithful reflection of reality, seems to be inspired by Pascalian meditation on a universe whose silent riddle the mind questions in vain. This ardent quest of the mystery comes out in the taste for the still-life: the mystery is felt to be contained in these ephemeral objects, pinned down by the image and asked to explain human destiny.

*310* ZURBARAN: *Citrons, Oranges and a Rose*

*311* HEDA: *Still-life*

*312* RUISDAEL: *Wheatfields*

# *Baroque Exuberance*

Life—its leaping symbolised by the rearing horse—carries all Rubens's forms along in a single whirlwind, which includes the tangled drama of the individual at grips with his fellow-beings. This trance finds resolution only in reunion with the flow of universal energy.

*313* RUBENS: *The Rape of the Daughters of Leucippus, 1618*

*314* RUBENS: *detail from the Battle of the Amazons, 1618*

*315* RUBENS: *Autumn, the Château de Steen, 1636*

# *Dreams of a Golden Age*

The painting of the classicists, which reaches its peak in Poussin and Claude, is an escape by heart and mind towards an imaginary world that claims, through Fable, to attain once more, across the ages, that mirage, the Golden Age—when men lived happily in a close alliance with a natural world still in its primordial innocence.

*316* Poussin: *The Birth of Adonis*

*318* Poussin: *Bacchanalian Revel before a Term of Pan* ▶

*317* Claude Lorraine: *Cephalus and Procris, 1645*

319 Claude Lorraine: *An Italian city*

# *Spirituality*

French spirituality forms a school opposed to the ecstatic mysticism exemplified by the Italian and Spanish schools: it seeks to climb towards God by a meditative ascent of mind and heart, setting all the faculties of a human being to work together in harmonious balance, in an atmosphere of extreme inner silence. The religious paintings of the time of Louis XIII express this withdrawal, in contrast to the passionate expression characteristic of Italian religious art at that time—perfectly typified by Bernini's St Theresa.

*320* JEAN TASSEL: *Catherine de Montholon, c. 1645*

*321* BERNINI: *Ecstasy of St Theresa, 1651*

*322* PHILIPPE DE CHAMPAIGNE: *Ex Voto, 1662*

323 GEORGES DE LA TOUR: *St Sebastian found by St Irene*

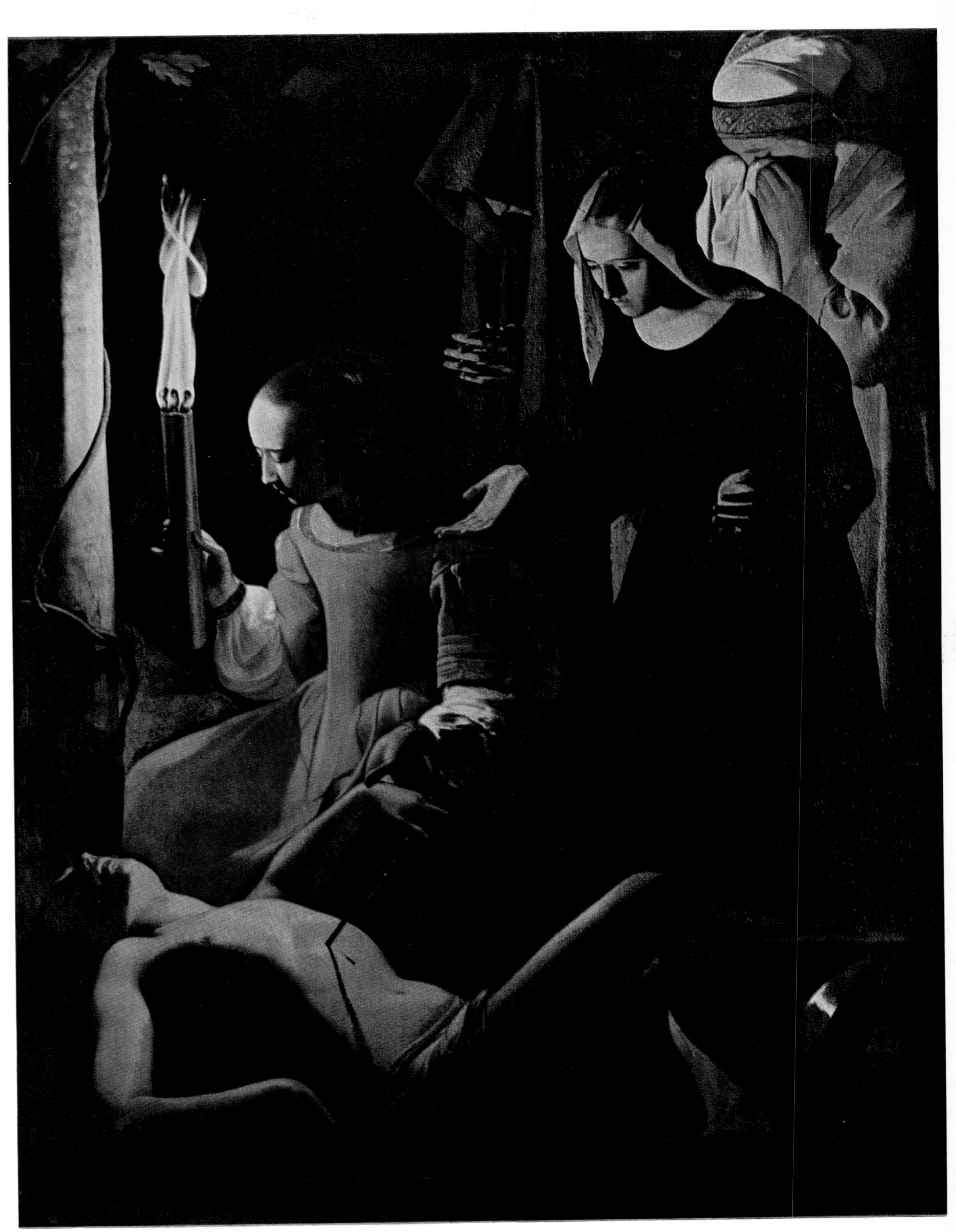

## *The 'Honest Man'*

The ethical ideal of the *honnête homme*, current in seventeenth-century France, transposes the classical ideals into conduct and self-government. 'Excellence' is accomplished in a balance of faculties that pre-supposes an exact self-knowledge, a consciousness of one's virtues as well as limitations. This balance is best realised in the *noblesse de robe*—the new nobility risen from the ranks of the French *bourgeoisie*—which, however, bows before the supreme virtues of the monarch, who possesses in full the attributes of excellence.

*324* LE BRUN: *Chancellor Seguier, c. 1660*

325 PHILIPPE DE CHAMPAIGNE: *Portrait of a man*

326 BERNINI: *Louis XIV*, 1665

# NOTES ON THE ILLUSTRATIONS TO CHAPTER VII

301 CARAVAGGIO (*c.* 1562–1609): *The Conversion of St Paul. 1600–1. Santa Maria del Popolo, Rome.*

302 VELASQUEZ (1599–1660): *Detail from the portrait of Philip IV of Spain. National Gallery, London.*

303 REMBRANDT (1606–69): *Detail from the portrait of Margarette de Geer, wife of Jacob Trip. National Gallery, London.*

304 VELASQUEZ (1599–1660): *The Toilet of Venus (The Rokeby Venus). National Gallery, London.*
*Photo: Zoltan Wegner*

305 PETER PAUL RUBENS (1577–1640): *Detail from the Judgement of Paris. National Gallery, London.*
*Photo: Zoltan Wegner*

306 FRANS HALS (*c.* 1580–1666): *Detail from The Repast of St Jorisdoelen in Haarlem. 1616. Frans Hals Museum, Haarlem.*
*Photo: A. Dingjan, The Hague*

307 JAN VERMEER VAN DELFT (1632–75): *Young Woman at the Virginals. National Gallery, London.*
*Photo: Zoltan Wegner*

308 REMBRANDT (1606–69): *Jeremias de Decker. 1660. Hermitage Museum, Leningrad.*
*Photo: Rijksmuseum, Amsterdam*

309 REMBRANDT (1606–69): *Detail from Jacob blessing the sons of Joseph. 1656. Museum, Cassel.*

310 FRANCISCO DE ZURBARAN (1598–1664): *Still-life: Citrons, Oranges and a Rose. Comte Alex Collection. Contini Bonacossi, Florence.*
*Photo: Giraudon*

311 WILLEM CLAESZ HEDA (1594–1680/2): *Still-life. Musée du Louvre, Paris.*

312 JACOB VAN RUISDAEL (1628/9–82): *Wheatfields. Metropolitan Museum of Art, New York.*

313 PETER PAUL RUBENS (1577–1640): *The Rape of the Daughters of Leucippus. c. 1618. Alte Pinakothek, Munich.*

314 PETER PAUL RUBENS (1577–1640): *Detail from The Battle of the Amazons. c. 1618. Alte Pinakothek, Munich.*

315 PETER PAUL RUBENS (1577–1640): *Autumn: le Château de Steen. 1636. National Gallery, London.*
*Photo: Zoltan Wegner*

316 NICOLAS POUSSIN (1594–1665): *The Birth of Adonis. Drawing. Royal Library, Windsor Castle. By gracious permission of Her Majesty the Queen.*

317 CLAUDE LORRAIN (1600–82): *Cephalus and Procris reunited by Diana. 1645. National Gallery, London.*
*Photo: Zoltan Wegner*

318 NICOLAS POUSSIN (1594–1665): *Bacchanalian Revel before a Term of Pan. National Gallery, London.*
*Photo: Zoltan Wegner*

319 CLAUDE LORRAIN (1660–82): *An Italian city. Drawing. Cabinet des Dessins, Musée du Louvre, Paris.*
*Photo: Archives Photographiques, Paris*

320 JEAN TASSEL (*c.* 1608–67): *Portrait of Catherine de Montholon, foundress of the Ursuline Convent in Dijon; died 1650. c. 1645. Dijon Museum.*
*Photo: Giraudon*

321 GIANLORENZO BERNINI (1598–1680): *Ecstasy of St Theresa. Finished 1651. Capella Cornaro, S. Maria della Vittoria, Rome.*
*Photo: Anderson*

322 PHILIPPE DE CHAMPAIGNE (1602–74): *Ex Voto. 1662. Musée du Louvre, Paris.*

323 GEORGES DE LA TOUR (1593–1652): *St Sebastian found by St Irene. Church of Broglie, France.*
*Photo: Zoltan Wegner*

324 CHARLES LE BRUN (1619–90): *Portrait of Chancellor Séguier shown as he appeared during the triumphal entry of Louis XIV and Maria-Theresa into Paris in 1660. Musée du Louvre, Paris.*

325 PHILIPPE DE CHAMPAIGNE (1602–74): *Portrait of a Man. Musée du Louvre, Paris.*

326 GIANLORENZO BERNINI (1598–1680): *Portrait bust of Louis XIV. 1665. Marble. Château de Versailles.*
*Photo: Alinari*

# VIII ENCHANTMENT—BAROQUE AND ROCOCO

# *VIII Enchantment—Baroque and Rococco*

*The Weltenberg St George, by the Asam brothers (327), really looks like one of Tasso's heroes just emerged from the enchanted forest*

THE TENDENCIES of the collective imagination in the West have varied very little in spite of changing history and fashions. From the thirteenth to the eighteenth century generation after generation took a passionate interest in the fortunes and misfortunes of Renaud de Montauban. Recharged with imaginative potential by Tasso in his *Gerusalemme Liberata*, the old *chanson de geste* received a second youth. Armida the enchantress became for two centuries a seemingly inexhaustible poetic theme with great theatrical possibilities: it produced, from Quinault to Rossini, a whole long chain of operas, including masterpieces by Lully and Gluck; and the art of painting was no less faithful to it—indeed the old poem which Poussin and Fragonard had loved was re-read by Delacroix at a time when it had collected a good deal of dust and when the novel was drawing its material from life, not from fancy.

Sometimes from pure caprice, sometimes to serve her designs, Armida with her sorcery confounded the various realms of Nature, imprisoning souls or releasing them as though the form of man or beast or monster was merely a transitory condition, a result of passing through an incessantly transformed world. One might be tempted to see in this one more example of the perpetual migration of souls through shifting forms characteristic of the Celtic stories, but the ramification of this fairy world is much wider; for while no doubt the Celtic spirit did inspire *Renaud de Montauban* its revival in the *Gerusalemme Liberata* was due to contact with Ovid's *Metamorphoses*. This perpetual search for escape went through many literary forms down to the end of the eighteenth century. In the theatre disguises, mistaken identities, men dressing as women and women as men, helped to produce a turbulent atmosphere in which every person takes the form of someone else, and by the eighteenth century disguise had become a theatrical convention: masters and lackeys, countesses and their maids were always exchanging roles—which enabled Marivaux and Beaumarchais to show, when they wished, that the valet was as good as his master and the maid as good as her mistress. Upon this sentimental labyrinth passion was superimposed: in the seventeenth century the hero remains constant in his love, which persists through all obstacles, metamorphoses, enchantments and ordeals; in the eighteenth eroticism has become no more than a means to self-forgetfulness in the play of bodies and souls. *The Marriage of Figaro* shows us an exhausted society in which everyone is playing at love but no one any longer knows very precisely who is loved by whom—or why and in what way one should love; and in this complex of feelings in fancy-dress even childhood, in the form of Cherubino, has exchanged innocence for dissipation. Love had been in the West, since the Middle Ages, a kind of ontological speculation, a passionate quest for a more intense being through another human being—and was to become so again in the nineteenth century; but in the century of Marivaux and Mozart it degenerated into a mere means to a change of fair.

Armida creates a magic garden in which she detains Renaud. This theme of the place of enchantment goes back well beyond the Middle Ages to Antiquity. It is the Castle of Love, to which Psyche is miraculously transported in Apuleius: 'For the embowings above were of Citron and Ivory, propped and undermined with pillars of gold, the walls covered and seeled with silver, divers sorts of beasts were graven and carved, that seemed to encounter with such as entered in.... The pavement was all of pretious stones, divided and cut one from another, whereon was carved divers kindes of pictures, in such sort that blessed and thrice blessed were they which might goe upon such a pavement: Every part and angle of the house was so well adorned, that by reason of the pretious stones and inestimable treasure there, it glittered and shone in such sort, that the chambers, porches, and doores gave light as it had been the Sunne.' Is it not easy, when one re-reads the poem of the second-century African rhetorician, to believe that one is stepping into the *Reichenzimmern* of some German palace or into some *Pfarrkirche* or *Stiftskirche* in Swabia or Bavaria? It is true that the walls are not of silver nor the columns of gold, nor the pavements of jewels, but thanks to the artifices of stucco-work, painting, mirrors, gilded woodwork, variegated marbles and lacquers, everything has been made to look like silver, gold or precious stones. Let us listen again to Apuleius as he describes, in *The Golden Ass*, the hall of Byrrhena's palace: 'On each side of her [Diana] were Dogs made of stone, that seemed to menace with their fiery eyes, their pricked ears, their bended nosethrils, and their grinning teeth, in such sort that you would have thought they had bayed and barked... I beheld the running water, which seemed to spring and leap under the feet of the goddesse... Moreover, amongst the branches of the stone appeared the image of Acteon: and how that Diana (which was carved within the same stone, standing in the water) because he did see her naked, did turne him into an Hart, and so he was torne and slaine of his owne hounds.' Could this not be taken for a description of the famous fountain in the gardens of Caserta?

*Plates 339–349*

*The finest of those rooms, known as* Reichenzimmern *and made of mirrors and of gilded wood and stucco reliefs, are those designed by Cuvilliés for the Residenz of the Dukes of Bavaria at Munich (335)*

*Plate 329*

Baroque art is Roman: at Rome it was born and at Rome it was to be reborn. Nero, in his Golden House with its portico a thousand feet long, its lake like the sea surrounded by cities and landscapes in miniature, its dining-room whose revolving dome imitated the revolutions of the celestial bodies, had made for himself, in imitation of the residences of the Oriental kings, a dwelling-place worthy of the Master of the World. Soon such palaces were made available to the urban populations in the form of public baths, just as, later, the princes were to transform the people's churches into palaces. Perhaps the most sumptuous of these public baths were those of Carthage, for it seems that Roman Africa cultivated this taste for architectural fantasy with particular intensity. 'Like the Italian Baroque of the *Seicento*, the African Baroque of the second century issues from classicism and opposes it, while continuing to feed on its substance', writes Gilbert Charles Picard, the archaeologist whom I shall also, at the risk of embarrassing him, call a poet, because he has contrived, by piously fitting fragments together, to call up before our eyes once more the mirage of that Roman Africa which was certainly the Empire's finest achievement.

It was in the building and adornment of his residence that the man of the sixteenth, seventeenth and eighteenth centuries succeeded best in his effort to recreate the life of Antiquity. The massive palaces of Rome and Florence are austere fortresses hiding their treasures from the outside world and retaining something of the feudal spirit: we must go to the villas, those palaces opening on to gardens that are themselves treated as palaces of greenery, if we wish to see how the humanist prince imagined his dwelling. These villas—those of the seventeenth century perhaps more than those of the sixteenth—were intended to be exact reproductions of the country residences of the Ancient Romans, of whose sumptuousness we can still form some idea through a few descriptions and from the ruins of Hadrian's villa at Tivoli, those of Pompeii and of Stabiae, or again those of the villas on Capri, which Augustus and Tiberius made into an enchanted island (recreated for us by Amedeo Maiuri).

All through their history the Romans remained closely bound to Nature, to its mysterious and deep-lying forces—which led them very quickly to religious syncretism. It was natural for them to create the humanistic garden, or rather what might be called the 'country palace', where the patricians came to enjoy some respite from the cares of business or the State by plunging into a fairy world peopled—both house and garden—by a thousand painted or carved images. These re-created, symbolically and still not without an element of magic, the order of the world as the gods had willed it, connected with men by a crowd of demi-gods and heroes. The ruling master here was Ovid, who in the twelve thousand lines of his *Metamorphoses*, passing through and exploiting the whole gamut of human passions, had systematised the world of mythology from chaos down to the metamorphosis of Julius Caesar into a star. In these gardens water, divided and made to play through many grottoes, basins and fountains—played a leading part, and Neptune, who was the god of springs before he was the god of the sea, presided over a world of water, the seminal element that produced a ceaseless rebirth of forms.

The Romans called such a residence an *otium*. Yet nothing is more foreign to our modern idea of repose than those country-houses. What we ask of the country is to restore us to ourselves by freeing us from the artificiality of our town life: the mere sight of some natural scene, looked at from a somewhat severe house, is expected to set us once more on the path of our own nature and to re-open its deepest springs. (Frank Lloyd Wright and Neutra have even balanced a house over a waterfall, or a mass of boulders.) The Romans expected the same thing from a country-house; but what they were in search of was '*Natura naturans*', not, as with us, '*Natura naturata*'. Reading Pliny's description of his villas at Lavinium or in Tuscany, one wonders how he could really find repose in those labryinths of artifice; and yet he speaks of the joy he felt at relaxing there and at putting off the toga, far away from his importunate clients. It was much the same in the West until quite recently, for the kind of garden known in Europe as English or Chinese merely replaced one artifice with another under the pretext of a return to Nature. What the aristocrat of the sixteenth, seventeenth and eighteenth centuries sought in the country was not Nature but the idea of Nature, or rather a fiction of the human and natural world that would enable him to escape from his day-to-day life by restoring him to contact with the order of the world. In his case, indeed, the deliberate unreality of all this contriving of Nature, architecture, pictures and sculpture was far more marked than in the case of the Ancient Romans; for the Romans saw in this man-made world a profound reality, and to them this landscape was a sacred landscape, whereas to a Roman of the seventeenth century it was a pure fiction that produced in his mind a transport, a genuine enchantment.

The Florentine villas of the fifteenth century, with their garden plots not far removed from the feudal orchard and their *casino* still looking like a fortress, were a long way yet from this ideal: it began to make its appearance in the villa built by Lorenzo the Magnificent at Poggio a Caiano. But it was at Rome that the Roman villa was reborn, along with so many other ideas of Antiquity, under the pontificates of Julius II and Leo X: Raphael, who was responsible for the decoration of the Farnesina and of the Villa Madama, was the arbiter of these new caprices. The Farnesina has long since lost its garden, and the Villa Madama, though it still has its country situation, offers us no more than an unfinished plan. In both of them the essential thing is the *loggia* which, laying the house open to Nature is adorned with forms and symbols that make it the court of the gods. In the Farnesina the allegory of Cupid and Psyche, completed by the story of Galatea in another room, celebrates Platonic *agape*, that apotheosis in which all creatures have a part and the soul is set free from the bondage of the senses. This 'rapture' of the soul is produced, for the visitor to the Villa Madama, by the marvellous world of the *grotteschi*—gods, demi-gods, fantasies of every sort—executed in stucco by Giovanni da Udine, who in the Farnesina had

*Plate 330*

*Plate 331*

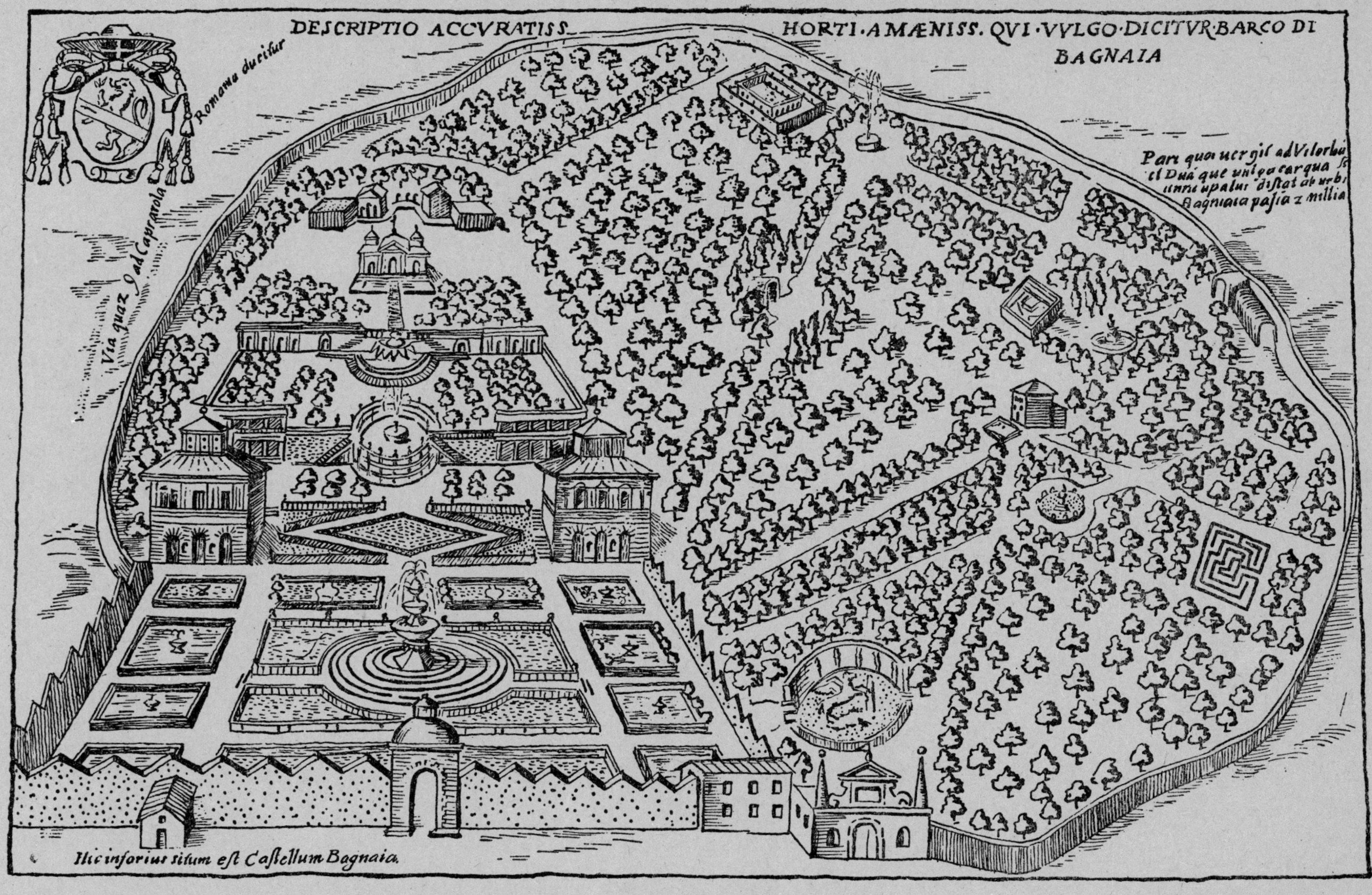


The Villa Lante, Bagnaia

painted amazing festoons of flowers, fruit and vegetables, an image of offerings to the gods in a country place. Even today, distant though we may be from the whole of that world, the charm of the Villa Madama and its setting works on us: the grace of its decorative fantasy, the ease of a free creativity that never goes astray, the enchantment of this play with allegories, of a 'thinking in forms' which fancifully juggles with beauty—all this makes us, for a moment live a radiant life that is above our own life, as though we were at last about to see mystery unveiled in full daylight. A morning spent at the Villa Madama, far away from the crowds trampling and jostling in the museums of Rome, is a moment stolen from the age of the gods.

This balance, the peculiar virtue of classicism, the power to set us free from the body without uprooting us, was broken by Giulio Romano. He transported the décor of the Villa Madama to the Palazzo del Tè at Mantua; but with him we pass into another world, that of Mannerism: the elegant play of the mind becomes an amusement of the imagination; what used to be merely suggested is now emphasised to the point of illusionism; the chimaera has become a monster, and in the Sala dei Giganti Titans are hurled to the ground all about us, while the chimney-piece imitates Etna. All that is left of the garden is an expanse of ground with some flowers, but the interest of the palace lies in the decoration, which is still perfectly preserved and unrolls before us a complete allegorical-cum-biographical story: the love of Prince Federigo Gonzago II for the Mantuan beauty Isabella Boschetto, and his accession to the ducal title conferred by Charles V, whose visit to the palace is recalled by obvious symbols. Thus, in this place of myths, the Prince's life is projected in fables and symbols, and he comes here in order to be face to face with himself—a place described in these words: '*honesto otio post labores ad reparandam virtutem*': to this fitting refuge the Prince, laying aside the burden of his office, comes to 're-make' himself; here the gods will help him to renew in himself the virtues of humanity.

After 1550 the villa develops in the form of grandiose schemes, of which perhaps the most vast was the Villa Giulia at the gates of Rome: its purpose was to provide Julius III with a magic palace concealed like some secret in the midst of huge gardens. Strange, too, is Pope Pius IV's conception of the *casino*, designed for his repose in the gardens of the Vatican: an enclosure over-populated with images, in which there is nothing to recall Nature except a few orange trees in pots and, in the background, the leafy trees of the great garden. Pirro Ligorio, who designed this Villa Pia, poured out a similar stream of images in the gardens of the Villa d'Este at Tivoli, which are still almost intact, the product of a Mannerist imagination. In the strange garden at Bomarzo, where one can feel the somewhat literal application of a plan dictated by some humanist with an extravagant mind, Mannerism develops towards monstrosity. Meanwhile at the Villa Lante at Bagnaia, Vignola took up the reins of imagination in a firm hand again and recovered the balance of classicism.

*Plate 332*

*Figure p. 227*

The walls of these villas are like an enormous picture-book—whose pages to this day have scarcely ever been turned. And yet in this prolix art (the Zuccari brothers come first to mind), is to be found the genesis of the future, especially the future of landscape painting. The aim of this decoration was to realise an encyclopaedia—what Vincent de Beauvais in the Middle Ages had called the *speculum majus*. In the castle of Caprarola, built and decorated by Cardinal Alessandro Farnese, the plan was drawn up by a committee of poets and scholars, Annibale Caro, Onofrio Panvinio and Fulvio Orsini: its central idea is the Prince's ecclesiastical dignity, and it depicts the contemplative life and the life of action; the life of action is shown in the summer apartments, where two rooms are devoted to tracing the important events in the history of the Farnese family in the service of the Church Militant; while the contemplative life is depicted in the winter apartments—contemplation of the cosmos in its celestial aspects (seasons, months and days) and in its terrestrial ones (the Sala della Mappamundi), God appearing in human life in the form of angels, and God's justice and the hermit's pure life of contemplation. At the same time the garden, which goes in terraces up the hill and joins the castle to the *casino*, is given up to pagan fantasies.

The villa underwent fresh developments in other parts of Italy. In the imperial villa at Pesaro, which Eleonora Gonzago had built before 1530 by Bartolomeo Genga in honour of her husband Francesco della Rovere, a pastoral spirit reigns and fills the decoration with plants and flowers: Nature here comes right into the house, and the demi-gods and sylvan gods take up their abode in it. On the other hand, the decoration of the palaces of the Veneto, following the influence of Veronese, uses the theme of the assembly of the gods with monumental nobility. Veronese—who was soon imitated by others—at Maser revived a very ancient idea, that of filling doorways with painted people; and so, in these houses designed for repose, the Italian, like the Ancient Roman, was so much afraid of being alone that, not content with surrounding himself with gods, he provided himself with painted visitors.

In France the *château* was ready to take up the idea of the villa. Already at Fontainebleau, in both palace and gardens, François I tried to fabricate another world and to make of this residence a 'Rome of the North'. When Louis XIV, tired of a work that had gone on from dynasty to dynasty and seemed to have no end, gave up the Louvre and decided to create Versailles, his ambition was not a merely personal one; he was tempted by the idea of creating a natural setting, a world in keeping with royal dignity, as Philip II had done at the Escorial but with the difference that it would use both the fictions of humanism and the resources of Nature. It was the hugest complex of terraces, groves, fountains, statues, galleries, marble halls and mirrors that had ever yet been put together, an Olympian residence, but with the symbolism centring on Apollo, the new royal emblem, instead of Hercules who had been the embodiment of the princely virtues during the sixteenth and early seventeenth centuries.

Versailles brought to France the enchanted palace, now a sort of sacred palace for the celebration of the religion of monarchy. Later, when Louis XV and Louis XVI withdrew into the secrecy of their small apartments, this masterpiece of royalty suffered a sad mutilation, completed by the Revolution, which reduced the grounds to a desert. But Versailles was copied again and again by the various European sovereigns who took up the royal legend. In some of them, ambition for royal grandeur seems even to have been a compensation for the limitations of their actual power, and the German princelings made the sumptuousness of their residences almost a principle of government. Since industrial stagnation offered capital only limited fields for investment, the wealth accumulated in a few hands had no other outlet than adornment. For centuries art profited from this economic situation, until in the nineteenth century the rise of commerce and industry slowed down, where it did not stop, this prodigality in non-productive investments.

From Versailles the idea of the enchanted palace transformed into a royal palace returned to Italy, where it was enriched by architectural resources that were lacking in the original which is, after all, a somewhat dull building that spreads out almost planlessly with its long façade giving on the gardens. The Stupinigi Hunting-lodge in Piedmont and the palace at Caserta near Naples are the finest realisations of this idea of the *reggia*, superb architectural poems in which complex and apparently arbitrary refinements of design provide beautiful exteriors for what are really functional purposes: for instance, at Stupinigi the arrangement of the accommodation for packs of hounds, for horses and for guests, and at Caserta the central entrance allowing the quickest possible access to all parts of the colossal building. One element of palace design, which developed in Italy and became the rage in Germany, remaining till the nineteenth century the symbol of monumental luxury, was the staircase. It was worked out by the Neapolitan school: grandiose as are the examples of it at Caserta, Pommersfelden, Brühl, Wurzburg or Schloss Mirabell at Salzburg, nothing will ever equal the fantasy, ingenuity and apparent spontaneity to be found in the staircases built by Sanfelice for palaces or villas in Naples, now fast disappearing—sacrifices to the modern city, which is on the way to deleting from the artistic map of Europe one of the great schools of Baroque architecture. Of the thousand and one ways of rising from one floor to another the most unexpected, cunning, 'Baroque' and witty were invented by Sanfelice and the Neapolitan architects. And what is one to say of that unknown architect's belvedere-staircase built by the monks of the Certosa of Padula on the borders of Calabria, simply that they might look out at the landscape?

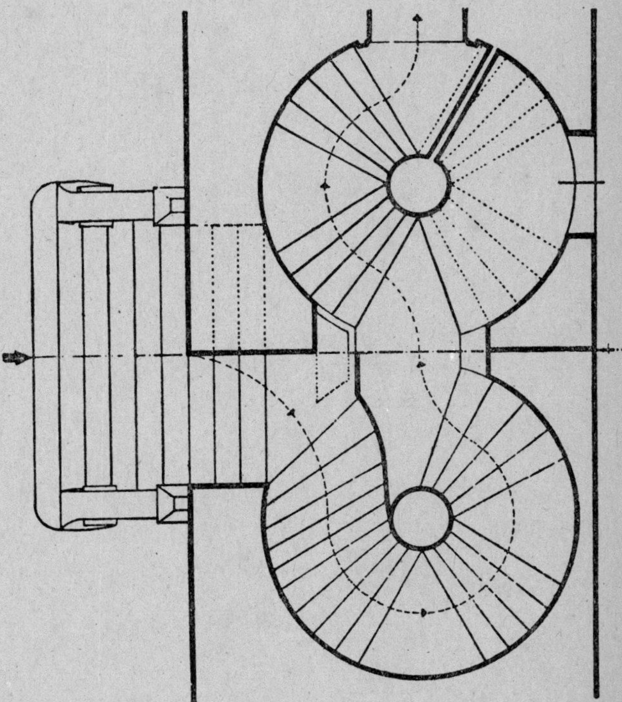

*Sanfelice: plan and perspective of a staircase in the Vergini Palace, Naples*

Arranged in terraces following the contours of the ground, the Italian garden is a kind of labyrinth, providing the visitor with surprises as he strolls about as though in the mazes of some secret place, never allowing itself to be grasped as a whole. But France returned to the perspectivist theme already so well exploited in the French medieval cathedrals, developing it at Versailles into a superb progress right to the horizon. The view from the windows of the Galerie des Glaces at Versailles is truly worthy of a royal glance. At Caserta Vanvitelli took up the theme again, but he Baroquised it by a disproportionate enlargement and, in the Italian manner, instead of making it lead away to the horizon pushed it up a hill, from which a cascade of water (repetition of Vignola's idea for the Villa Lante and for Caprarola) fed huge fountains that were made the excuse for orgies of mythology. France, with her mania for destruction, now offers no more than poor remnants of her fine gardens, and even the gardens of Versailles are no more than a shadow of what they were: one must go to Eastern Europe, to Germany, Poland and Russia, to find intact (when not devasted by the last war) those '*bois sacrés*', those Arcadias peopled with statues, temples, aqueducts, baths, arbours, hermitages, open-air theatres, 'wetting sports', Palladian bridges, mosques and Chinese pavilions which transformed them into something decidedly foreign to Nature, into a miniature cosmos where the sovereign is shut up within his own majesty as in a magic circle.

On the interiors a more and more fantastic luxury was lavished, as though with the intention of really bringing the fairy palace of Apuleius to pass on earth. To break off all contact with reality the Italians—and even more so the Germans—made a fetish of mirrors. Lafont de Sainte-Yenne, though noting with disapproval that they have taken the place of paintings, concedes that they have great charm: 'I admit,' he wrote in 1746, in his *Réflexions sur l'état de la peinture en France*, 'that these mirrors have advantages that are almost miraculous, in many ways deserving the favour bestowed on them by fashion. A device that can pierce the walls so as to enlarge the rooms and add fresh ones to them, that can return with interest the rays of light it receives, whether from the windows or from the candelabra—how could man, the enemy of darkness and of everything that can cause sadness, have helped loving such a device, such an embellishment, which both gives him light and leads him astray and which, in the act of deceiving his eyes, gives him a pleasure that is no deception.' The same idea of multiplying light, but this time with a symbolical intention, governed the use of mirrors in religious art, as for instance in the Spanish altarpieces inlaid with mirrors and in the pendentives of the domes of Mexican churches in which mirrors—mirrors of truth—serve as emblems for the Evangelists. At Palermo in the eighteenth century, for the festival of St Rosalia, the vault and walls of the cathedral were covered with fragments of many-coloured looking-glass placed at different angles and set in gold and silver paper: the light came from a thousand chandeliers, each with six candles. In the fantastic Villa Palagonia at Bagheria near Palermo the ballroom has a ceiling of mirrors: these have now gone dim and give the visitor the strange illusion of watching himself walking on his head at night. In the Rosenborg Castle in Copenhagen one room is decorated with a marquetry floor reflected in a mirror ceiling, the image being sent back to an oval mirror let into the floor: in this make-believe space there is no longer any above or below. In the mirror rooms and *galeries des glaces* of the German palaces, the mirrors, facing each other or multiplied at every conceivable angle are obviously intended to dislocate, break up and pulverise any image of the real world and to give the dweller among them doubts of the reality of his own existence, which has suddenly become innumerable, repeated *ad infinitum*: never has the passion for escape from oneself and from the world and for projecting one's life into a world of fiction achieved more insensate expression. Leonardo da Vinci, the old wizard, had indeed thought of these illusionist tricks, for there is in his notebooks a design for an eight-sided mirror chamber.

*Plates 339, 340*

*In the 19th century, in the Gletschergarten at Lucerne, an Irrgarten (garden of errors) was constructed: the varied play of mirrors made it seem as if you were entering a mirage*

Into this world of the fantastic everything that could serve these orgies of the imagination converged, especially from those countries whose distance gave them a dream quality. Although the Americas—still known as the West Indies—contributed few forms to the plastic arts, Turkey and (above all) China were the main sources of Rococo forms in the eighteenth century. The first cases of porcelain from Cathay had already reached Lisbon in the time of King Manuel the Fortunate, but the Renaissance was too self-absorbed to let itself be tempted by horizons beyond the Mediterranean. It was the Dutch (the Netherlands East India Company was founded in 1602) who began to import Chinese pottery for the decoration of their houses, and later traded in it. The *Compagnie des Indes*, founded in Paris in 1664, intensified this commerce, aided by agents among whom there were missionaries. But it was soon found to be less expensive to imitate than to import: this was the origin of Delft blue, and very soon Nevers and Rouen followed suit. Thus the extraordinary development of the ceramic art in the seventeenth and eighteenth centuries has its origin in plagiarism. Till then Italian pottery had been the main source, imposing everywhere its characteristic curves and its narrative or grotesque decoration; but suddenly, in the second half of the seventeenth century, the direction changed, and China communicated to the potteries of Europe its forms and its vocabulary of ornament. Soon it even stimulated them to imitate porcelain, which had been made in China since the T'ang Dynasty: Böttger, one of the jewellers of the King of Saxony, discovered the secret of it in 1709, and founded the first factory at Meissen as early as

*Plates 361–367*

*Plates 354, 355*

1710; the other countries of Europe tried in turn to steal the secret from Meissen. First soft-paste, then hard-paste factories were founded all over Europe and flooded the market with their products: in Germany, Berlin, Höchst, Nymphenburg, Ludwigsburg, Frankenthal, Furstenberg, Ansbach and Fulda; in Austria, Vienna; in Denmark, Copenhagen; in Sweden, Stockholm; in Russia, Saint Petersburg; in Holland, Loosdrecht, Amstel and The Hague; in Switzerland, Zürich, Schooren and Nyon; in Belgium, Brussels and Tournai; in Portugal, Lisbon; in France, Saint-Cloud, Mennecy, Chantilly, Vincennes, Sceaux, Lunéville, Strassbourg and Sèvres; in England Bow, Derby, Chelsea, Bristol, Worcester, Plymouth and Liverpool; in Italy, Doccia, Rome and Capodimonte; in Spain, Buen Retiro and Alcora. After a while, not content with making vases and table-ware, the potters produced figurines embodying mythology, the *commedia del'Arte* and picturesque aspects of the life of the times—or again crucifixes or even reproductions of pictures. Porcelain cabinets in the Chinese style were also manufactured, the finest examples being in the Capodimonte Museum at Naples, at Aranjuez and in the royal palace at Madrid.

The artistic value of these products is very unequal. The art of modelling clay and decorating it had for long been a pilot art, one of those in which men carry through their experiments in forms, diagrams and rhythms: it had been so from Neolithic times down to the Greek period; but in the Hellenistic era pottery became no more than a derivative art, and in the Roman world it disappeared as an art, experiencing, in the West, a long night until its revival in Italy in Renaissance times. Decoration was condemned to take second place to the fine arts, at a moment when those also, in most European countries, were thought of as servants of a setting. The best of the inventions of Rococo pottery are those that are not enslaved to the figure, those in which the potter and the painter give free rein to their decorative fantasy.

Woven materials, painted wallpapers, silks, bronzes and so-called Coromandel lacquer-work continued to flow in from China, together with the porcelain which was produced in increasing quantity for export under the reign of the emperors K'ang Hsi (1662–1722), Yung Ch'eng (1722–35) and Ch'ien Lung (1736–96). This flood of *chinoiserie* certainly influenced the evolution of Rococo taste by providing the artists with a vocabulary of forms much better adapted to their aspirations than the Graeco-Roman ones. Fiske Kimball attributes to the decorative craftsmen of the Late Louis XIV and Regency periods the formation of the Rococo style, which he considers the product of a slow evolution of the decorative repertoire from Berain onwards, reaching its climax in Pierre Lepautre, Audran and Oppenord. French art historians who despised the Baroque were not pleased with this compliment and have violently rejected a hypothesis according to which their country played a part in creating this 'impure' style; none the less, Fiske Kimball was right in his view of the preponderant role of the decorators in the elaboration of Rococo. Rococo is an art of the pen and graving tool transposed into wood, stucco and—very soon—stone. The engravers in their turn took up the speculations of the decorators at the point where these had been left by the last Mannerist engravers of Flanders (Vredeman de Vries), Germany (Lukas Kilian, Friedrich Unteush, Dietterlin and Johan Smieschech) or even France (Callot). Mannerism might have evolved spontaneously into Rococo, but for the braking action exercised by the Counter-Reformation architects in their return to the Graeco-Roman monumental tradition—in which they were really following Bernini at a time when Borromini in Rome, Guarino Guarini in Turin and the sculptor Serpotta at Palermo were already, in the seventeenth century, creating all the elements of Rococo: its fragmentation of space, which is rendered vibrant by the multiplication of axes and the warping of planes, its linear continuity obtained by asymmetrical forms compensating one another, and its loosening of structure, which is made subordinate to effect.

*Plate 367*

*Plates 349–352*

*This asymmetrical balance of forms, achieved through contrapuntal compositions, recurs throughout the Rococo, in its architecture (344), its sculpture (350, 351) and its painting (352, 353)*

With Rococo there developed an art which had remained, till then, really 'minor'—that of furniture-making. All through the Middle Ages and during the Renaissance, people had

*Plates 341–344*

remained content with a rudimentary equipment in furniture—some chests, beds, tables, tapestries, and not many chairs. The man of those times lived on his feet, on horseback or lying down—he scarcely ever sat; the ladies of the reign of Louis XIII held their literary receptions in bed in their *ruelle*; and the kings of France, until the early part of the reign of Louis XIV, lived a wandering life inherited from feudal times, carrying around with them the minimum of furniture. To these circumstances is due the birth of Louis XIV. When Louis XIII was passing through Paris on his way from Saint-Germain to Fontainebleau and a storm prevented him from travelling on, he had to sleep at the Louvre and found no bed available except that of the Queen, whom he had left some years ago; nine months later, to the day, the future *Roi Soleil* came into the world. What would have been the history of France without that storm? No one can say, but the arts would have been considerably the poorer.

The refinement of furniture came from the changes in social life. From that time onwards pieces of furniture were made for all the attitudes of men and women at work, in repose and in conversation: furniture lost the monumental appearance and the outlines imposed by the Renaissance, which it had kept during the whole of the seventeenth century and became more and more elaborate in its forms, more in keeping with the lavishness of its surroundings both in finish and in the beauty of its materials. Craftsmen worked at one piece of furniture for years, as in the case of Oeben and Riesener who laboured for nine years on that masterpiece of French furniture-making, the cylinder writing-table known as the *bureau du roi Louis XV*. Chests-of-drawers, wardrobes and escritoires were enriched with lacquer-work, with marquetry and also with carved bronze, drawing on the new skill in the goldsmith's art.

*Plates 345–348*

This prosperity in the decorative arts reflected the important part now taken by women in the refinement of civilisation—a moral influence which they had exercised in the West since the Middle Ages and were now to maintain until the moment when, having won equal rights with men, they abdicated the power belonging to their femininity. Women, whether princesses or of lesser rank, were honoured by the painters and it was they who governed the 'arts of the interior'. It was they—queen or favourite, Pompadour or Marie-Antoinette—who set the tone of the court and contributed their elfin talents to the fantasies of the Rococo. A sister of Frederick the Great, educated in the French manner, arrives in a semi-barbarous Principality, and the result is the blossoming of artistic refinement at Bayreuth. Another German woman, Catherine II, makes the court of Saint Petersburg the rival of the other European courts, and masterpieces of art leave France and England for the Hermitage, where she holds her philosophic *salon*. Women mould men and make them more civilised. Under the influence of women the eighteenth century saw a decline in sports: formerly, to please a woman, a man had to show his strength in the tournament, but now she found these outdoor games less attractive than the *ieux d'esprit* displayed in the drawing-room.

Romain Rolland, that witness of a time that has disappeared, wrote in 1901 to Sofia de Gonzaga words that would apply perfectly to the society of the eighteenth century: 'Women make men. Think what power it must have over a man—that daily, indeed hourly, influence exercised throughout his life by his mother, the girls who are his friends in childhood, his mistresses, his wife, the women he confides in and those who give him intellectual company . . . Who can reckon the influence radiated over literature, art and the tone of public life by certain *salons*, certain actresses, certain society women? . . . If ten women, five women, or *only one* arises in this medium with a healthy and constant intelligence and moral energy added to her natural seductiveness, I guarantee that there will be a change in the whole spirit of the time.'

# *Baroque Drama*

327 EGID-QUIRIN ASAM: *St George overcoming the dragon,* 1721

330 GIOVANNI DA UDINE: *detail of stucco work, 1519–25* ▶

*328 Piazza Armerina, Roman mosaic, 4th century* A.D.

*329 Fountain of Diana and Actaeon at Caserta, 1790*

# *In the Gardens of Armida*

Renaissance Italy revived that Roman idea, the 'villa'—a place of delight set in the country, a small world filled with images and symbols that re-create a mythical world or order. There the prince relaxes from the cares of authority, finding him-self once more in the company of the gods and heroes, his peers.

*331* RAPHAEL, GIULIO ROMANO *and* GIOVANNI DA UDINE: *Venus and Psyche, 1517–18*

*332 The Villa d'Este in the sixteenth century*

# Courtly Art

Louis XIV turned the Italian 'enchanted palace' into a 'sacred palace', scene of the ritual of monarchy. All the European sovereigns, small and great, imitated this example, and in the service of these ambitious architects and decorators created magnificent edifices and interiors of a sumptuousness that will never be surpassed.

333 VANVITELLI: *Staircase of Palazzo Reale, Caserta*

334 *Schloss Mirabell, Salzburg: detail of staircase, 1721*

335 CUVILLIÉS: *bedroom in the Residenz, Munich*

336 *'Galerie des Glaces', Versailles, by* MANSART *and* LE BRUN

337 JUVARRA: *Stupinigi, near Turin*

## *Play with Mirrors*

Mirrors face to face, or placed in large numbers in every conceivable plane, break up and pulverise each image of the real world, launch those who live and move among them into a world of fiction, and express the strange passion for self-escape that is at the heart of the Baroque period.

*339 Mirror of Marie de Médicis, c. 1600*

*340* Augsburg Workshop: *Mirror, 1699*

◀ *338 The Queen's Dressing room, Royal Palace, Turin, 1737*

*341 Medal cabinet from Stupinigi, 1739*

# *The Art of Living*

In the eighteenth century the furniture-maker's art, born of the refinement of social life, begins its great development. Furniture loses the monumental appearance it has kept since the Renaissance, and becomes more elaborate in its forms, the finish of its workmanship and the beauty of its materials.

*343 English mahogany armchair: detail, c. 1760*

*342 Cylindrical top desk, Louis XV style, 1769*

*344 Salon of the Château de Champs, French, 18th century* ▶

345 CHARDIN: *La Pourvoyeuse*, c. 1738

In the eighteenth century society takes its tone from women. Princesses or commoners, they are given pride of place by the painters, and it is they who govern the arts of indoor life. They mould men, making them more civilised, presiding over the games of wit played in the *salons* and even contributing to the development of philosophy.

*346 Chelsea porcelain figure, 1725*

*347* JEAURAT: *The Needlewoman: detail*

*348* GAINSBOROUGH: *Mary, Countess Howe*

*349* ZIMMERMANN BROTHERS: *ceiling of the church at Steinhausen, 1746–54*

*350* SERPOTTA: *Putti, from the Oratorio S. Lorenzo, Palermo, 1699–1707*

*351 Putti from Ottobeuren, Bavaria, 1767*

# Rococo

The contradictions of the Baroque are resolved in the Rococo: there the restlessness of curve and counter-curve is controlled by principles of rhythmic compensation. In the superabundance of ornamentation, unity is achieved through the convergence of all those vibrant elements towards a harmonic centre—an ideal point situated in the space defined by the setting.

352 TIEPOLO: *drawing for a ceremonial gondola*

353 FRAGONARD: *Bathers*

*354 Meissen chandelier, c. 1741*

All over Europe the refinement of the arts of living gives a new impulse to that of porcelain, stimulated also by the knowledge of Chinese examples.

*355 Rouen dish, 18th century*

# *Gold and Silver Work*

The inflow of precious metals from America caused princes to have whole suites of furniture made for them in silver, of which the most famous was that of Versailles; it was finished in 1660, but the vicissitudes of the war against the Augsburg League forced Louis XIV to have it melted down in 1689. Lords and wealthy commoners ordered gold and silver vessels for use or ornament, the finest examples being produced in France, Germany and the British Isles.

*356 Portuguese silver dish, Manueline style, late 15th century*

357 London Workshop: *Tea-caddy, 1748*

359 *Centre-piece from Augsburg, 1775*

358 Charles Kandler: *Samovar, 1727–37*

360 Thomas Germain: *Silver wine cooler, 1727–8*

# *Chinoiseries*

Countries situated as far away as dreamland entice the imagination. China in particular brings to the West a flood of brocades, silks, wall-papers, bronzes, porcelain and so-called Coromandel lacquer-work—produced for export and supplying the rococo artists with a vocabulary of forms much better suited to their needs than that of Greece or Rome.

*361 Summer residence near Peking, built in imitation of Versailles, 1747*

*362 Chinese red and gold lacquer, showing the arrival of a European mission*

*363 Detail of tapestry: English Soho factory, c. 1730*

*364 Chinese bowl with European inscription, 1557*

*365 London coffee pot, 1769–70*

*366 Chinese cabinet belonging to the Duc de Choiseul, 18th century* ▶

*367 Ch'ien Lung, porcelain objects, 18th century*

# NOTES ON THE ILLUSTRATIONS TO CHAPTER VIII

327 EGID-QUIRIN ASAM (1692–1750): *St George overcoming the dragon. The paintings behind the statue are by Cosmas Damian Asam, his brother. High altar of the Benedictine church of Weltenburg, Bavaria. 1721.*
*Photo: Hirmer*

328 *A Roman villa on the sea-shore. Detail of mosaic from the Roman villa of Piazza Armerina, Sicily. 4th century* A.D.
*Photo: A. Balbo*

329 *Fountain of Diana and Actaeon by* PAOLO PERSICE, ANGELO BRUNELLI *and* PIETRO SOLARI. *1790. Gardens of Palazzo Reale, Caserta.*
*Photo: Brogi*

330 GIOVANNI DA UDINE (1487–1564): *Detail of stucco-work at the Villa Madama, Rome. 1519–25.*
*Photo: Anderson*

331 *Psyche gives Venus the draught of immortality. Detail from the Psyche Loggia, Villa Farnesina, Rome. Figures by* RAPHAEL *and* GIULIO ROMANO, *decoration by* GIOVANNI DA UDINE. *1517–18.*

332 *View of the Villa d'Este, Tivoli, as it was in the 16th century. Painting, after the engraving by Dupérac. The Villa was built 1550–86, after the plans of* PIRRO LIGORIO. *Acton Collection, Florence.*

333 *Staircase in Palazzo Reale, Caserta. Built after plans made in 1751 by* LUIGI VANVITELLI.
*Photo: Georgina Masson*

334 JOHANN LUCAS VON HILDEBRANDT: *Detail of staircase, Schloss Mirabel, Salzburg. 1721–7.*
*Photo: Dr Alfred Nawrath, Bremen*

335 F. DE CUVILLIÉS (1695–1768): *Bedroom, decorated for the Elector Maximilian Emmanuel II (1679–1726). Residenzmuseum, Munich.*
*Photo: Courtesy, Department of Castles, Gardens and Lakes, Munich*

336 JULES HARDOUIN-MANSART *and* CHARLES LE BRUN: *Galerie des Glaces, Versailles. 1678–84*
*Photo: Alinari*

337 *Aerial view of the Stupinigi Palace, Piedmont, built after the plans of* FILIPPO JUVARRA. *Made in 1729 for Vittorio Amadeo of Savoy.*
*Photo: Pizzi, Milan*

338 *The Queen's dressing-room. Marquetry of rare woods, ivory, glass and chased bronze-gilt. Designed in 1737 by* BENEDETTO ALFIERI. *Royal Palace, Turin.*

339 *Mirror given to Marie de Médicis by the Republic of Venice in 1600. Agate, onyx, emerald, cameos. Musée du Louvre, Paris.*
*Photo: Archives Photographiques, Paris*

340 *Mirror in silver, silver-gilt, mother-of-pearl and engraved glass. Augsburg Workshop. 1699. Seligmann Collection, Paris.*
*Photo: Eileen Tweedy*

341 PIETRO PIFFETTI: *Medal cabinet. Wood marquetry and ivory. Queen's bedroom. 1739. Stupinigi Palace, Piedmont.*

342 *Desk with cylindrical top. Marquetry and bronze-gilt. Belonging to Louis XV. Made in 1769 by* RIESENER *and designed by* OEBEN. *Cabinet de Louis XV, Versailles.*
*Photo: Archives Photographiques, Paris*

343 *Detail of mahogany arm-chair. English, c. 1760. Untermyer Collection, New York.*

344 *Salon of the Château de Champs; the chair-backs are covered in Beauvais tapestry; the painted panels are the work of* CHRISTOPHER HUET. *French, 18th century.*

345 JEAN-BAPTISTE CHARDIN (1699–1779): *La Pourvoyeuse. Another version of the picture painted for the* Salon *of 1739. Musée du Louvre, Paris.*

346 *Chelsea porcelain figure. English, 1725. Untermyer Collection, New York.*

347 ETIENNE JEAURAT (1699–1789): *The Needlewoman. Private collection.*

348 THOMAS GAINSBOROUGH (1727–88): *Mary, Countess Howe. Kenwood, London.*
*Photo: Eileen Tweedy*

349 *Ceiling of the church at Steinhausen, Bavaria. 1746–54. Architect,* DOMENIKUS ZIMMERMANN, *frescoes by* JOHANN BAPTISTE ZIMMERMANN.
*Photo: Hoffman and Campe, Hamburg*

350 GIACOMO SERPOTTA (1656–1732): *Putti. Oratorio S. Lorenzo, Palermo. 1699–1707.*
*Photo: Anderson*

351 JOSEPH CHRISTIAN *and* JOHANN MICHAEL FIECHTMAYER: *Putti from an altar of the church at Ottobeuren, Bavaria. 1767.*
*Photo: Kohlbauer, Allgäu*

352 GIAMBATTISTA TIEPOLO (1696–1770): *Drawing for a ceremonial gondola. Duke of Talleyrand Collection.*

353 HONORÉ FRAGONARD (1762–1806): *Bathers. Musée du Louvre, Paris.*

354 *Chandelier, with gilded bronze and porcelain ornaments; at the crest a golden oriole modelled by* J. E. ENDER. *Meissen, c. 1741. Untermyer Collection, New York.*

355 *Large dish with lambrequin decoration. Faïence. Rouen. French, 18th century.*
*Photo: Eileen Tweedy*

356 *Silver dish, decorated with wild beasts and men. Manueline style, late 15th century. Fundaçao Ricardo Espirito Santo, Lisbon.*
*Photo: Photo Studios, London*

357 *Tea-caddy. London Workshop. 1748. Worshipful Company of Goldsmiths, London.*

358 CHARLES KANDLER: *Samovar. 1727–37. Victoria and Albert Museum, London.*
*Crown Copyright reserved*

359 *Table centre-piece. Augsburg, 1775. Weimar.*
*Photo: Bildarchiv Foto Marburg*

360 FRANÇOIS-THOMAS GERMAIN: *Silver wine cooler. French, 1727–8. Private collection, Paris.*

361 *South wing of the Summer Residence at Yuan Ming Yuan, near Peking, built in imitation of the Palace of Versailles for the Emperor Ch'ien Lung, by two Jesuit priests in 1747. From a Chinese engraving after 1783.*
*Photo: Connaissance des Arts, Paris*

362 *Chinese red and gold laquer, showing the arrival of a European mission in China. Dr Pedro Batalha Reis Collection, Lisbon.*
*Photo: Photo Studios, London*

363 *Detail of an English tapestry with chinoiseries. Wool and silk. Soho Factory. English, c. 1730. Guldenstein (Ostholstein), Sk. H. Erbgrossherzog Nikolaus, Herzog von Oldenburg.*

364 *Bowl. The earliest Chinese bowl with a European inscription, made for a Portuguese customer in 1557. Chinese, Ming Dynasty. Junta de Baixo Collection, Beja, Alentejo, Portugal.*
*Photo: Photo Studios, London*

365 *Coffee-pot. London mark 1769–70.* C. W. *Collection. H. Farmer, Victoria and Albert Museum.*
*Crown Copyright reserved*

366 *Chinese cabinet belonging to the Duc de Choiseul, bearing the mark B.V.R.B. (Bernard II van Risen Burgh). Panels in red, black and gold Chinese laquer. 18th century. Musée du Louvre, Paris.*

367 *Ch'ien Lung porcelain objects. 18th century. Museum of Eastern Art, Oxford.*
*Photo: M. R. Dudley* A.I.B.P., A.R.P.S.

# IX REALITIES OF YESTERDAY

# IX Realities of Yesterday

IN FRENCH ART the grave and the gallant form a continuity. The eighteenth century joins hands with the sixteenth across the seventeenth, but the nineteenth century contains all: grave in its first half, in the second it is all smiles; it ends with its contrary, for the great debate that had nourished European art in the seventeenth century constitutes the richness of this period also. Perhaps nowhere else, in this century, were the aesthetics of the Ideal and of Nature so violently opposed: this time the struggles were ferocious, and the high-priests of the Ideal, monopolising honours, position and the employment on which livelihood depended, denied the votaries of Nature the right to live. And yet—leaving aside the fossils who occupied the official scene—all through that century the idealist and naturalist aesthetics managed to live in concert.

As Goethe had already noticed, in the epistemology of Western civilisation Antiquity plays a part analogous to that of Nature. Everything can be derived from both—the object and its contrary, the Baroque and the classical, the fantastic and the rational—so that our civilisation consists of one 'Renaissance' after another. Every time an artistic crisis looms up, two ways of solving it lie open—Antiquity or Nature: the two are indeed complementary; Nature solves the crisis produced by Antiquity, and Antiquity goes to the rescue of failing naturalism. The eighteenth century presents a profound conflict between art, more heavily engaged than ever in the service of fantasy, and thought, pressing onwards towards modern positivism and rationalism; the conflict is resolved by Antiquity bringing art back 'to reason'. What is most remarkable is that the fantasy itself draws its nourishment from a source in Antiquity, namely Fable: Antiquity supplies everything (swap Fable against History and art is turned upside-down); two sides of the same coin, Brutus and Andromache follow Venus and Bacchus. And Antiquity, though this was not always apparent, even opens the way to Realism. We need only examine how the hands are painted in David's picture of the *Horatii* and compare them, for instance, with Tiepolo's. Winckelmann has left his traces there, teaching artists once more to look at the human body: if they look at it through the Greeks, so much the better—it is a good school and, if the model in the studio is made to take up poses in imitation of the antique, the model is still a living one. The power of David lies precisely in this fresh harmony between *Natura* and *Idea* which is the very principle of classicism. Some have tried to make a distinction between David as portrait painter and David as classicist, but one need only look at the way in which, in his *Sabine Women*, he caressed with his brush the delicious curves of the ladies of Bellegarde to see that this painter of history was no mere 'history-painter'.

*The mania for Antiquity, which Winkelmann aroused, is expressed—perhaps with a certain irony—in the picture of Charles Towneley amid the accumulation of marbles in his gallery (369). Imitation of the Ancients is pushed to every kind of eccentric extreme. While a Wedgwood vase (371) with its pure curves has retained the Hellenistic grace that was rediscovered at Herculaneum and Pompeii, what is to be said of a chair (373) imitated from a Roman chariot?*

But this reuniting required a Frenchman: the neo-classicists who blazed the trail for David—

Anton Raffael Mengs, Angelica Kauffmann or Benjamin West—are only classicists: in Antiquity they sought only the antique. David had Antiquity in his head but reality in his hands: he could do nothing without a model, and so weak was the imagination of this historical painter that, when he needed Roman furniture for his picture of the *Lictors bringing the body of his son to Brutus*, he had it made according to his ideas by the furniture-maker Jacob so that he might 'pose' it in the studio!

*Plate 370*

*Plate 372*

As for Ingres, his head was so poor in ideas that he had to extract the dreamed-of form painfully from the real by means of a ceaselessly renewed series of studies, each of them an approximation. There has never, certainly, been an artist with so little imagination to start with; to get him going he had to have some visible object; and he has left behind him a strange body of work, in which an oppressive sensuality wears the mask of the ideal.

Géricault had learnt the right habits in the studio of Guérin. To paint the *Raft of the Medusa*, it is true, he set up a studio close to the Hôpital Beaujon in order to have at his disposal fragments of human anatomy that were still fresh; then he painted English thoroughbreds, taking his inspiration from sporting prints; but of the Barbary horses he saw racing at Rome he made classical metopes.

* * *

Between 1820 and 1860, a time when everyone claimed to be classical and usually achieved only academicism, the only truly classical painter was Delacroix—Delacroix the romantic! It was a strange century, in which the label did not fit the goods; a tormented century, in which man, born in the midst of griefs, had to contradict himself if he was to say anything at all. No artist's work is less the result of chance, more deeply thought out or longer thought over than the impetuous and palpitating work of this suffering genius; but this demi-god who was at the same time a sensitive human being disdainfully rejected the restrictions of classicism as imprisoning the artist within the gilded circle of an ideal. David requires that we should know Roman history, Ingres that we should know mythology; but to understand Delacroix one must have '*lu tous les livres*'. He is the 'historical painter' of all history, dreamt of by classical and Baroque artists alike from Titian to Rubens.

Delacroix dedicated his work to death, that terrible divinity. There is not one of his heroes, from Christ to Sardanapalus, who does not feel its menace hanging over him indistinguishable from a promise of glory. The epiphany of death is accompanied by all the pomp of light and colour—the purple of blood, the amber of the twilight, the flash of a dagger tearing apart the drapery of the night, a face lit up by cruelty, by grief or by fear, the streaming gold of women's hair, and the roses and lilies of lovely flesh tints trembling beneath the point of the sword. *Thanatos* inspires in his votary a holy intoxication: 'Oh, smile of a dying man, grief-stricken gaze of a mother, despairing embrace—precious domain of painting,' he cried one day in a transport of adoration. Does not death, violent death, the kind that is received and given in battle, which strikes in a duel, an assassination or an act of treachery, force the powers in us to their paroxysm? Perhaps, in the human being stricken by the arrows of death, it is merely a seething of life that, by being too intense, kills. Nietzsche was to say: 'To beget, to live and to murder are one.' In both animals and men Delacroix loved the struggle that stretches their energies to the full, twists their bodies and ensures the triumph of the strong over the weak—that *mêlée* of life and death in which death always gets its prey. *Moira* strikes terror into the pusillanimous human being whom she has vowed to extinction; but to her glory-conferring kiss the hero presents his radiant brow, seeking in danger, and finding, that trance in which a being transcends itself, and which makes the last breath the most living. For the lover as well as for the martyr, the only fulfilment of the sublime is

*With Delacroix this* mêlée *often takes shape as a whirlwind, that form familiar to the romantics especially in music. Turner uses it in a famous landscape where he tries to convey the* mêlée *of the elements (380)*

death. The man who takes the sword and perishes by the sword fixes his statue in a mad gesture, a superb attitude, which casts upon the future a giant's shadow. Delacroix's massacres have their epilogue on the peak of an Olympus where those who have fallen victims to steel, to fire or to poison receive as reward for their death the crown of immortality.

In the *Sardanapalus* death strikes one of its finest blows. What a magnificent harvest it is—all that flesh like a great cluster of fruit, carried away on the waves of a torrent of purple and gold! Those courtesans, their throats devoted to the knife, never tasted such rapture from the pleasures of love. The Olympian satrap looks down upon that vision of delight which is immolated to his greatness: by a final gesture of his power he will make heroes out of the effeminate flock of odalisques and eunuchs. Like Nero watching Rome in flames, he is a cruel aesthete, discerning in that tragedy the secrets of beauty and silently savouring the pride of dying as master rather than living as slave.

And so, at a moment when battalions of pedants in the schools and academies had for thirty years been imagining that they were finding Antiquity by ransacking tombs, Delacroix at one stroke of his genius rose to the height of Aeschylus and Euripides: an ardent disciple of Byron, he found the superhuman at the sources of tragedy before Nietzsche did; and to Barrès he handed on the message of Hamlet. A whole century palpitated in that ardent soul.

* * *

*Plate 383*

Corot is not Nature, he is *the natural*—perhaps the most natural of all the French painters, a complete man in his directness, in his lively senses, brain and heart: without complication, the sensation transmitted to him by his eyes became an appeal of thought and feeling. He went to look for Antiquity in its natural setting, in Italy; and when, in the second half of his life, he abandoned it, his art at once grew lax.

* * *

*Plate 382*

And now we come to the real man of Nature. In his own time Courbet ran the same risk as he does in ours—that of being judged by his ideas rather than as an artist. Held up to execration by the conventional spirits of his own period on account of his Socialist convictions, Courbet is now treated by some critics as the revolutionary painter *par exellence*; have not the Communists even made him into the precursor of Socialist realism? In reality it is curious that so much importance should be attached to the ideas of a man whose art contains so little thought: he put far fewer explicit intentions into his painting than did Daumier or Millet. When he did try to express ideas in his pictures, the result was so lacking in spontaneity that a dictionary is required to decipher them. This is the case with *L'Atelier*, that '*allégorie réelle*' which certainly forms an astonishing collection of portraits; but it adds nothing to our pleasure or understanding to know that the couple passing in front of Baudelaire symbolises '*l'Amour libre*'. In contrast, the woman of the people trampling the dead bodies in Delacroix's *Liberté sur les Barricades* is the incarnation of revolution, far more so than any of Courbet's peaceful labourers; for with Delacroix the idea is plastic—it is born with the form, whose soul it is, simultaneously in the imagination of that visionary painter.

This absence of the intellectual element governs all Courbet's work: it explains the extraordinary poverty of his drawing, also the absence of composition in his pictures—the largest ones are made up of juxtaposed fragments. His art brings us the embodiment of a sensation in the crude state: in this it is very different from that of the Impressionists, who are town-dwellers and do not so much surrender themselves to Nature as observe her, gathering their slightest visual sensations like specimens and submitting them to delicate analyses. In the whole of our Western civilisation Courbet is perhaps the only peasant painter: he is certainly far more so than Brueghel, who was deeply influenced by humanism, or than the Le Nain brothers, who became town-dwellers and producers of genre painting. Courbet's painting is a soil and a race, it is the earthy Franche-Comté, that mountainous province, that rough land with its unforthcoming population who borrow something of their mixture of the sensual and the truculent from neighbouring Burgundy. The great Courbet must be looked for in his landscapes, portraits, nudes and animals: he was the only one of the painters of the French school to have felt the power of Nature in its virginity and primordial force—certainly far more than Théodore Rousseau, who was a thinking painter. And man, like the natural scene and like animals, appeared to him in his elemental, clean and healthy power as a rustic being, not contaminated by civilisation. What Millet tried to express (and failed because he put into his paintings too many explicit intentions)—the greatness of the life of the people—Courbet attained effortlessly, thanks to the magnificent purity of his instinct. His masterpiece is that sombre picture, *Enterrement à Ornans*, which draws together the whole population of a village, its theme suggesting one of the subjects that came most gratefully to the French medieval spirit, the Entombment of Christ; for to find a precedent for the simple and direct art of Courbet one must pass over the whole of the court painting and *bourgeois* painting produced in Europe during more than three centuries and go back to the image-makers of the Middle Ages.

Courbet was self-taught—he was free from all school tradition but had to create his own technique. Ignorant of the '*beau métier*' of painting which had been, since the Van Eycks, the ability to paint in transparent layers, he crudely accumulated *impasti* laid on with the knife, one on top of another, leaving unsmoothed the defects and accidents of each successive layer so that the roughness of the layer underneath shows through. In this way he obtained effects of depth and density that the earlier painters (and Delacroix, following their example) had attained by transparent painting. Without actual recourse to scumbling he was sometimes tempted, principally in his nudes, by the punctilious method of the academics, which he reproduced by means of *demi-impasti* well tied together; but Courbet's real and impressive technique is produced by the spurting and spattering of colours that seems as if they had been mixed with earth. It is this technique, invented by him (for he did not know the work of his predecessor Constable) that enables him to express his sensual joy at living in communion with Nature. When he came out of the Saint-Pélagie prison after serving a long sentence, Courbet (at the age of over fifty) said that he would like to 'pick up the earth of the fields in fistfulls, sniff it, kiss it and chew it, smack the bellies of the trees, throw stones in the puddles, muddy the stream, chew and devour Nature'.

Impressionism proclaimed the end of everything in painting that was not either painting or Nature. Monet was even more daring than Manet, in overturning the idols. But in less than twenty years they were back on their pedestals: Cézanne was the first to protest against their abandonment and tried, by a purely visual effort (a superhuman enterprise), to remake classicism, starting from sensation. He devoted a considerable part of his life to measuring his strength against the anti-Impressionist theme *par excellence*, the mountain: form and matter at the same time, a jutting upwards of the earth at the expense of the sky, a pedestal of glory, the mountain is to Nature what the hero is to the human; and of this the Montagne Sainte-Victoire supplied the Aix painter with his model. At other times he celebrated the cerulean calm of the sea of the gods in forms and images that suggest Valéry.

The painters who can be grouped together in the '*mouvement de 1889*' had a clearer idea of the reform to which Impressionism needed to be subjected. Van Gogh, that wild and lonely spirit, must be set apart. As for Seurat and Gauguin, they took up positions clearly against the pure naturalism of Impressionism and tried to return to intellectual painting.

Gauguin's rebelliousness, his drinking and debauchery, his venereal diseases, his taste for

*The extreme of naturalism is the attempt, which was made, to infuse it into architecture, so as to rid this of Graeco-Roman formalism and eclecticism. The results were* le modern style *(France), Art Nouveau (England) and the* Jugendstil *(Germany), in which the forms are directly inspired by vegetation (397). Its influence can be felt in some of Picasso's early pictures (400). This direct recourse to natural forms had already tempted some earlier artists, as is shown by the strange resemblance between a vase by the Renaissance potter Bernard Palissy (398) and a Lalique vase (399)*

native women, his Bohemian life, his marital troubles and his flight into exoticism—all this left its mark on his real nature, but many people, misled by the enthusiastic partisanship of the Symbolists and by Gauguin's own longing for the mysteries of primitive life, have tried to see in him an 'oneiric' artist, the man who introduced into painting the data of the subconscious, a kind of forerunner of Surrealism. Some have even detected in his art a trace of mysticism and of some sort of '*frisson du sacré*'.

*Plate 390* The truth is that what Gauguin brought back into art was the 'subject'—the literary basis which the Impressionists had banished. The explanations of some of his pictures, which are so frequent in his letters, reveal the 'intellectualist' nature of his inspiration. The violence of his verbal opposition to classicism has concealed the way in which he restored its values by such roundabout ways, it is true, that criticism was easily misled. In fact, although Gauguin does battle against the inspiration from Antiquity which had nourished generations of artists before the rise of Impressionism, he was deceiving himself when he thought he found an antidote to it in Breton or Polynesian primitivism, for what he was doing was to restore to painting a mode of poetical expression that had belonged to Poussin and to Claude Lorrain. To realise that there is nothing *Plate 389* primitive in his style one has only to compare Gauguin with the Douanier Rousseau: the Douanier rediscovered instinctively the stylistic devices and the state of mind of primitivism, and through his *Charmeuse de serpents* there breathes that mystery of primordial life which was later to inhabit the *Forêts* of Max Ernst; but in front of a picture by Gauguin, if one cuts out everything literary one cannot feel, even mimetically, the '*transe du sacré*'. What indeed do we see in this artist's pictures of Tahiti or the Marquesas Islands? Beautiful, healthy creatures with robust bodies, their eyes filled with a happy languor, living calmly in the midst of flowers, in radiant and delicately coloured landscapes that suggest the Age of Gold, which is one of the myths most firmly anchored in the human heart. The decorative feeling takes away from these creatures all fleshly feeling, and one wonders how these nudes, so free from suggestiveness, could have scandalised Gauguin's contemporaries. The way in which they are composed in independent groups, organised in verticals and horizontals, is completely classical. As for the Polynesian inscriptions, in spite of all the artist's ardent desire to convey a meaning, they add nothing to the mystery when not understood, and when translated they throw no light on the subject. These pictures, in fact, overleap the centuries and group themselves with Poussin's *Bacchanales* or Claude's *Danses des Nymphes*: the subject is the same (even if the myth is not)—the happy blossoming of human beings in a scenery of Eden.

Gauguin lulls our imagination in that remoteness which gives the human spirit the illusion of some state of original perfection, capable of making the sad realities of mortal life bearable to him. To achieve this, or rather to give glimpses of it, is the very aim of painting, as it is of poetry. Paradoxically, it can happen—and often does in the course of Western civilisation—that Nature itself is called upon to provide this mirage of something beyond: with Van Eyck, as also with the Dutch or Flemish still-life painters in the seventeenth century, a flower or a shell or an ewer—any object from the external world faithfully reproduced as it appears, but losing, by this likeness, its quality of crude reality—carries in it a message from the infinite, giving the spirit access to the threshold of the great problems of consciousness and of the world. The Impressionists discovered in light the means of piercing through appearance to reach essence; but in general, since the Renaissance, it was Antiquity that was called upon to transport the mind into the world of imagination. The myth of Antiquity seems to have acquired for mankind, at least in the West, a primordial value—it is an archetype; and just when it was believed to be moribund, it was born again, stronger than ever, thanks to Winckelmann and to David, one of whose last words to his students was: 'Re-read your Plutarch.' And what did Napoleon ever do except try to add a chapter to Plutarch's *Lives*? The example of Caesar tormented this modern builder of empires.

The myth was to prove more lasting in poetry than in painting: Leconte de l'Isle and the other Parnassians tried to revive it by adding the ferment of barbarism; but in our own century it has been reborn in rhythms of Greek purity with Paul Valéry, and in its narrative magic with André Gide, while a whole people, intoxicated with Utopian visions, has thought it its duty to lay claim to the hereditary rights of the Roman Empire at the international conference tables. Have the horrors of the Second World War thrown that fabulous period back into some sort of human prehistory? Camus, the greatest French writer of our time, had recourse to it, none the less, to express the anguish of modern man.

In the nineteenth century Antiquity was no monopoly of the classicists: the dream of some of the romantics was to achieve the synthesis of Homer and Ossian, Shakespeare and Sophocles. Goethe was more successful at this than Delacroix; in painting, the last exhalations of the Age of Gold are to be found in Ingres and Corot. But at the end of the century it had produced such a spiritual sclerosis that Gauguin, paradoxically, was forced to do battle against it in order to achieve its metamorphosis—into the last primitive peoples living beneath a sky of Paradise. To him, anti-culture gave the equivalent of what earlier men had had from culture. The whole Symbolist movement in literature is permeated with the culture of the Ancients; and the painters whom the critics consider attached to that movement certainly did not reject it: Odilon Redon in his reveries saw the leaping horses of Apollo, and as for Puvis de Chavannes, he tried to give style again to the old themes of '*l'Ecole*', which had become academic. Gauguin's passion for primitive life never prevented him from appreciating Puvis, whom the Symbolist critics also praised as a representative of their aesthetic. Indeed Gauguin took Puvis as a model: 'It is odd,' he wrote to Emile Bernard in 1889 from Arles, 'what Vincent finds to do here is work like Daumier's, while I find Puvis.' Later the two men—one celebrating the Greeks, the other the Kanakas—held each other in mutual esteem, having felt their deep affinities: both of them were 'ideist' painters, reducing form to surface, depriving it of its value as 'tangible' reality and transposing it into the decorative and plastic realm. Akin in their treatment of form, the two painters differed only in their degree of talent and inspiration and in the plastic source of their art—which was for one of them academicism, for the other Impressionism. Gauguin always excepted Puvis from his diatribes against the academics, while he thundered against Degas 'who always went for the bad smell of the model'.

*Plates 377, 383*

It may well be that too much importance has been attributed to Gauguin's epigram about preferring 'the hobby-horse of our childhood' to the horses of the Parthenon. He did say that 'the great error is the Greek', but he added 'for all its beauty': thus he recognised its value and turned away from it only by discipline. He re-established the idols not so much to replace the gods as to replace God. Gauguin's anti-cultural reaction is aimed much more against Christianity than against the paganism of Antiquity, to which he is allied by his cult of Nature.

Gauguin made Fable bloom again in the fragrant islands of the Pacific; and the words used by Bernini to describe Poussin might be applied without change to him: '*Veramente quel uomo e stato une grande istoriatore e grande favoleggiatore.*'

In Gauguin there was a magnificent understanding of how surfaces should be organised: it might have made a great monumental painter of him if the public authorities, in whose hands the commissions lay, had been aware of him. Here we touch on the immense loss we have sustained through the backwardness of the *bourgeoisie* of the last century: they had Gauguin available, and it was to Puvis de Chavannes that they handed over the walls of public buildings. However, sympathetic his effort may be, the art of Puvis, though it gained a slight breath of life from his having rubbed shoulders with Symbolism, was doomed to failure because its basis was artificial. Gauguin might have sunk in the mud of literary painting, but was saved by his Impressionist starting-point, which enabled him, 'ideist' though he was, to practise the method of direct observation. In this way, while abandoning the subjects of Antiquity, he was able to recreate them from Nature. Has enough thought ever been given to the fact that those strange compositions of his, with their usually arbitrary colours but always harmonious arrangement, were all painted from Nature or from the posed model? Is not this the true attitude of a classic painter—to start from observation of Nature in quest of 'the idea' which constitutes the deep-seated reality underneath the singularity of appearances?

What renders classical painting out of fashion nowadays is the fact that, to the eyes of most of us, now that we have lost most of our humanistic culture, a large part of its charm, which lay in its intellectual content has evaporated: the mythical world in which men formerly moved with ease is something that we can no longer even perceive as a faraway mirage. The mystery of the Polynesian idols says more to our imagination—but how long will this last? Primitive life is fast disappearing from the earth, and when man is travelling in interstellar space the ancient Polynesian religion will seem to him even more incomprehensible than that of Apollo or Orpheus. When that happens the subjects of Gauguin's pictures in spite of their '*paroles du cru*', will seem as boring as those of Poussin; but in so far as people are then still interested in art, they will always be enchanted when they look at Poussin's pictures or at Gauguin's by the one authentic magic a work of art contains—that of art itself.

*Plates 391–393*

Seurat went even further. His *Dimanche d'été à la Grande Jatte*, which was preceded by an extraordinary mass of drawings, sketches and studies after Nature, exercises the fascination of the absolute masterpiece. This picture took him two years to do, and in it he accomplished what he sought—to pin down the eternal in the instant. Who else, except Leonardo, ever painted with such 'obstinate rigour'? Seurat is indeed the French Leonardo: like the great Renaissance painter, he tried to rescue painting from empiricism, to make it a re-creation of the world by an implacable method, based on knowledge of Nature, knowledge of the laws of harmony and a scientific study of technique. His paintings, like Leonardo's, are very few, and his highest quality is realised in that masterpiece, *La Grande Jatte*. What would Seurat have become if he had not died at thirty-one? Could *La Grande Jatte* be surpassed? The *Poudreuse* and the *Cirque*, his last works, suggest a development towards a kind of academic drying up of his style—which is, alas, what lies in wait for every art that has attained perfection.

Thus a whole century leads us, after a long *détour* through Nature, from the Idea back to the Idea: the wheel comes full circle. But then came Van Gogh, falling like a meteor and setting the world on fire. The fire has not yet gone out.

Some twenty painters, spread out through the nineteenth century, handed the torch from one to another; twenty painters of genius tried to save the spirit in an age dominated by the tyranny of matter. The destiny of a civilisation with a long past rested on them: architecture was dead and sculpture in its death throes, while the decorative arts were degenerating through an uninspired imitation of earlier styles: all the forms of beauty that require a social impulse for their blossoming were perishing. Music and painting alone prospered, since their nature fitted them to receive the confession of the individual: at the keyboard and at the easel the hand lends itself to the impulse of the heart. Thanks to German music and French painting, the modern world can still hold its own in the competition for artistic glory between the centuries.

Coarsened by more than a hundred years of *bourgeois* stupidity and Socialist barbarism the modern Sodom displays its obscene ugliness before our eyes with indecent complacency; but within its walls it has preserved some temples sheltering the works of a few just men, on whom it relies to bear witness in its favour in the Day of Judgment. As if to increase their merit, it has made martyrs of them: in accordance with an unwritten law of this egalitarian civilisation, every genius, before being raised upon the altars, must be crucified—'thrown to the wild beasts', as Delacroix put it. 'O multitude!' cried Vigny in the person of Doctor Noir in *Stello*, 'nameless multitude, you were born an enemy to names!' The man with great gifts has a choice of two paths: one of them, strewn with money, decorations and position, ends in oblivion, while he who is not afraid to face hunger and public ridicule may hope for immortality.

The solitary of Heilingenstadt and the hermit of Barbizon learned what it costs to bring men a new form of beauty and of love. Berlioz ended his days as a King Lear, howling with the pain of loneliness. Even Ingres, *ce bon bourgeois arrivé*, came to avoid the *Salons* and to despise the public, as though he too felt that in that century it was impossible to create without keeping somewhat aloof. As his death approached, Delacroix realised that he owed his place in society to his good connections rather than to his works.

The artist tormented by genius must accept unflinchingly the Promethean destiny prefigured by Rembrandt: in a steep wide ravine, apart from the herd, he must gird himself to wrestle with the angel. A man's value, in the century of Vigny and Nietzsche, is measured by the quality of solitude in him, of which he will fashion his work. He will be forced to separate it from the rough ore in order to extract the gold. Nietzsche and Van Gogh purified it in the flame of madness; Gauguin, suddenly stricken with grace, abandoned family, reputation and *bourgeois* position and fled from civilised men, setting his course for poverty and death; Cézanne, a new Moses, ended in a titanic colloquy with a mountain; like some old alchemist, in his laboratory of sky, flowers and water, Monet shut himself up at Giverny; and the aged Degas, walled up within himself by being half blind, wandered for hours frowning through the streets of Paris, like a bear in a cage. All of them lived as though searching for a secret that is not to be found in the society of men. Even Delacroix, that man of the world, was a hermit living in the midst of secular life, affiliated to some lay Order in which his peers in genius were joined together across the centuries. He grieved over his uniqueness, and this suffering was itself a pleasure: that a man should never be able to be known and understood by the same friend was bound to sadden him, and yet he disdained love—such self-alienation was against his conscience. At all costs, at the cost of harsh suffering, he had to preserve the virtue of silence.

*Plates 394–396*

Deprived as they were of witnesses to sustain their judgment, and surrounded by contempt and indifference, these men had to find the principle of their strength in themselves alone. Under the breath of solitude, burning and icy by turns, by what a bitter insistence on being themselves were they driven onwards—heroes preserving themselves from contamination by the crowd! Each of them suffered from the self-doubt that ravages great spirits determined to attain their most fully authentic form. Cézanne, Monet and even Corot complained of never being able to achieve what they imagined: to them each of their masterpieces was a failure. Gros committed suicide rather than survive his failing genius and with what lucidity did Delacroix, so impartial, yet so conscious of his worth, appear every evening before his inner tribunal. The most heroic of all these hermits was Théodore Rousseau, banished in perpetuity by the *Institut* and labouring during his whole life in the pursuit of the impossible. If one finds in the painters of that period a more authentic feeling of the creative artist's problem than one does in the writers, the reason perhaps is that the writers suffered from a lack of misunderstanding: indeed they were so conscious of this that at the end of the century they took refuge, beyond the reach of the vulgar, with Mallarmé upon his glaciers of Symbolism.

368 DAVID: *unfinished study of Bonaparte, 1797–8*

*369* JOHN ZOFFANY: *Charles Towneley in his antique gallery*

# *Return to Antiquity*

In Western civilisation Antiquity acts as a kind of permanent reservoir, much as Nature does. The conflict that arose at the end of the eighteenth century between art—enjoyed more than ever in the service of the fantastic—and thought—well on its way towards positivism—is resolved by a return to the influence of Antiquity, which brings art 'back to reason'. For a moment art recovers that balance between Nature and the Ideal which is the principle of classicism.

*370* ANTON RAFFAEL MENGS: *Jupiter and Ganymede, before 1762 (imitation antique)*

*371 Wedgwood vase, 18th century*

372 DAVID: *Lictors bringing back to Brutus the body of his son, c. 1789*

373 *French armchair, Empire style, early 19th century*

374 SCHOOL OF PRIMATICCIO: *drawing for the Diane d'Anet, 17th century*

375 CANOVA: *Pauline Borghese*

## *Neo-Alexandrianism*

The development of the classicist style from David to Ingres is similar to that which led from Pheidias to Alexandrian art. Ingres thought he took his principles from Raphael, but his refined mannerism (shared by the sculptor Canova) has the same relation to Raphael as that of Primaticcio or Jean Goujon.

376 RAPHAEL: *'La Fornarina' (detail of head, reversed)*

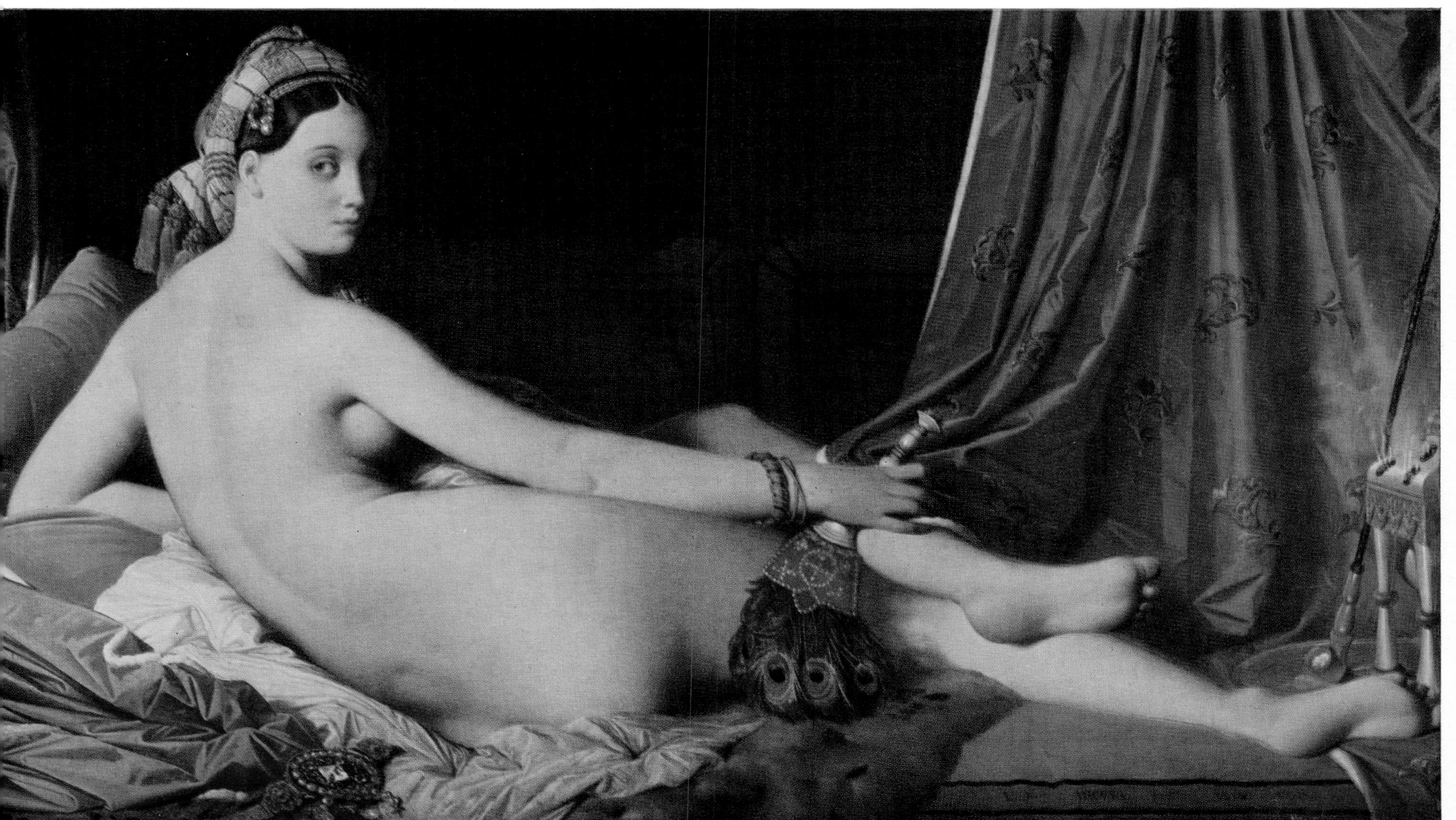

377 INGRES: *La Grande Odalisque, 1814*

## *Beauty in the Whirlwind*

The syncopated rhythm of the galloping horse that haunts the romantic composers inspires the painters too. But these are even fonder of showing forces in conflict, human or animal energies stretched to the full in a supreme effort to escape death in the midst of the fight, elements unchained, oceans turned by the hurricane into giant whirlpools.

379 DELACROIX: *drawing for Arab on horseback attacked by a lion*

378 DELACROIX: *Arab on horseback attacked by a lion*

*380* TURNER: *Steamer in a snowstorm, 1842*

*381* DELACROIX: *study for the Death of Sardanapalus, 1827*

## *Nature and The Natural Man*

Nature, always in the end triumphing over the Ideal in art, yields up her soul to Corot, and to Courbet her body. Corot, the most natural of the French painters, surrenders to her by an impulse of the heart: Courbet, having felt Nature's power in its primordial instinctiveness, corners her in her most secret lairs. To Corot, in accordance with French tradition, she never ceases to be gentle and civilised, and to paint her he scarcely strays at all from inhabited places.

*382* COURBET: *The Haunt of the Deer, 1866*

383 COROT: *Souvenir de Marissel, 1866*

## *Impressions*

Impressionism proclaims the end of everything that is not painting or nature. The painter shakes himself free from the literary or sentimental heritage of Romanticism, and takes a fresh look at the spectacle of people and things. He rediscovers the spontaneous genius of the eighteenth century in the sketch, and bases his aesthetic on a hedonistic ethic—on the *douceur de vivre*.

384 MONET: *Field of Poppies*, 1873

*385* MANET: *Nana, 1877*

## *Recreating Poussin from Nature*

Less than twenty years after the overturning of the idols, they are back on their pedestals. Cézanne is the first to protest against such an abandonment. His is a superhuman enterprise: he attempts, by a purely visual effort, to remake classicism, starting from sensation. He bends bodies into a melodious arabesque; and at his call all the elements of a landscape order themselves in a strict architecture, built up slowly by his hesitant hand with generous but controlled *impasti*.

*386* CÉZANNE: *La Lutte d'Amour*

*387* CÉZANNE: *Bay from Estaque*

*388* CÉZANNE: *detail from Rocky Landscape at Aix*

## *New Golden Age*

By the détour of exoticism Gauguin re-introduces 'subject' into art, restoring to painting a mode of poetic expression that once belonged to Poussin and to Claude: through Tahiti he evokes the Golden Age—one of the myths most firmly anchored in the human heart.

After him, by pure play of imagination, the Douanier Rousseau goes back even further, and invents a virgin Nature that has not yet known the presence of man.

*389* DOUANIER ROUSSEAU: *Le Repas du Lion*

390 GAUGUIN: *Maternity, 1896*

391 SEURAT: *Sketch for La Grande Jatte*

392 SEURAT: *Lady fishing*

# *A Fin-de-Siècle Leonardo*

Like Leonardo da Vinci, Seurat tried to wrench painting away from empiricism. He turned it into a re-creation of the world, by means of an implacable method based on knowledge of nature, knowledge of the laws of harmony and a scientific study of technique. With Seurat the 'century of nature' comes to an end in one of the most highly intellectual of all the enterprises of painting.

*393* SEURAT: *La Grande Jatte, 1885*

# *The Flame of Reality*

Nothing is more traditional than Van Gogh's compositions in his black period. First he borrows his way of seeing from the Romantic tradition, then joins the Impressionists; but in the end a fiery star falls and sets fire to the world. The naturalistic universe of the nineteenth century perishes in a cosmic cataclysm.

*394* VAN GOGH: *Grove of Cypresses, c. 1889*

*395* VAN GOGH: *The Starry Night, 1886*

*396* VAN GOGH: *Road with Cypresses, 1889*

# *Art Nouveau*

The century ended also in a last recourse to Nature to regenerate the forms of architecture and ornamentation, brought to degeneration by imitating the styles of Antiquity. This ephemeral movement was called *modern-style* in France, *Art Nouveau* in England, *Jugendstil* in Germany: it borrowed its forms and sinuous energy from the life of plants. There had been precedents: for instance, the ceramics of Bernard Palissy (which indeed were often copied in and about 1900) and certain aspects of German rococo art.

*397* Guimard: *Castel Béranger, 1897–8*

*398* Palissy: *Ewer, late 16th century*

*399* René Lalique: *Vase*

# NOTES ON THE ILLUSTRATIONS TO CHAPTER IX

368 JACQUES LOUIS DAVID (1748–1825): *Unfinished study of Bonaparte. Sketch for part of a large picture showing General Bonaparte looking at the Alps from Rivoli. 1797–8. Musée du Louvre, Paris.*
*Photo: Giraudon*

369 JOHN ZOFFANY (1734–1810): *Charles Towneley in his antique gallery. Towneley Art Gallery, Burnley.*
*Photo: Gabinetto Fotografico Nazionale, Rome*

370 ANTON RAFFAEL MENGS (1728–79): *Jupiter and Ganymede. Painted to pass as an antique, and certified as such by Winckelmann. Before 1762. Galleria Nazionale, Rome.*
*Photo: Gabinetto Fotografico Nazionale, Rome.*

371 *Vase. Wedgwood. English, 18th century. Victoria and Albert Museum, London.*
*Crown copyright reserved*

372 JACQUES LOUIS DAVID (1748–1825): *The Lictors bringing back to Brutus the body of his son. Smaller version of a picture exhibited in 1789. Wadsworth Athenaeum, Hartford, Connecticut.*
*Photo: Anna Wachsmann*

373 *Arm-chair. French, Empire style, early 19th century. M. Douchet Collection, Paris.*

374 *School of* PRIMATICCIO: *Drawing for the Diana of Anet. 17th century. Cabinet des Dessins, Musée du Louvre, Paris.*

375 ANTONIO CANOVA (1757–1822): *Pauline Borghese, sister of Napoleon (or Venus Victrix). Marble. Galleria Borghese, Rome.*
*Photo: Alinari*

376 RAPHAEL: *La Fornarina (detail of the head, reversed). Galleria Borghese, Rome.*
*Photo: Anderson*

377 JEAN AUGUSTE DOMINIQUE INGRES (1780–1867): *La Grande Odalisque. 1814. Musée du Louvre, Paris.*

378 EUGÈNE DELACROIX (1798–1863): *An Arab on horseback attacked by a Lion. Art Institute of Chicago.*
*Photo: Anna Wachsmann*

379 EUGÈNE DELACROIX (1798–1863): *An Arab on horseback attacked by a Lion. Drawing. The Fogg Art Museum, Harvard University, Cambridge, Mass.*

380 J. M. W. TURNER (1775–1851): *Steamer in a Snowstorm. 1842. National Gallery, London.*
*Photo: Zoltan Wegner*

381 EUGÈNE DELACROIX (1798–1863): *Study for the Death of Sardanapalus. Drawing. 1827. Cabinet des Dessins, Musée du Louvre, Paris.*
*Photo: A.F.I., Venice*

382 GUSTAVE COURBET (1819–77): *The Haunt of the Deer. 1866. Musée du Louvre, Paris.*

383 JEAN BAPTISTE COROT (1796–1875): *Souvenir de Marissel. 1866. Musée du Louvre, Paris.*
*Photo: Jacqueline Hyde*

384 CLAUDE MONET (1840–1926): *Field of Poppies. 1873. Musée du Louvre, Paris.*

385 EDOUARD MANET (1832–83): *Nana. 1877. Kunsthalle, Hamburg.*

386 PAUL CÉZANNE (1839–1906): *La Lutte d'Amour. Mrs Averell Harriman Collection, New York.*

387 PAUL CÉZANNE (1839–1906): *Bay from Estaque. Art Institute of Chicago.*

388 PAUL CÉZANNE (1839–1906): *Aix: Rocky Landscape (detail). Tate Gallery, London.*

389 DOUANIER ROUSSEAU (1844–1910): *Le Repas du Lion. Metropolitan Museum of Art, New York.*

390 PAUL GAUGUIN (1848–1903): *Maternity. 1896. Private collection, U.S.A.*

391 GEORGES SEURAT (1859–91): *Sketch for La Grande Jatte. Metropolitan Museum of Art, New York.*

392 GEORGES SEURAT (1859–91): *Lady Fishing. Drawing for La Grande Jatte. Metropolitan Museum of Art, New York.*

393 GEORGES SEURAT (1859–91): *La Grande Jatte. Exhibited 1886. Art Institute of Chicago.*
*Photo: Anna Wachsmann*

394 VINCENT VAN GOGH (1853–90): *Grove of Cypresses. Drawing. c. 1889. Art Institute of Chicago.*

395 VINCENT VAN GOGH (1853–90): *The Starry Night. 1888. Drawing from a letter.*

396 VINCENT VAN GOGH (1853–90): *Road with Cypresses. Saint-Rémy. May 1899. Kroller-Muller State Museum, Otterlo.*

397 HECTOR GUIMARD (1867–1942): *Castel Béranger. Paris. 1897–8.*
*Photo: Hubert, Paris*

398 BERNARD PALISSY (1510–89): *Ewer. Late 16th century. Musée du Louvre, Paris.*

399 RENÉ LALIQUE (1860–1945): *Vase. Musée des Arts Décoratifs, Paris.*
*Photo: Eileen Tweedy*

# X ANTI-REALITY OF TODAY

# X Anti-Reality of Today

Now that the Impressionists are becoming rare, American collectors are looking eagerly for the canvases of Bonnard, whom they carefully place among the painters of the joy of living, the lovers of naturalism of the 1900 sort. This is rather a short-sighted view, due to the fact that all contemporary criticism tends to centre around the so-called figurative problem. Actually Bonnard brought into painting new spatial relationships that were to open the way to modern art. This starting-point is usually traced back to the 1890 generation: no doubt it was more 'modern' than Impressionism, in that it opposed the *mimesis* which was Impressionism's aesthetic theory; but it can also be considered as having tried to revive the traditional values of the Idea, and therefore as being opposed to the dissolution of the real which was Claude Monet's aim from his *Meules* (1891) onwards to his *Peupliers* (1892) and his cathedral pictures (1895)—and which was to lead this painter to the dreamy contemplation of the grey or sunny pools in his garden at Giverny. Monet's anti-figurative influence is realised by our contemporaries—so much so that some see in the painter of the *Nymphéas* the predecessor of the *Informel*. Gauguin tried to restore a soul to the '*tableau-objet*' which Cézanne had rendered sterile; Seurat aimed at studying, analysing, ordering and re-creating, all by himself, all the resources of painting; as for Van Gogh, nothing is more traditional than his arrangement of a canvas, but when the building is finished he sets it on fire. But Bonnard, following Degas, dared to lay hands on the sacrosanct laws of classical perspective—which the Impressionists had taken care not to destroy, which Gauguin had neglected but not transgressed, and which Cézanne had craftily evaded in order not to have to obey them. Bonnard deliberately looked at the world with a modern eye: making horizontal space unroll itself over the vertical space of the canvas, he discovered that in practice objects do not recede along the controlling lines like a platoon at the command 'By the right . . . quick . . .march!' Such a thing would only be true if we were Cyclops, and if our single eye were motionless and we looked at the world from a constant angle; but our capricious eyes are essentially mobile, ceaselessly scanning space in all directions. There is, in particular, a rising movement of the eyes from the ground to the horizon, which unrolls vertically on the retina the whole of the slanting space between our feet and the distance: the eye rises along the table from the floor, slides over the corner of the wall, prolongs beyond measure the body of the girl standing in her bath-tub, takes unconnected 'cuts' out of the real world and juxtaposes them. Thus the painters at the end of the century —Degas, Lautrec, Bonnard—rediscovered the perspective with several vanishing-points. This is the perspective of the Oriental paintings and in the West certain primitives had found it by intuition before Renaissance intellectualism imprisoned the external world in the cage of linear perspective—into which painting shut itself anew in the nineteenth century after having enjoyed a certain liberty in Baroque space.

The first compositions of the Fauves—those of Matisse in particular—are really much less bold. I imagine that one day, when the eye trained by the *Informel* has become entirely free from the realism habit, Matisse will pass for a naturalist and will be classed among the followers of Impressionism. Matisse's revolution—which gained for him and his associates in the 1905 *Salon* the name of 'Fauves'—was based on a purely arbitrary distortion of the real: applied mainly to the human figure and achieved by a kind of use of colour in reverse, its aim was simply to liberate the artist from naturalist—in this case Impressionist—forms. This exercise in pure destruction lasted until 1919; after that, Matisse, freed from all allegiance to Nature or to any aesthetic theory, found his true path, which was to order the canvas in accordance with simple and harmonious colour relationships, borrowing from reality merely what he needed to serve his designs—that is to say, less and less as he matured, for, after a few years in which the pleasure of painting does not seem to have been the only one for him, he progressively purified his art, reducing it to the minimum of means and yet not altogether abandoning reference to Nature. The fact that in his pictures of Oceania he is akin to Gauguin shows the part played by natural 'data' in the work of both these two artists, the one an 'ideist' and the other aiming at being a pure plastic artist. But is not Matisse also—with all the difference there is between a genius and a failure—akin to Puvis de Chavannes? By constant purification he arrived at that exalted spiritual masterpiece, the chapel of the Dominicans at Vence, which was built from his indications and decorated by him. Matisse's stylising economy found its true place in the monastery, that clinic of souls; and anyone entering that small space feels a thrill of awe, coming, within the abstract enclosure, upon the high glaciers of the spiritual life where the soul must venture before it receives the warm breath of the divine love.

*Plate 402*

This success gives us the standard by which to measure how grave is the responsibility of a society that leaves the artists to themselves and fails to stimulate inspiration in them by contact with the realities of life. The relations between society and the artist have been, as it were, reversed: it is society that expects inspiration from the artist; it is he who must fill out its culture. In this solitude, the 'reference to the work' has lost all its operative value, giving place to a 'reference to one's own self'—a self built up into a hero-prophet from whom the crowd expects a sort of magical revelation of the absolute. In this way artistic creation tends to resemble a neurosis, obliging the creator—separated as he is from men and from the world—to fashion and live in what the psychiatrists call a 'world of substitution'.

Looked at with the eyes of 1961, the art of Matisse is still, for all this, a picture-book; and the great enterprise that was to give the death-blow to those ideas of plastic space on which men had lived for centuries is to be sought elsewhere—in Cubism.

In 1906–7 Picasso, painting *Les Demoiselles d'Avignon*, imposed on the human figure a distortion inspired by negro sculpture. All the artists who eventually practised Cubism adopted geometrical stylisation gradually, claiming support from the example of Cézanne. It answered to a need so universal that practically no artist between 1907 and 1914 escaped it. But in Picasso the barbarous distortion inflicted on the human body was more an expression of rebelliousness than the result of a will to construction: while Derain and Modigliani found their inspiration in masks from the Ivory Coast, which attracted them by their purity, Picasso's choice went to Congolese carving with its bestial muzzles and animal snouts. During 1907 he executed a whole series of more or less negroid heads. It was in the next year that Braque, in his series of landscapes of l'Estaque, imposed on Nature a Cubist stylisation that was very different from the distortion conceived by Picasso at that moment. While the example of Picasso, with his natural taste for taking risks, was a stimulant and a confirmation to Braque's more timid spirit, Braque's example made Picasso see the virtues of system and discipline, and the Catalan's wandering spirit found a support in the industrious

*Plate 401*

strength of the Frenchman. The association of two such opposed temperaments is one of the most remarkable facts in the history of art. From 1908 to 1914 the two artists shared their aspirations, researches and discoveries—they were like two mirrors exchanging light. By the time Braque left for the Front, their seven years of collaboration had borne fruit. The two artists had destroyed painting as representation. They moved further and further away from the observed fact towards an autonomy of the plastic fact: by a whole system of analyses, cuts and reassemblies, which remind one of descriptive geometry, they contrived to *render down* reality; the forms on the canvas are associated by means of analogies, assonances or rhymes, no longer by 'pictorial memory'; the picture is now governed solely by its intrinsic form, and seems to be a system of relays between painter, spectator and Nature. Sometimes fragments of objects are left intact, but they are now only signs, chosen for formal reasons. The pieces of material stuck on to the canvas (*collés*) from 1912 onwards are surely a clear indication that the only thing sought for now in any object that is painted is a 'surreality' that has no relation with the usual, natural appearance of the real object.

No doubt, if the two artists had remained united, they would have moved straight to constructivism. But they separated. Braque, when he returned from the War, began to flirt with reality: he painted still-lives which Chardin would not have repudiated as descendants of his; his grapes are eatable and his pears juicy. Later on he returned to more abstract conceptions, but this never stopped his art from being a sort of speculation *hovering over real things*. As for Picasso, he returned to his native errancy, to that revolutionary temperament of his that insisted on manifesting itself at the expense of any- and everything—of the forms of Greek art, those of China, and even those of Nature. Clouzot's film has revealed to us where Picasso finds the stimulus to creation: an act of destruction is necessary to give him the impulse. He works at the expense of some classic form, which, most frequently, he himself sets up, in a spirit not far from that of Antiquity, only to hack it to pieces gradually with determined application; and sometimes, after passing through two or three masterpieces and destroying them *en route*, he arrives at a dead-end, as in the case of the picture *without* which the film ends. Picasso cannot invent without a substratum upon which he sets up his destruction-creation system: he is essentially a figurative painter. When he is at a loss for inspiration, he chooses some ancient work on which to exercise his talents as vivisector: in recent years this has been a common proceeding with him, the best-known example being the series of variations after Velasquez's *Las Meninas*, in which the spirit of *Les Demoiselles d'Avignon*, the picture that is pivotal to his life-work, recurs. This obsession with massacre, when stimulated by the Spanish Civil War, led him to produce what will no doubt remain his masterpiece *Guernica*, in which the vivisection process (revealed in his numerous preparatory studies) perpetuates in painting the crime then committed by man against himself.

During and after the Second World War Picasso pursued the style characterised by these massacred human figures. The painter reassembles the pieces of the human figure that has been burst as though by a bomb, and in doing so follows no law except incongruity. The puzzling objects grinning there are perhaps the most typical expressions of the chaotic discontinuity, at enmity with unity, that is the very essence of the demoniac style. The red constellations that are the sign of Satan in our time have reappeared over the horizon of history: the lampshades made of human skin from Buchenwald are more demoniac than the human soup drunk by the Ch'in generals or the Aztec carnivals of flayed human beings—these at least had the excuse of being magic rites. After the War Picasso did indeed try to find peace again: his use of this theme is not, as some have affected to believe, merely political propaganda. In the Antibes period he sought from Antiquity—Antiquity yet again—an idyllic inspiration; and yet his canvases display only fragments of free forms, with no suggestion of the unity from which harmony springs. He is happier in his drawings, which play a curious compensatory part in his work: in the grace of an arabesque

*Picasso: Drawing of the Antibes period*

that reminds one of the beauty of Greek vases or Chinese paintings, he finds respite from his vocation as a prophet of human bloodshed.

The drawings of the Antibes period seem indeed to have the opposite meaning to the paintings inspired by the same themes in the same period. In the drawings a few figures—a man piping, a girl dancer with a tambourine, a satyr, a goat, a lamb, a centaur, now and then a snake, a fish, some marine monster, the sun, a starfish and an owl (closing the sequence like some enigma of wisdom)—set the artist's imagination on fire. In this quest of forms his pencil darts onwards, now nonchalant, now possessed, lingering in amorous curves and lines, fondling the breasts of the dancing-girl, rounding her voluptuous thighs like the belly of a vase, ruffling the fawn's fleece, tying together the moving figures as if by the tendrils of a creeping plant, or on the contrary letting the fragments of a shattered hope fall like a rain of stars from fireworks bursting into the night—or even destroying the form at its birth with an angry scribble and beginning all over again. So, between accomplishment and destruction, these sheets of paper display Picasso's special art of metamorphosis which, instead of showing us the successive incarnations of a form, usually catches it at the instant of its change. At the sound of a pipe the dancing-girl grows more and more excited, and soon the frantic rhythm will set the swaying buds opening; the lamb moves us by its inimitable sweetness, then the more lusty sweetness of the goat, then comes a centaur galloping madly; and here is an owl to haunt us—a strange creature, alive and yet like a construction in geometry, with only its eye escaping from the form to participate in the game of life. These drawings are available to the public in an album of facsimiles, and there are two ways of enjoying them: one can turn over the plates one by one or, better, one can spread them out on the floor and walk about among them—and one is then truly under the spell of that musician of myth, caught in his network of lines. These sheets of drawings from the Antibes studio show us Picasso in the youthfulness of creation, in one of the happy moments of his life, trying after the War to forget the cruelty by conjuring up, on the shore of the civilising sea, the ancient idylls—those dreams to which men always return after having shed their brothers' blood. How does it happen that this enchantment of Fable, when transposed into painting in the pictures that hang in the Antibes Museum, changes in spite of the painter's intentions, into a diabolical magic? Here we are close to the mystery of Picasso's creative activity: the hardened outline, bristling with corrections that break the spontaneous movement, becomes a contour that is deaf to the spell of rhythm and transforms it into jerks; the gracious tarantella becomes a negro tom-tom; here the style that consists of cutting out bits of reality and reassembling them is dominant. This strange reversal of values in the passage from drawing to painting reveals Picasso's deep-seated nature, which is based on *ambivalence*: it is this tension of contradictory elements that cannot be resolved into unity that has made him the man of his time, the example in whom the modern world has recognised itself. By contrast, at the same moment, Matisse, whose line of development is continuous and whose work has a perfect equality of inspiration, remains to a considerable degree psychologically integrated.

What genius, in its full power, had laid down in a single individual (producing that superb pulsation of forms born pure, entering into ferocious conflict, becoming reconciled and then clashing again) was also expressed, as it were, collectively by the great mass of the Surrealists, under the guidance of a theoretician and poet who was regarded, after the First World War, as a kind of wizard—André Breton. Restoring the Idea as the generating force in a work of art, Breton tried to give new strength to the Symbol. The Symbol always comes into the open in the periods when, more or less empirically, mankind feels that appearance does not correspond to reality, but it effaces itself in the realist periods when thoughtful men can believe in an equivalence between the world and the mind's picture of the world, and when truth stands for reality. The Symbolist movement had prepared the way, setting language free again through the emotional power of words; but it lacked a philosophical basis and rested on a confused and vague cult of mystery. In restoring transcendent value to the Idea in painting, Surrealism had the merit of being based on much sounder ontological and metaphysical foundations by a man who was, in a way, the 'Descartes of the irrational'. The Surrealists have insisted that the power of the Symbol depends on the strength of contradiction it contains: 'The image', says Pierre Reverdy, 'cannot be born of a comparison, but of bringing together two more or less distant realities. The more remote and yet definite the relations between the two realities that are brought together, the stronger will be the image.' André Breton, in the *Manifeste du Surréalisme poisson soluble*, goes even further: 'It is from the, so to say, fortuitous bringing together of the two terms that a special light has spurted, the light of the image, to which we are infinitely sensitive. The value of the image depends on the beauty of the spark obtained; it is therefore a function of the difference between the two conductors.' Further on he speaks of the 'lightning relation' between the two poles of the image, and takes pride in the obscurity of the Symbol: 'The most beautiful night is the night in which there is lightning.' Surrealism is a kind of conscious exercise of the a-logical relations perceived by the subconscious; the knot, the symbol of the enigma, occurs again and again in his vocabulary; and Paul Klee shows it to us as a disquieting personage, like some Irish arabesque come alive.

The doctors of Surrealism proclaimed that they sought their truth in the doctrines of Freud, and it is therefore only natural that we should be tempted to apply Freudian methods of analysis

*André Masson: 'Il n'y a pas de monde achevé'*

to their movement. At the end of his life Freud believed the deepest psychic reality to consist in two fundamental and complementary urges—the life urge, which he called *Eros*, tending to unite the parts together, and the death urge, which he called *Thanatos*, tending to dispersion and eventually to the inertness of the non-living, a state anterior to the living. Are not these two powers a rebirth of Manicheism in the thought of the Viennese doctor in his old age? Certainly the love urge and the death urge reign over the Surrealist world: each of them asserts its independence, its triumph; they join battle, or else mingle in monstrous couplings. Max Ernst, in his forests crawling with a viscous life that still has in it something of the primordial waters, and in which the serpent, the lizard and the grub dominate, and Salvador Dali, obsessed by the symbol of the egg and by the soft, mucous structures of an intestinal life, have certainly proved the best at expressing the power of the *libido* over human life—to which others have sometimes given a more emphatically sexual character. The coupling of life and death produces the monsters of Picasso or of Miró, creatures shattered as soon as created. Sometimes André Masson makes explicit this conception of the world as a failure: '*Il n'y a pas de monde achevé*', is the title he gives to one of his finest drawings. Possessed by a passionate desire for life, this artist has shown the two urges in conflict in scenes of carnage where the smoking and palpitating guts spurt from disembowelled bodies. In the work of Delvaux death takes the form of petrified phantoms, statues of phantoms in an indifferent world. And Coutaud, at the end of the War, showed a world bristling with darts, spikes, bayonets and barbed-wire.

*Plate 409*

*Plate 408*

When death has done its work it gathers in its harvest, raises the corpses to make of them fresh monsters: it assembles—in the pictures of Chirico for instance—the works of trampled civilisation, to make of them ridiculous panoplies and trophies. In a picture explicitly entitled *Guerre civile*, Salvador Dali raises loathsome anatomical fragments towards the sky in a hideous defiant claim. André Masson, in whose work the symbol is often so legible that it comes nearer to Expressionism,

*Plate 407*

paints in his *Héraclite* a picture of universal life in the process of self-dislocation, vanquished by the powers of death; and in his *L'Aube à Montserrat* the stars have gone mad, they no longer obey the laws of gravity, but explode and, carried along in a mad rush, collide. The universe is consumed, and what is left after it? Nothing. Is not this what the paintings of Yves Tanguy show us—nothing but a frozen and fossilized landscape, a world whose sovereign ruler is the inertness of *entropy*, that degradation of energy which is one of the most desolating scientific notions of our time? And yet a few grubs seem still to be crawling about in the limitless expanse: are they germs of species to come, the hope of future life, or are they life's last manifestations?

*Plate 406*

Turning from the cosmology of Surrealism to analyse its ontology, one finds a state of mind just as desolating, dominated by Existentialism, of which the painters had a presentiment before the philosophers made it explicit. Since things have no existence except through ourselves and our consciousness has no existence except through things, and each term annihilates the other, we are struggling and revolving incessantly in the vicious circle of the *néant*.

And so, like the world, being is rejected. André Masson writes, '*Dans le néant à la cime de l'être*' ('In nothingness at the summit of being') under one of his drawings: is not this a title for a book by Jean-Paul Sartre? Man is driven out of the comfortable ontological home where he lived, just as he is driven out of the world, and thrown into a solitude as absurd as would be that of a man living on his own body. He has broken the bond with the world that was provided by the sympathy of love—which inhibits aggressiveness because it is based on an unconditional re-valuing of its object. This aggressiveness is the only bond or attachment that is left to him, leading him in self-defence to seek mastery, by means of science, of a universe which rejects him. Now that 'nausea' has produced in him a conviction of the non-existence of the Other (regarded as a value), he finds that he is, as Doctor Etienne de Greef puts it, 'like an amoeba in a dry medium'—an image that might well be derived from the pictures of Yves Tanguy.

*The only great French Expressionist, so far, is Rouault (404), who stems from the tradition of Daumier*

What is expressed by Surrealism in cipher is stated by Expressionism *en clair*—perhaps in a more superficial way, but generally with a more valid artistic quality; for Surrealism works chiefly as imagery, and few of its votaries were real painters. Is it not symptomatic that while the word Impressionism is a term of French origin, Expressionism is a neologism born in Germany? The movement is a rebirth of the dramatic instincts that were native to Germany, whose artists all through the nineteenth century had known only the subject-matter of romanticism, not its form. German painting had thus been on a wrong track during the whole of that century: although Philipp Otto Runge, a powerful personality whose rise was cut short by an early death, had indeed tried to break these bonds, the Nazarenes had steered German painting into an exercise in archaeology, succeeded by a platitudinous realism that had lost even the charm of paradox. It was Impressionism that rescued German artists from this aberration by at last putting at their disposal a painterly technique supple enough to serve their purposes; but they hardly had time to practise it as such before they began to use it as a means for elaborating that modern form of romanticism, Expressionism. In the ten years before the First World War, the German artists covered the same ground as Fauvism, freeing themselves from art based on observation in order to lay claim to the artist's right to express his temperament: they were, in this, protesting against pure painting (then being developed in Paris), while at the same time, on occasion, using its technical devices, but distorting them to their own ends. The Expressionism that flourished in Germany, Belgium and Holland answered to Nordic instincts which were stimulated by contributions from the Slav and Balkan countries flowing in to join the Munich and Paris movements. The Austrian painter Kokoschka is perhaps the most representative of all these artists: he painted the barons of crime, and, after the First World War, took pleasure in flying over the great cities of Europe that were to be annihilated by the Second.

*In Kokoschka's work, even the lovers are tragic (403)*

Thus, between the two world wars, the various forms of play with reality—massacre play, image play, or flirtation at a distance—were continued; but meanwhile the movement towards integral abstraction, which had been smouldering since 1910, was prepared by a few precursors, and immediately after the Second World War it burst out. Following the years of horror, it took on the meaning of a final rejection of the world, an attempt to live in an artificial universe that should owe nothing any more to the system of relationships and exchanges upon which the organisation of art and human life had always been based. Sometimes, then, this rejection took an aggressive form. 'But against whom is such an arsenal directed? Simply against space,' wrote Pierre Guéguen, discussing the sculptor Giorgio de Giorgi. The painter Mathieu likewise speaks of 'the coffins of space'; and if one looks for a point of reference, it must be chaos. Speaking of the same artist René Berger writes: 'Stripping man of the successive deposits with which civilisations have loaded him and purifying history of the chronologies that encumber it, the artist makes prehistory actual again.' He means the prehistory of the world, not of humanity, for he quotes the Sumerian poem that sang of the world at the moment of the creation:

> 'When heaven on high was not named
> And the earth below had no name.'

Others have not broken with the real: they take it as a starting-point of a slow elaboration which, by a system of deduction analogous to the reduction of fractions of which the pebbles of the Mas d'Azil provide us with well-known examples from prehistory, results in a system of formal equations more or less analogous to Nature. Thus Manessier, Bazaine, and Maria Elena Vieira da Silva quite rightly protest that they are not 'abstract artists': they still remember the objects from which they drew their forms, and these have become signs decipherable not only by them but also by some members of the public who, being trained to this sort of vision, are capable of capturing the reality that still emerges from these paintings. Others play hide-and-seek with Nature, producing pictures that can be read either *en clair* or in cipher: Jean Paul Riopelle's native Canadian forest, the stony and bushy hills of the Dalmatian artist Zoran Music, and the cockfights or Channel waves of the Flemish painter Pignon can be made out by 'objective reading' in the systems of spots of which their pictures consist. There is in these cases a play of forms, analogous to word play or, again, to the plastic anamorphoses of earlier painters; and abstraction is sometimes produced simply by suppressing all discontinuity between the various forms, creating an effect like that obtained by running together all the words of a phrase.

*Plate 418*

Some artists, noticing that painting reduced in this way becomes a kind of writing, fall back upon the example of calligraphy, as is evident in the drawings of the French artist Michaux or of the American Tobey, whose scrawls and dots are almost indistinguishable from the ideograms of the Japanese calligraphists of the fifteenth to the eighteenth centuries. Sometimes in these calligraphies the figure reappears—in the work of Genovés or of Tobey, for instance—as though the other way round: in such cases it arises from a caprice of the artist, not from Nature.

As a result of an exhibition in 1951 the term '*Informel*' came to be used for those forms in which all reference to Nature is abolished. It is certainly not a very suitable term for the geometrical variant of abstraction (Magnelli, Kerrowe, Herbin, Arp, Marcelle Cohn, Chodar) which is on the contrary a rigorous formalisation; but it surely applies to the Tachism of Pollock (when he laid his pictures on the ground and poured colour on them by the bucketfull in a frantic dance) or, again, to the works of Mathieu in which he introduces what one might call the dimension of speed into painting.

*Plate 419*
*The real predecessor of the* Informel *is the Russian, Kandinsky, who made his appearance in the midst of the German school, and whose paintings remind one of the spirit of certain Oriental forms (417)*

In this lyrical kind of form, derived from Surrealist and Dadaist automatism, the artists and their critics hoped to find 'oracles'—an emergence into the visible of that 'world of possibles' into which man, in flight from our world, plunges like a submarine fisherman, hoping to catch *pure* messages stripped of the human and moral significance that Surrealism gave to its automatisms.

*To Maillol, still, sculpture is essentially volume (413). The sculptors who derive from Cubism break up volume within a fragmentated space. The most recent ones imagine a space in tension (411), which also inspires some of the creations of architecture today (410)*

Some artists, in order to stimulate the oracle, paint under hypnosis (Marcel Caille), or take hallucinogenic or 'psycho-dyspeptic' substances, as in the case of Michaux who drugs himself with mescalin. They imitate what certain poets had done before them.

Abstract sculpture is even more 'significant' than painting; for, whether constructivist or lyrical, engaged in re-creating pure forms (Pevsner, Lippold), going back to the rocks or to minerals (Giorgio de Giorgi), finding elements of form in the scrap-heap in the manner of Picasso (Paolozzi), cutting sections out of space (Lardera, Müller), or concentrating the density of matter in the manner of Brancusi (Giglioli), all these artists achieve a more complete abolition of the classical object than any picture can, since it remains dependent on a surface with its limited dimensions.

The speed with which so-called abstract art has spread all round the world, establishing a uniform style, is not due merely to the fact that it is easy: its absolutism expresses the determination to reject what has gone before, in an effort of anticipation that leaves the spirit trembling on the borders of the unformulated. The enormous amount of exegesis that pullulates about this art has become, paradoxically, a fresh instance of the interaction of art and literature. It is a literature at large, which in its efforts to transpose the *Informel* into words, merely repeats the discarded terminology of a fossilised Surrealism. To quote an example:

> 'Blues with false looks, haggard light of stemlike greens, and those madly barking yellows. A tall bitch, that heaven-studded pulp flung on canvas. With sword and torn-out vitals in the stir of all colours.
> 'Colours thunderstruck into those gigantically demiurgic tubes. Detonated message of the unprecedented with seven-fold murder in itself. Ah! the apocalypse of the foaming Beast, rearing in epilepsy!
> 'Dagger survival, in Karel Appel an impossible trembles.'
>
> (Emmanuel Looten)

Sometimes literature and painting are done together, as with Gisèle Prassinos commenting on Mario Prassinos.

Again, Michaux's fundamental difficulty is that of being, of really having a substance: 'It is his ontological vacancy,' says Robert Bréchon, and he goes on to analyse 'lack of being', thesaurus in hand: '*trou, vide; état gazeux, nuageux, nébuleux, vague, informe, flou, flasque; ou liquide déliquescent, dilué, flottant, coulant, diarrhéïque, vilaine eau sans bord ni fond*'.

'*L'Impasse d'Impossible*'—'The dead-end of the Impossible'—is the phrase used by Emmanuel Looten (quoted above) about Karel Appel. The present situation of art is in many ways comparable to that of Italian Mannerism around the year 1560: it too was an '*impasse d'impossible*'. Will a new Caravaggio soon arise to open up the *impasse*? Unless the Sputniks solve the problem on some other planet.

## *The Harbinger*

Painted by Picasso in his Blue period, this harlequin—whose gesture and sinuous pose still attach him to the *Art Nouveau*—seems to announce the extraordinary adventure in which Man is about to engage, calling in question all the principles by which he has lived till now.

400 PICASSO: *The Actor*, 1905

401 PICASSO: *Les Demoiselles d'Avignon, 1907*

402 MATISSE: *Tree near Trivaux Pond, c. 1916* ▶

## *Expressionism*

Developing in the Germanic countries and stimulated in Paris by the contributions of Slav, Jewish and Balkan artists, Expressionism gives romantic and tragic utterance to the deep disquiet tormenting humanity on the eve of the First World War.

*403* KOKOSCHKA: *The Bride of the Wind*

*404* ROUAULT: *Aunt Sallies, 1907*

*405* CHAGALL: *detail from The Poet Reclining, 1915*

# Surrealism

Inspired by Freud's psychoanalytical doctrines, Surrealism is a kind of conscious exercise in a-logical relations stemming from subliminal depths. It displays the struggle between the life-impulse and the death-impulse, which between them dominate the life of the self.

406 TANGUY: *Le Palais aux Rochers de Fenêtres*

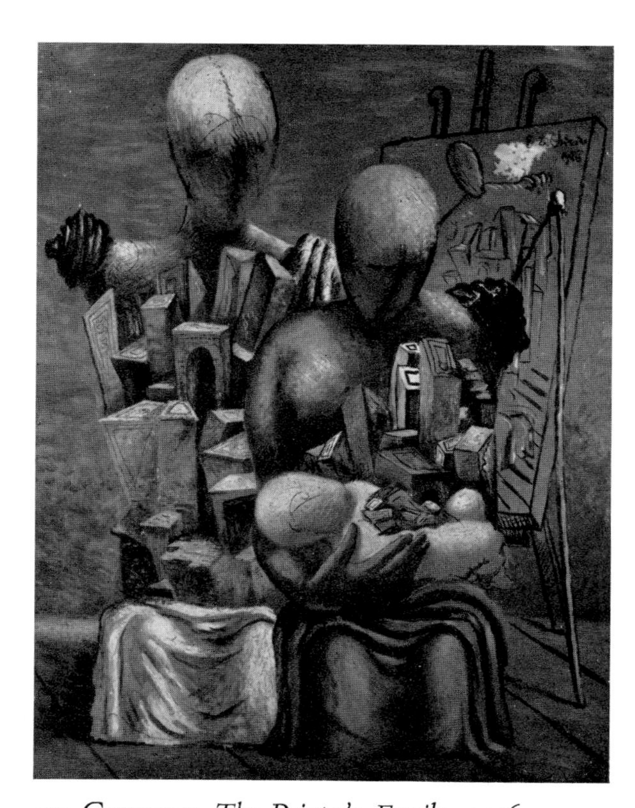

407 CHIRICO: *The Painter's Family, 1926*

*408* DALI: *Apparition of face and fruit-dish on a beach*

*409* ERNST: *Europe after the Rain*

*411* REG BUTLER: *Model for the monument to an unknown political prisoner*

*410* LUCIO COSTA *and* OSKAR NIEMEYER: *part of Brazilia*

*412* LIPCHITZ: *Melancholy*

## *Towards a New Space*

Maillol seems intoxicated by the density of volumes swollen to excess. After him, both in sculpture and in architecture, we see a real dislocation of space, possibly the premonition of new relationships between Man and the Universe.

*413* MAILLOL: *Torso, Monument to Blanqui, 1905–9*

414 *Fresco from Palestine, c. 3000* B.C.

The movement towards total abstraction, for which Cubism prepared the way in 1910, moves onwards slowly, then explodes after the Second World War. It passed, first, through a phase in which the artist still started from observed objects, arriving by progressive elaboration at a system of signs. There have been many precedents in history for this abstract art, as for example, on this page, a painting of the year 3000 B.C., found at Ghassul in Palestine, and an object from ancient Mexico.

415 MONDRIAN: *Rhythm of straight lines*

*416 Feather shield from ancient Mexico, 15th century*

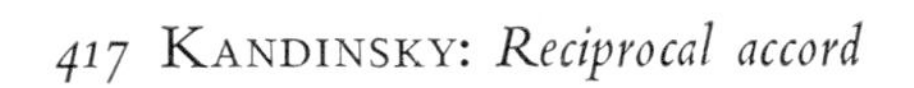

417 KANDINSKY: *Reciprocal accord*

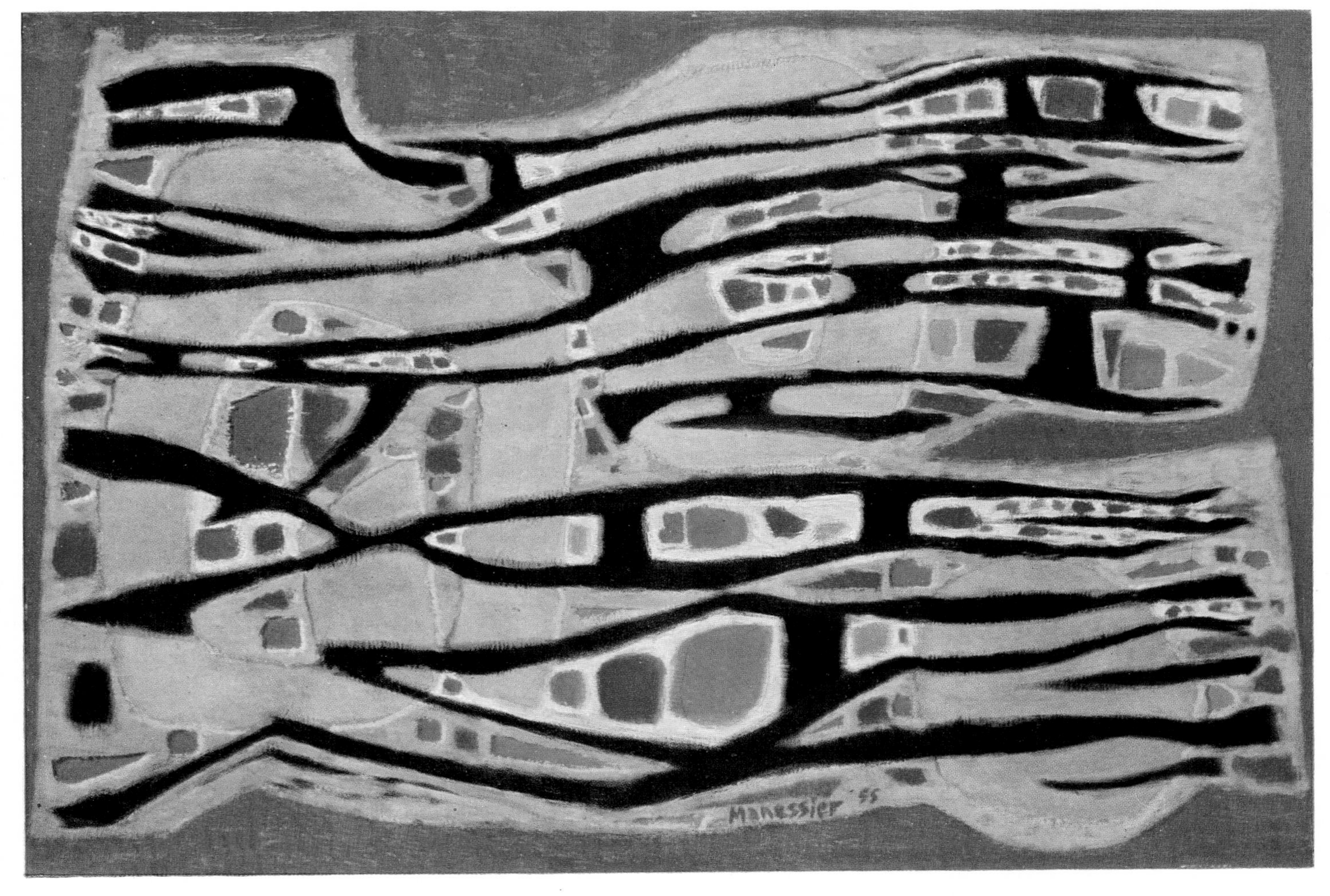


418 MANESSIER: *Plain Chant, 1955*

## *'Informel'* End of quest—dead end—'l'impasse de l'impossible'.

*419* JACKSON POLLOCK: *Painting, 1948*

## NOTES ON THE ILLUSTRATIONS TO CHAPTER X

400 PABLO PICASSO (*b.* 1881): *The Actor. Paris, 1905. Metropolitan Museum of Art, New York.*

401 PABLO PICASSO (*b.* 1881): *Les Demoiselles d'Avignon. 1907. Museum of Modern Art, New York.*
*Photo: Anna Wachsmann*

402 HENRI MATISSE (1869–1954): *Tree near Trivaux Pond. c. 1916. Tate Gallery, London.*
*Photo: Zoltan Wegner*

403 OSKAR KOKOSCHKA (*b.* 1886): *The Bride of the Wind. Kunstmuseum, Bâle.*

404 GEORGES ROUAULT (1871–1958): *Aunt Sallies. 1907. Tate Gallery, London.*
*Photo: Zoltan Wegner*

405 MARC CHAGALL (*b.* 1887): *Detail from The Poet Reclining. 1915. Tate Gallery, London.*
*Photo: Zoltan Wegner*

406 YVES TANGUY (1900–55): *Le Palais aux Rochers de Fenêtres. Musée d'Art Moderne, Paris.*
*Photo: Jacqueline Hyde*

407 GIORGIO DI CHIRICO (*b.* 1888): *The Painter's Family. 1926. Tate Gallery, London.*

408 SALVADOR DALI (*b.* 1904): *Apparition of face and fruit-dish on a beach. Wadsworth Athenaeum, Hartford, Connecticut.*
*Photo: Anna Wachsmann*

409 MAX ERNST (*b.* 1881): *Europe after the Rain. Wadsworth Athenaeum, Hartford, Connecticut.*

410 LUCIO COSTA *and* OSKAR NIEMEYER: *Chapel of the Alvorada Palace, Brazilia.*

411 REG BUTLER (*b.* 1913): *Model for the monument to an unknown political prisoner.*
*Photo: Pantlin, Radlett. Copyright, Architectural Press*

412 JACQUES LIPCHITZ (*b.* 1891): *Melancholy. Mr and Mrs Bernard J. Reis, New York.*
*Photo: A. Studly, New York*

413 ARISTIDE MAILLOL (1861–1944): *Torso, Monument to Blanqui. Lead. 1905–9. Tate Gallery, London.*
*Photo: F. L. Kenett*

414 *Star with eight branches. Detail of a polychrome fresco at Ghassul, Palestine. c. 3000* B.C.

415 PIET MONDRIAN (1872–1944): *Rhythm of straight lines. Henry Clifford Collection.*
*Photo: Anna Wachsmann*

416 *Feather shield from Ancient Mexico. 15th century. Würtemburgisches Landesmuseum, Stuttgart.*

417 WASSILY KANDINSKY (1866–1944): *Reciprocal Accord. 1942. Nina Kandinsky, Paris.*

418 ALFRED MANESSIER (*b.* 1911): *Plain Chant. 1955. Galerie Änne Abels, Cologne.*

419 JACKSON POLLOCK (1912–56): *Painting. 1948. Paul Facchetti Collection, Paris.*
*Photo: Eileen Tweedy*

## NOTES ON THE TEXT FIGURES TO CHAPTERS I, II, IV, V, VI, VIII AND X

*page*

15 *Eannatum's stele. Drawn by Shalom Schotten. Musée du Louvre, Paris.*

19 *Pebbles from Mas d'Azil. From André Varagnac: 'L'homme avant l'ecriture.'*

19 *Garland-dancers. From André Varagnac: 'L'homme avant l'ecriture.'*

40–1 *Chinese Bronzes. From the catalogue to the exhibition 'L'évolution des arts chinois archaïques', Paris, 1937.*

101 *Altar of Ferentillo. Drawn by Ian Mackenzie Kerr.*

103 *Altar of Cividale. Drawn by Ian Mackenzie Kerr.*

105 *Bogomil sarcophagus. Drawn by Ian Mackenzie Kerr.*

125 *Plan of St Gall. Redrawn from the plan in the Chapter Library, St Gall.*

132 *Stone head from Heidelberg. Redrawn by Margaret Scott from P. Jacobsthal, 'Imagery in Celtic Art', 1941.*

162 *Plan by* LEONARDO. *Redrawn by Shalom Schotten. From MS. B, Institut de France, Paris.*

164 *Elliptical church plan. From* SERLIO: *'Tutte l'opere dell'Architettura', Book V.*

227 *The Villa Lante. Redrawn by Shalom Schotten. From* JACOBUS LAURAI: *'Antiquae Urbis Splendor', 1612.*

229 *Vergini Palace staircase. From Roberto Pane, 'Architettura del' età barocca in Napoli'.*

293 MASSON, *'Il n'y a pas de monde achevé'. From J. L. Barrault and others: 'André Masson', 1940.*

# CONCLUSION: MUSEUM TIME

## *Conclusion: Museum Time*

THE NEED to use the past as some sort of counterpoise seems vital to modern man, plunged as he is into the futurist world of science which had already alarmed Châteaubriand, astounded by the beginnings of steam navigation, and which made the Comte de Laborde say, as early as 1865, that the discoveries of chemistry and physics were throwing the society of his time into 'a whirl of novelties and of reversals that might well turn one's head or drive one mad'.

Of all the creatures in the world, man seems to have been the one intended by Nature to experience the consciousness of time. Like every other living thing, he is a blend of past, present and future—of the done with, the immediate and the possible. Before the rise of scientific civilisation the majestic march of time set men in an atmosphere of continuity: manners, customs and institutions did not develop fast enough to give an individual, during his lifetime, the feeling of any profound change. Man's strong consciousness of the present was a harmonious articulation between past and future: the past was not 'time past' or that which passes, but, on the contrary, tradition, or that which endures. The various parts of a social body based on the dynastic principle, the family unit and the eternity of religion, were cemented together in a continuity.

To the romantics, drawn as they were towards the past by the trauma caused by the political events that had just shaken Europe, the sense of days gone by had given a sharp awareness of death; and they tried to escape from it through love, which was cultivated in their time as the individual's own ethical principle—through love which, based on vows that were a commitment for life, gave to the instant an eternal value.

As the memory of the holes torn in the tissue of time by the Revolution and the Napoleonic Wars began to fade, the period that followed romanticism recovered the feeling of continuity. Between a past considered as a guarantee and a future that was a promise, the men of the West found they could linger and live the pure present. Of this happiness Impressionism is the image. Never was the triptych of time so well balanced; never perhaps had its centre been so beautiful.

The world catastrophe of 1914–18 smashed this harmony: death, becoming legion, gave man once more an anxious consciousness of time; and he tried to escape from the nightmare of a horrible past by throwing himself breathlessly into the future—a course that in the end gnawed away his feeling of the present, for to get into the state of living in the morrow is to stop living in the present and leads us by the shortest way to the fatal moment.

The belief in progress goes back to the origins of Western civilisation. This idea of time as rectilinear—in opposition to the myth of cyclical time which has flourished in the East—was created by the Judeo-Christian tradition, though the Greeks show traces of both: by subjecting the world (now regarded as *creature*) to the decrees of a Providence-God whose destiny was to achieve final victory over evil by raising man from his original fall, both the Old and the New Covenants gave the march of time a direction and made it a progress. Isidore of Seville in the seventh century invented the new universal chronology, making the birth of Christ the turning-point of history. Modern society as it became secular, inherited from Christianity this idea of progress, but changed it by substituting for the heavenly Paradise the earthly one, which it made the aim of Science. The obligation for man to evolve ceaselessly towards perfection became then an inevitable destiny.

Soon history was invaded by the idea of speed, and its rhythm accelerated. The last War, reaching a world scale, made more havoc of the map in a few years than centuries, even millennia, had done. The individual had now cut the thread that bound him to the past, and become himself the agent of discontinuity. Now began that feeling of the precariousness of life with which we are all familiar—a feeling of being perpetually menaced by change, made even more terrifying by the sudden speeding-up of the whole process in the last half century. Who, among those living today, can be sure of living tomorrow? What man who has worked throughout his life to assure himself a happy old age and a good use of his few remaining years can be sure that he will not be baulked of it by one of the laws now known as 'social'? Not that political events are needed for his ruin: it is enough for him to have invested his savings in what are so curiously called 'securities'. The present is now simply a maturing past: at the moment when an aircraft prototype reaches the production stage, its replacement is having its trials and the replacement of the replacement is on the drawing-board, so that all the aircraft in use by our commercial lines and by the world's military forces are junk, whose place in the museum is already waiting for them. The toys that were our childhood pleasure are now appearing in the windows of the antique shops—the precious lead soldiers that I broke so gaily as a child! Has not one of the shops in the rue Jacob been displaying as an antique one of the acetylene lamps formerly used by motor-cars? And did I not, in the Belo Horizonte Museum come across a tile made at Marseilles at the beginning of this century? But indeed the museums are not content with giving house room to the past—they include in their welcome that past-in-the-making, the present; and we have science museums where designs for technical marvels that have not yet seen the light are exhibited.

Modern man, fallen from the eternity which the religions promised him, has tried to satisfy his inner need of continuity by balancing his break into the future with an equal delving into the past. And indeed this need to 'step back' is part of the same instinct as that of progress. This 'perspectivist' tendency permeates the whole of Western civilisation and makes it regard even space as a progression in time: science now, by introducing a new idea of time and showing that human time does not apply on the scale of the universe, has developed still further in Western man the feeling of a temporal dimension that is man's own and is, so to speak, the conductor, the live wire of his life. America—in which the European, when he lands, feels he has suddenly had one of his dimensions, the past, amputated—is the part of the world where the museums, the only witnesses to the human past, are given the greatest importance by society.

This passionate attachment to the human past, which is becoming rather like a new religion, shows clearly in the increasing care taken to preserve the evidences of the past from devastation by war. It was in the eighteenth century, during the Seven Years War, that the first passive defence measures were taken to bring threatened works of art into safe shelter. After the Austrian soldiers of the Prince of Zweibrücken had forced the Prussian garrison of Dresden to surrender on September 4th, 1759, the works of art accumulated by the two Augustuses were packed up for removal to the fortress of Königstein. Johann Anton Riedel, Inspector of the Gallery, has left us a journal of this operation, for which he was responsible; it did in fact save the celebrated collection of pictures, later admired by Goethe, for during the bombardment of July 1760—which caused the first destruction of Dresden, the second being in 1944—the Gallery and the Judenhof, where the pictures had been exhibited, were very badly damaged. On the other hand almost all the two hundred and eighty-six pictures at Hubertursburg, near Oschatz, which was pillaged by Frederick's armies, were lost. Later the Austrian Emperor carried out a large-scale strategic withdrawal of works of art threatened by the French armies as they marched across Europe. In 1794 the Treasure of the Golden Fleece was evacuated from Brussels to Austria through Holland and Germany. In the same year the regalia of the Holy Roman Empire, which were kept partly at Nürnberg and partly at Aix-la-Chapelle, fled before General Jourdan: evacuated from town to town they reached the Schatzkammer of the imperial capital in 1800 and 1801 respectively. In 1806 other treasures converged on Vienna in order to escape from the victorious armies of Napoleon or his allies. The famous collection brought together by Archduke Ferdinand of Tyrol in the castle of Ambras in the sixteenth century left that province by water, when it was occupied by Bavaria, and was installed in the Lower Belvedere in Vienna. All these art treasures remained in the capital: the Austrian sovereigns were no doubt not displeased by circumstances that favoured their idea of centralising the Empire's masterpieces in Vienna, an 'imperial' idea which the French Directoire and Empire tried at that same period to realise for the benefit of Paris.

In 1870 there were proposals to evacuate the contents of the Louvre: the *Venus de Milo* was actually sent to a vault in a cemetery. The exodus was more pronounced in the First World War, when the church of the Jacobins at Toulouse received works of art from the Louvre. At the same time some belligerents asserted, as one of the aims of a war that must be total, a determination to destroy the enemy's works of art—which is one way of recognising their value. The Germans aroused the indignation of the world by bombarding the cathedral of Reims; they blew up the Château de Coucy, the finest feudal monument in Europe; and during the 1918 retreat they made preparations to do the same to the cathedral of Saint-Quentin. Did not the Austrian *Fremdenblatt* (in its issue number 315 of November 14th, 1915) justify the bombardment of Venice—which cost the world Tiepolo's ceiling in the Scalzi—by the need to ruin Italy's economic wealth, to which the tourist traffic was one of the main contributors? In contradiction to this attitude, the measures taken by the military authorities of Nazi Germany to protect from destruction the works of art of the countries they occupied are well known—at least in the West, for in the East, in Poland and in Russia, destruction was systematic, and that magnificent ring of palaces built by Peter the Great, Catherine II and Paul I around Leningrad was demolished by conscious vandalism. These facts illustrate the perpetual instability of the German soul, which finds room at one and the same time for every sort of contradiction.

But in a war today, which of the belligerents—of the civilised countries at any rate—would take responsibility before history for destroying works of art? Huge movements of works of art over the roads of Europe during the Second World War, including such large-scale operations as the exodus of the Leningrad collections to the Urals, proves the value attached nowadays to the work of art and to the historical document.

It might indeed seem surprising that men should have become so suddenly conscious that the legacy from the past is irreplaceable, were there not, at the origin of this feeling, an obscure inferiority complex. Our forebears, when some building was destroyed by accident or war, had the impression that what replaced it was at least as good, if not better. How unjust the people of Brussels are when they reproach the Maréchal de Villeroi for the 1695 bombardment which destroyed the Grand Place of their city, since this destruction obliged their ancestors to build what is one of the marvels of Europe, a jewel of Baroque art!

This inferiority complex is at the origin of every enterprise in museum making. It was the motive of the Hellenistic tyrants when they collected Greek statues of the 'good period'—including the archaic—as the Attali of Pergamo did in their museum. As for the Romans, convinced as they were that beauty was fixed once for all between the fifth and first centuries B.C., they limited their ambition to copying its prototypes. What despair is expressed in Hadrian's insensate effort to withdraw from time by reproducing the most beautiful sites and monuments of Greek art in his villa at Tivoli, the first 'open air museum'!

When the Renaissance princes collected ancient statues with such passion, when the artists from the *Quattrocento* to the *Seicento* looked for and pored over beauty in the *antiquaria* set up by the Medici, by the Popes, or by the Gonzagas, was it not because they were ashamed of the legacy of the preceding age and had caught from Rome the feeling of an aesthetic inferiority of the present as against the past? The excavated remains of Antiquity were venerated like the gods of some new religion: the *Laocöon* group, found in a vineyard in 1506 and bought by Julius II, was transported to the Vatican in an atmosphere of triumph, to the pealing of bells and the firing of salutes, and the people of Rome had the day off as though for a saint's day. The Popes lost little time in establishing a system of export licences to protect the artistic patrimony of the Papal States; but, like all edicts of that kind, it was not much observed, and had no more luck than the sumptuary laws. In 1627, when the Flemish antiquary Daniel Nys managed to seize the collection of the Gonzaga for Charles I of England, there was consternation throughout Italy. In the eighteenth century the capture of Raphael's *Sistine Madonna* (sold by the convent at Piacenza which owned it to the Elector of Saxony, Augustus the Strong, in 1754) was considered as an exploit, exciting envy and admiration all over Europe. All Europe, in fact, took part in this movement of veneration for the past. But it was unquestionably the Swedes who led in the protection of the past as such—that is to say, of the historical document considered apart from its artistic value: is it not surprising that a soldier-king, Gustavus Adolphus, should have taken the trouble to publish on May 20th, 1630, an edict urging historians and antiquaries to search out ancient monuments, runic inscriptions, tombs and the ruins of old castles? In 1643 there was even organised in Sweden a Department of National Antiquities with regional inspectors.

Nowhere has the rise of the museum-making phenomenon been so clearly bound up with a feeling of inferiority towards the past as in France. In 1744 Lafont de Sainte-Yenne published his *Réflexions sur quelques causes de la décadence de la peinture en France*, in which he advocated that the royal collections should be publicly exhibited: the spirit of this pamphlet comes out well in its title—the good models, which had been forgotten, must be placed before the eyes of artists in order to cure what the author believes to be the decline of painting, that is to say of historical painting. The same spirit led to the foundation in 1850 of the museums of '*Arts Décoratifs*', one of the main stages in the formation of our museums. The first universal exhibitions, those in London in 1851 and in Paris in 1855, had made people conscious of the decadence of the arts of furniture and ornament, and it was considered an imperative necessity to show modern artists the masterpieces of earlier times; but the initiative defeated its own end—it merely succeeded in stimulating *pastiche* and eclecticism, which flourished at the end of the last century. In the same period the nostalgia for the poetry that had filled the immemorial life of the people and been killed by modern standardisation likewise gave rise—especially in the Scandinavian countries, with their strong love for their national antiquities—to the great movement for creating museums of folk art.

* * *

A newspaper—provided it is not a 'progressive' one—cannot go far wrong if it commissions an article on the 'dehumanisation' of the modern world. But the term is an absurd one seeing that in no other age has humanism been so widespread or been pushed so far. Never has man taken such an interest in man: following the advance of the Natural Sciences, which went on at breakneck speed for a whole century (1850–1950), there is a sudden and noticeable intensification in all the various sciences of man whose abnormal backwardness was noted by Doctor Carrel in 1935, retarded as they were for so long by ethical or metaphysical considerations inherited from religion. Now the most modern techniques are being placed at their disposal—card indexes and, very soon, computors. While there is no reason to suppose that the limits of the technical conquests of the Natural Sciences are in sight, it is possible that speculative knowledge of the external world may for a time and provisionally be slowed down after its recent formidable progress and that the future is open to the sciences of man.

Looking at the past and future of our Western civilisation, without going further back than the Christian era, it seems that in the development of man's attempt at self-knowledge one can distinguish three ages—the age of theology, that of biology and that of psychology. Psychology, including sociology, appears to be in the forefront of the preoccupations of our contemporaries, who argue about man as people used to argue about God. The Existentialism of Jean-Paul Sartre, in bringing to human beings the sad realisation of the 'dereliction of God', contains in its very pessimism a nostalgia for the divine, yet is a last fling of metaphysics that sets the human soul free from metaphysics.

For the last twenty years the epistemology of history has been deeply affected by this forward movement of the sciences of man. The French school of historians, in its reaction against the fallacies of the German followers of Hegel (who indeed were always to some extent influenced by pan-Germanism), has prudently kept within the traditional disciplines; but thinkers like Sorokine or Toynbee, helped by the powerful means of investigation possessed by British and American institutions, have devoted themselves to efforts at synthesis, in which factual knowledge is simply a collecting and classifying of the kind of material from which sociological laws can be worked out. The aim of history now becomes not so much to establish the chronological succession and the temporal factors involved in the development of civilisations as to look for constants, for cyclical principles, for progressive or retrograde movements, for oscillatory rhythms—for anything that can throw light on the content of the human soul. Even the study of the divine has come down from the heights of metaphysics to psychology: what now interests the philosopher is how man made his god.

From the day when factual knowledge, though still of primary importance as a means, became secondary in relation to the ends of historical study, the work of art acquired a considerable value in the eyes of the historian and the sociologist: the enormous mass of inscriptionless documents yielded by excavation, our only source for the periods before writing, necessarily taught the historian to consult the work of art as a human specimen, even apart from the temporal circumstances of its birth.

Thus the value of a work of art has come to seem all the greater in that it is in itself a significant part of history. The notion of an object that has utility independent of any artistic purpose belongs to our own time: most of the objects handed down to us by the past have an artistic value, whether mediate (motivated by some magical, theological, spiritual or social purpose) or immediate (caused by an intrinsic purpose). It is therefore impossible to deny the importance of a factor so basic to the study of man as aproducer or creator. In the sciences of man the interpretation of forms is bound to take a place as great as that which for the last century has been assigned to philology.

The museums offer the sociologist the formidable arsenal of their treasures: these are still classified chronologically by the historian, but they may one day be submitted to other rational systems of classification that will answer to a synoptic vision of man, if indeed the predominance of sociology brings about a kind of eclipse of history in its hitherto accepted meaning and causes all the acts of man to be considered as though present in the light of a definition of the human.

As it happens, the 'archaeological phenomenon', the conscious research into antecedents in order to bring out origins, has always meant decadence. This was so in the seventh and sixth centuries B.C., when the knell sounded for the old world—the Middle East—whose efforts during millennia had created civilisation. The Saitic pharaohs of the Twenty-sixth Dynasty tried to go back to the Age of the Pyramids; the last kings of Babylon, in their nostalgic return to the past, resuscitated a dead language, ancient Sumerian; Nabonidus, whom Cyrus defeated, went so far as to have the temples excavated to find out the names and dates of their first builders. The past is expected to be surety for the future. One is strongly tempted to see in our own curiosity about the past—about all the past—a premonitory sign of the end of a world. Yet truthfulness forces one to recognise that, as the sociologist gradually takes the place of the historian, the consciousness of the past which oppressed the century of romanticism, is becoming less vivid: recorded, riddled with queries, classified and interpreted, the human facts appear as parts of the 'present' of science; the sociologist is interested merely in the reality and psychological bearing of the observed phenomenon without regard to its age, in the same way as it matters little to the astronomer that the image reflected in the mirror of his telescope now brings him only the message from a star that is dead. It is as if thought conferred on its object the power of being, in a way, extra-temporal.

* * *

Interpretation of the work of art as that and nothing more—begun by the German thinkers Riegl and Wölfflin at the end of the century and brilliantly continued by historians or essayists writing in French, Waldemar Déonna, Elie Faure and Henri Focillon—crystallised this character of timelessness. But formal criticism of this kind carried with it the danger of a dehumanised formalism. In various ways writers and art historians of our own time are trying to restore to the work of art its human significance. The working out of André Malraux's thinking in his various writings on art during the last ten years is a movement upwards towards the absolute. After first laying down a *Musée Imaginaire*, to whose walls and shelves the works of art are summoned from far and near in space and time, André Malraux studied the sources and powers of that phenomenon, *La Création Artistique*, and he found a fine field of experiment in the complex phenomenon of stylistic 'regression' which, at the beginning of the Christian era, made the immemorial forms of the ancient magical Orient burst forth again. The revival of humanist sentiment within Christianity, when it was refreshed by contact with the youthful forces of the West, provides a kind of counter-proof. Enriched by these researches, Malraux penetrated to the very heart of artistic creation: he analysed the vision of the artist in its essence, contrasting it with ordinary vision; he unmasked the all too persistent deception of realism; to his way of thinking, the artist never seeks a representation of the world, he seeks a system of meaning. Facing up to his time and to his own living character, he makes the work of art an eternal challenge to death, renewed by successive generations. The crown of Malraux's *Psychologie de l'art* is its third part, *La Monnaie de l'Absolu* (*Currency of the Absolute*) in which the work of art is shown as a constant state of metamorphosis: in succession it is the currency of God, then of Poetry, then of the Nation, the People and Nature, those false gods of modern times; after the 'death of the eternal', this is reborn in the form of the 'immemorial' in the popular arts; and finally, in our own time, the work of art accomplishes its supreme metamorphosis by becoming 'pure currency of the absolute'. Under the influence of this state of mind a phenomenon of integration transforms, before our eyes, all the works of art of the past—in which we are now ready to see nothing but evidence of the absolute that haunts us.

Early Christian art is an example of a metamorphosis in the making, just touching on meaning before it actuates the form itself—the coins of Gaul show it spurting out and are direct expressions of instinct, literally 'currency of the absolute'.

Thus the work of art *in se* is a thing we can never catch: moreover it comes to us—from the past—profoundly changed, and we value its mutilation as much as the work itself, for it is this that has uprooted it from its own time and made it live in 'time', which is equivalent (for our illusion) to throwing it 'out of time' into our own.

The essay on Goya, called *Saturn*, is another example of metamorphosis, this time provided by Malraux himself—a metamorphosis from plastic into literary form: the best—the only—equivalent to a work of art is another work of art. Only the writer's thinking is capable of transcribing the mystery of the painter's work into another and more explicit significance, that of words. This literary masterpiece, a prolongation of masterpieces in paint, is clearly the result of the man's adequacy to his subject: the novelist of *La Condition Humaine* (*Man's Estate*), inspired by truly saturnine insight, has found the best possible stimulus for him in tragedy—in which indeed he has often been drawn to take an active part.

The style itself reveals the author's spirit: it is a conqueror's style, one that corresponds to an ardently active mind that has the quick nervous reactions of a fighter and then, gradually, dominates the ground it has won and organises it. His *Musée Imaginaire* had a tone of prophetic improvisation, on which gradually his intelligence, growing more self-assured, imposed, in *La Création Artistique* and *La Monnaie de l'Absolu*, a straightforward progression well served by a supple dialectic; and now in *Saturn*, which is more specifically literary, this tone has given place to a continuous style and a self-contained thinking that derives its shapeliness from an assurance of logic intimately, almost essentially, bound up with its poetic quality. The organisation of the conquered land is presented to us in *Les Voix du Silence* (*The Voices of Silence*): here the thoughts which, at the stage of discovery, had had the incantatory character of a prophet's utterance, tend to fall into ordered logical series, aesthetic categories and human instances—these being not so much items of historical evidence as means for the investigation of the depths.

René Huyghe's *Dialogue avec le visible* (*The Discovery of Art*) is a work in which painting is isolated as a fact of experience: its quality is that of an exercise in 'expertise' upon works of art to which the author claims to submit with humility—an expertise of the intellect and of the senses, based on the primacy of visual examination, as the title stresses. René Huyghe aims at rescuing criticism from its blindness by forcing it to do without the ideological veil that modern man in his mania for mental categories, throws over facts; he wants to 'blast away these agglomerations of ideas . . . so as to open in them breaches through which air and sight may circulate'. His method is 'the approach by looking'. After a chronological survey which provides a kind of historical ground-plan for his exegesis, Huyghe places painting firmly outside time, and, having analysed the various elements of a painting with the scrupulous conscientiousness that comes of a museum director's close and daily contact with works of art, he shows artistic creation as the connecting link between two incommunicable and impenetrable worlds, 'which never couple except through points of clash and interaction'—the worlds of spirit and of matter. Artistic creation is thus a thing close to love 'and to its effort to reach what is none the less, by nature, distinct'; but the work of art goes further than love because it is 'an object' and takes root. Like love, it is something in the physical world that tends to escape from time; it offers firm ground to 'human beings in their grief at witnessing the crumbling away, without respite, of what they know and what they see, what they think and what they feel, in a dissolving, universal relativity—human beings whose one longing is to escape from a drift that is even more cruel than that of time'.

While the writers were thus extracting the work of art from history, certain scholars were bringing about a similar change, sometimes even without realising it. The formalism that has attracted critics and art lovers during the last half century has masked the continuous development of the *Geistgeschichte*, which was started by Dvorak in Vienna and, before him, by Emile Mâle in France, both of them in an effort to integrate art history with spiritual history. One of them took the world of the Renaissance as his field of experiment, the other Christianity. For both of them the work of art is an *image*, the clothing of an idea. As the Middle Ages provided the stimulus for

Emile Mâle, the Renaissance gave rise to *Studies in Iconology*. Fritz Saxl (1890–1948), who had been a pupil of Dvorak in Vienna and Wölfflin in Berlin, founded in 1912, with the Hamburg banker Warburg, a study centre whose aim was to elucidate the ideological content of works of figurative art; and it was here, at the University of Hamburg that Erwin Panofsky made his *début*. This research centre started by Germanic thinkers was forced to move to Great Britain and America by the hazards of political history: in 1937 London gave a home to the Warburg Institute, driven from Germany by the Nazi violations of liberty of thought; and in 1939 Erwin Panofsky published in English his *Studies in Iconology*, in which he defined the method and laid down the idea of 'planes of significance'.

What strikes the reader of Emile Mâle's books on Christian art or of the studies published in the *Journal of the Warburg Institute*, is the feeling that the work of art, taking off from the idea, parts company with the temporal; and this is all the more surprising since in both cases the method consists in justifying the work of art by close comparison with contemporary written evidence. With Emile Mâle, whether visiting the Gesù in Rome, Santa Maria in Trastevere or the cathedral of Chartres, one has the impression of living in one and the same epoch, enclosed in an enchanted circle—that of Christian civilisation; the grace of his thought and the charm of his narrative style succeeded in raising studies based on the strictest historical accuracy to the plane of legend. The *Studies in Iconology* also take us into a closed world of pagan or neo-pagan myths, with complete correspondences between one time and another, but it is a world with a rarefied atmosphere, that of pure erudition. Unity might be given to this world by a recognition of the archetypes hidden under the various myths—archetypes of which the authors of these studies do not seem conscious.

It is surprising that the discoveries of Jung's psychology have still hardly passed beyond the world of specialists in psychiatry, by many of whom it is contested. In itself it abolishes history, by showing basic human nature as constant through time—founded on the mental archetypes deposited in the collective memory by the earliest civilisations: according to it, the movement of the psyche consists of bringing these idea-forces up from the depths to the threshold of consciousness. A work like Mircea Eliade's *Treatise on the History of Religions* is an attempt to reduce the innumerably various forms of religion to the unity of archetypal functions. In the field of creative art—not only poetry but also the fine arts—books like the *Introduction to the Essence of Mythology* by C. G. Jung and Carl Kerényi, or Georges Dumézil's studies on the Indo-Europeans could help the *Iconology* to emerge from the monotonous round: 'written thought=painted thought'. Written thought and painted thought neither cause nor explain one another. What is needed is to go beyond them, back to the archetypal world of the collective unconscious. This contact between artistic interpretation and the psychology of Jung is bound to take place, and unquestionably the future for art criticism lies there.

* * *

The past has to some extent lost its savour, and it has already had an influence on the museums, which are highly delicate sounding-boards for the sensibility of a period. In romantic times all pictures were given a coat of bitumen or varnish, to increase their share of the 'colour of time' which in those days touched people's souls. The moderns were not exempted from this treatment: how otherwise can one explain the fact that David's great compositions in the Louvre, which were painted in bright colours, were artificially browned—no doubt in about 1830? Indeed the Barbizon school openly used 'museum varnish'. In our day, on the contrary, and particularly in Great Britain and America, we expect works of art to be as clean as our houses. Greek marbles, stripped of their crust oxidised by the centuries, are beginning to look like the dull academic imitations to which they gave rise; the Sassanid or Early Christian silver objects are scoured till they shine like those of Puiforcat and are gradually, in the course of these successive cleanings, losing the bloom of their relief; the pictures of the Old Masters are scraped and brought into line with those of Matisse, Derain, Rouault or Van Gogh—they must at all costs (even at the cost of their original paint) acquire the discordant colours, improvised modelling and harsh surfaces of these. As for books on art, the great public is coming to prefer to the traditional 'history of art' a synthesis that looks at the works of all the ages in an eternal present.

* * *

What we now require of a work of art is that it should be not so much a message from the past as a specimen of man's creative powers: the public is more interested in its aesthetic and psychological value than in its quality as a historical monument. Through this specifically human power, provided it is intense, we enter directly into contact with it, without having to have recourse to the intermediary of the man who produced it or had it made. Fifty years ago Romain Rolland approached Michelangelo as a man of destiny: in our time Charles de Tolnay is interested not so much in the man as in the eternal human content of his work, to which, as a disciple of Dvorak, he tends to attribute a real symbolic function. The revival of Platonism in present-day studies of the Renaissance is symptomatic of this tendency. The meaning of a work of art can be appreciated in its essence and totality, thanks to the enormous increase of skill in the reading of it achieved in the last half century. From being an image it has become a sign.

The secondary masters—those who bear witness only to their period and who enjoyed citizens' rights in the museums of Taine's period with their emphasis on history—are disappearing from the walls of our present-day museums and are shut up in the reserves. Only the masterpiece, which communicates the human vision, is now tolerated: isolated from context of any kind on a light, abstract wall, it takes on the value of an absolute. There is a grave danger in this—that of a diminution of knowledge, a weakening of the historical apparatus that has served as foundation for psychological interpretation. The nineteenth-century '*connoisseur*' is tending to disappear, giving place to the '*amateur*' who is now, indeed, no more than an amateur of sensations. As a result there may come a day—it may be nearer than people think—when the immense prestige nowadays enjoyed by the work of art will dwindle: by dint of making itself unreal and becoming timeless, it will snap its roots in the living. In judging works of art young people display an appreciation that might well make their elders blush: trusting to their taste, they base their judgment on pure sensation. But culture cannot come of this: feeling is not enough to produce love, let alone knowledge; and when old age diminishes this power of feeling, nothing is left in the soul but the ash of memories. To adapt a saying of Bossuet's: 'Woe to the sensation that does not turn to knowing.'

* * *

The art history offered to us by the pared-down museums of today is coming to resemble, to a certain extent, that which was formerly inspired by the biographical method: in those days the history of the masters was set forth, and the evolution of forms emerged as a succession of 'strokes of genius': nowadays we are given a series of works of genius and, since the 'conjunctive tissue' of art constituted by the lesser masters has thus been torn to shreds, the mechanism of art history is in danger of becoming as motionless as a machine whose connecting parts have been removed; or it might be compared, again, to a mountain range with only the peaks emerging from the mist, or to a collection of precious stones torn from their carefully worked settings. Can Rembrandt be understood without Seghers, Claude Lorrain without Elsheimer, Poussin without Domenichino, Corot without Valenciennes and David without Vien? Let us simply try to imagine how false would be our picture of Italian painting in the *Seicento*, reduced to its 'great masters'. No doubt this simplification of art history was stimulated by the peculiar situation in the nineteenth century, especially in its second half, when the artists of genius were men isolated in the midst of an abyss of mediocrity. This dichotomy of artistic production into two halves, one addressing a public which was quite unaware of the other, affected all forms of culture in the nineteenth century; and before Impressionism the greatest artists themselves succumbed to it—for instance Corot, whose work divides into two parts, one of which, designed for the *Salon*, was meticulously painted and is generally mediocre or merely respectable, while the other is the spontaneous expression of his genius. And indeed for a long time Corot kept this intimate part of his work to himself, not daring to believe that it was 'art', and yet obscurely convinced of its authenticity. Before him, Valenciennes had kept hidden, all his life long, his exquisite studies of the Roman *campagna*, of which he made use in the painting of his boring 'neo-Poussinist' compositions. Corot lived long enough to become established and was able to bring his marvels out of what he called '*l'armoire*'.

The Germans have given a name—*kitsch*—to this aspect of collective culture, really a by-product of culture, which for a long time took, for the *élite*, the form of academicism. *Kitsch* is the result of the democratisation of culture: formerly the people approached the culture of the *élite* from the outside only, being subjected to the prince's display or the Church's world of wonder, while in a closed circle it went on with its own culture, whose immemorial forms were handed down without change from the times when the barbarian migrations settled; even today, in carving the yokes for their oxen, the peasants in the north of Portugal use a decorative vocabulary that goes back to the Visigoths. The promotion of the people to the culture of the *élite* was done through the *bourgeoisie*, which taught it realism, so that the popular imagination, which for centuries had produced only the abstract suddenly found itself unable to apprehend forms except naturalistically.

*Kitsch* indeed ends up by drawing its nourishment from the creations of the *avant-garde*, being in a way their commercial product. The 'low-brow', though scandalised by the anti-realism of modern art, submits to being seduced by abstraction in advertisements: from them, indeed, it would not tolerate any other kind of image, and the realistic posters of some time ago would make any business that used them now go bankrupt. The silhouette of Nicolas, with his '*fines bouteilles*', has become more and more stylised till it is no more than an outline. In 1925 there began to appear in French houses and flats wallpapers inspired by Cubist artists or by Fernand Léger, whose pictures were laughed at by the very people who lived between those walls. *Kitsch* now enjoys an amazing prosperity, thanks to the cinema, which seems to have been invented expressly to propagate it. The works of the Old Masters are themselves becoming accessible to the widest public, introduced to them by the fictional biographies that are also by-products of artistic culture: Van Gogh's suicide and Goya's affair with the Duchess of Alba will always bring crowds to the exhibitions of those masters, while the austere Poussin—who, unlike Caravaggio, never killed anyone—will not be a great draw.

The growing number of the public interested in art is misleading: this public, in comparison with the total populations, is still insignificant and constitutes the *élite*. The notion of an *élite* in our time is no longer dependent on fortune or social class—indeed *kitsch* has its privileged position in the ruling classes. The grace of culture can touch individuals in all classes: added together, these make the crowds that frequent our museums, and we marvel at them; but the churches too are well filled on Sundays and our age is godless.

* * *

Our museums have become the sanctuaries of that 'universal humanism' which is the major gain of our period—a gain which it is absurd to deny. This humanism, though threatened, is none the less vital and active: it draws from what is opposed to it a livelier consciousness of what determines it. Graeco-Roman humanism invented a word for everything that was foreign to it, the word 'barbarian': the greatness of modern humanism—but also its weakness—is that it has proved capable of including what was opposed to it—that is to say, the 'barbarian reality' as a genuine human reality therefore worthy of scientific study and even of admiration. The civilised man of the West has gone beyond the barbarian, deeper still into the infinity of human nature, to search out in their deserts, islands, jungle and bush, those whom we no longer dare call 'primitive'. Claude Lévi-Strauss, in a book that is a confession, maintains that this is done from a bad conscience and is an attempt at escape from oneself: 'The reason why the West has produced ethnologists,' he says in *Tristes Tropiques* (*A World on the Wane*), 'must be that it is tormented by a strong feeling of remorse, which drives it to confront its own image with those of societies different from it, in the hope that they will reflect the same blemishes or will help it to explain to itself how its own have grown up within it.' And yet it was not blemishes that Lévi-Strauss found among 'these primitives whom one has only to visit to return sanctified'. This activity of knowledge is one that kills its object: it has taken just half a century to prepare the way for the suppression of that 'sanctified way of life'; and less than that will be needed to make it vanish altogether from the globe, thus completing the levelling of humanity to one standard type—a ridiculous result of all the efforts to define 'Man' as a quasi-deified entity—unless a third world catastrophe by annihilating both the neo-civilised and the old in civilisation produces chaos, a field for new beginnings in the future.

No doubt it is disgust with history—that story of lost opportunities, that recitation of the political and social messes ceaselessly made by humanity, which creates only to destroy without delay—that has unconsciously stimulated the admiration for the works of the spirit—the only human creations to be really accomplished, which have succeeded one another from metamorphosis to metamorphosis, in a chain with no link missing from the remotest ages down to our own times. But to modern men this transcendence can only be manifested through great numbers; and to show their veneration for the new idols the American art lovers have set a price on them. I am well aware that works of art have always commanded high prices—the Romans paid absurd sums for Greek works of art or for certain '*curiosa*'; but there has never before been the same alarming spectacle of customers outbidding the dealers themselves, forcing the prices up by a hundred thousand dollars a time!

These idols require temples: *Die aesthetische Kirche* was the title given in 1935 by a German author to a book on museums. But the idea goes back much further. Already at the end of the eighteenth century it was felt by Goethe, who was 'transported' by the sight of the Dresden picture gallery, and he expressed it in the clearest terms in *Dichtung und Wahrheit*: 'The time for the gallery to open, impatiently awaited, came at last. I entered that sanctuary, and what I saw surpassed all that I had imagined. That hall going round in a full circle, magnificent and well cared for, in which there reigned a profound silence, with its dazzling, recently gilded frames and its well-polished floors; had the effect of a spectacle much more than of a place of work and produced a solemn impression, unique in kind—all the more like the emotion with which one enters the house of God since the adornments of more than one church, things that had been objects of adoration, were exhibited anew in this place for the holy ends of art.'

And so, right at the beginning of the movement, the supreme metamorphosis was accomplished in the thoughts of Goethe, that man of genius: deconsecrated, the works of art were destined, by a final metamorphosis, to re-enter the sacred—the human sacred. *Quis ut deus?* Man, the creature, driven mad by the dizzy contemplation of cosmos and glory, turns to his own work (which, though mortal, is less so than he is) and pronounces the words that the Psalmist, trembling, addressed to God: 'Thou art the same, and thy years shall have no end.'

# INDEX

# Index

*Numbers in italics refer to plates*